About Island Press

Since 1984, the nonprofit organization Island Press has been stimulating, shaping, and communicating ideas that are essential for solving environmental problems worldwide. With more than 1,000 titles in print and some 30 new releases each year, we are the nation's leading publisher on environmental issues. We identify innovative thinkers and emerging trends in the environmental field. We work with world-renowned experts and authors to develop cross-disciplinary solutions to environmental challenges.

Island Press designs and executes educational campaigns in conjunction with our authors to communicate their critical messages in print, in person, and online using the latest technologies, innovative programs, and the media. Our goal is to reach targeted audiences—scientists, policymakers, environmental advocates, urban planners, the media, and concerned citizens—with information that can be used to create the framework for long-term ecological health and human well-being.

Island Press gratefully acknowledges major support of our work by The Agua Fund, The Andrew W. Mellon Foundation, The Bobolink Foundation, The Curtis and Edith Munson Foundation, Forrest C. and Frances H. Lattner Foundation, The JPB Foundation, The Kresge Foundation, The Oram Foundation, Inc., The Overbrook Foundation, The S.D. Bechtel, Jr. Foundation, The Summit Charitable Foundation, Inc., and many other generous supporters.

The opinions expressed in this book are those of the author(s) and do not necessarily reflect the views of our supporters.

Design Professional's Guide to Zero Net Energy Buildings

Design Professional's Guide to Zero Net Energy Buildings

CHARLES ELEY, FAIA, PE

ISLANDPRESS

Washington | Covelo | London

Island Press is a trademark of The Center for Resource Economics.

Keywords: Carbon emissions, climate change, BREAM, energy efficiency, green building, Green Globes, high-performance building, LEED, Living Building Challenge, renewable energy, smart grid, solar energy, wind energy, zero-energy buildings (ZEB), net-zero energy (NZE) buildings

Library of Congress Control Number: 2016938768

♻ Printed on recycled, acid-free paper

Manufactured in the United States of America
10 9 8 7 6 5 4 3 2 1

Contents

List of Figures and Tables

Figures

Tables

Preface

Tomorrow's Child

_Without a name; an unseen face
and knowing not your time nor place,
Tomorrow's Child, though yet unborn
I met you first last Tuesday morn.
A wise friend introduced us two,
and through his shining point of view
I saw a day that you would see;
a day for you, but not for me.
Knowing you has changed my thinking
for I never had an inkling
That perhaps the things I do
might someday, somehow, threaten you.
Tomorrow's Child, my daughter/son
I'm afraid I've just begun
To think of you and of your good,
though always having known I should.
Begin I will to weigh the cost
of what I squander; what is lost
If ever I forget that you
will someday come to live here too._

© Glenn C. Thomas, 1996
Used by permission of the Ray C. Anderson Foundation.

The world has changed from the days when I grew up in rural Tennessee in the 1950s and '60s. A long-distance telephone call to the next community or state cost a lot of money and was a rare event. Today, with the Internet and Skype, we can easily, inexpensively, and instantly have face-to-face conversations with friends and acquaintances all over the world. Television was just beginning to emerge in the fifties and the technology was pretty primitive, compared to today. We watched newscasters like Walter Cronkite and David Brinkley, who spent some time with each story and provided impartial coverage of the events of the day. Today we have Netflix, YouTube, and on-demand entertainment at our beck and call.

Computers as powerful as the smart phones we now carry in our pockets filled rooms, and only a dozen or so existed in the whole state of Tennessee. Instead of swiping a screen or clicking a mouse and getting immediate results, we prepared a deck of punch cards that contained data and Fortran programming instructions. The card deck was hand-delivered to the university computer center and we got our results the next day—unless we made an error, in which case we had to repeat the whole twenty-four-hour process until we got it right.

Freeways were just beginning to be constructed, so most communities were compact, organized around a courthouse or municipal building, and surrounded by locally owned and operated cafes, banks, drugstores, dry goods stores, and hardware stores. Town folks lived mostly within walking or biking distance from the square, and the countryside was dotted with small farms. Today, thoroughfares bypass the historic town centers and commerce is clustered around the exits in the form of multi-ethnic supermarkets, restaurants, fast-food joints, and "big box" retail. A car is required for the simplest of errands.

My first job was working as an "ice puller." I used a hand winch to lift 300-pound blocks of ice from a vat of 26°F brine and move them to an "ice house" where they were divided into smaller pieces and delivered to homes and businesses. Yes, some folks in my town were a little late in buying electric refrigerators, which had been around since the 1920s.

I have a son and a daughter in their early thirties. When they reach my age, it will be the middle of the twenty-first century (about 2050). If my children choose to become parents, by the time my grandchildren reach my age, we will be beginning the twenty-second century. The world has changed since I was a child; what will life be like for them and for their children as they live their lives and become senior citizens? Will the Earth's resources support the 9.6 billion or so humans that are expected to inhabit our planet in 2050?[1] Will we have enough fresh water? Will soil depletion be curbed so that our farmland can provide enough food to feed us? Will our atmosphere be resilient enough in light of massive pollution to continue filtering out harmful ultraviolet light, regulating temperature, and performing other critical functions essential to human life? Will the Earth's supply of minerals and especially rare-earth metals be adequate to accommodate continued economic growth, especially in the information-technology industries? Will we continue to rely primarily on oil, gas, and coal to power our economy, or will we finally wean ourselves from the pollution of fossil fuels and enter a new era of wind, solar, and other renewable resources?

In recent decades, we have witnessed the beginnings of climate change. Hurricanes have devastated the East Coast, the Gulf, and the Philippines. Tornadoes are more frequent and more powerful. California and much of the West suffer from drought while other areas are being drenched with flooding rains. Carbon dioxide (CO_2) exceeded 400 parts per million in 2013, and CO_2 concentrations would be even higher were it not for the ability of our oceans to absorb much of the CO_2. However, as the oceans absorb CO_2 the waters are becoming more acidic, and this chemical change is affecting the ecology of the oceans in ways that we are only beginning to understand. Most fish species are declining in number and some are endangered from overfishing. Coral reefs, their health so sensitive to water temperature and chemistry, are being bleached and are dying throughout most of the world.

We are on a treacherous path, but I believe that we can change that path and build a more sustainable future for our children and grandchildren. The inspiration for this book springs from a lifelong awe toward nature. Its beauty, resiliency, complexity, and diversity are magical. I am motivated to try and protect our environment as I listen to songbirds, hike in the wilderness, and enjoy the greenbelts that separate some of our cities and towns.

There are lots of ways to address climate change and environmental problems, but my perspective is that of an engineer and architect who has spent most of his career working to make our buildings and communities more energy-efficient. Through this lens, I see that much of what we do is inefficient and wasteful. We have the potential to design our communities, homes, and businesses to use much less energy and have a much smaller environmental impact. We can do this while at the same time improving our quality of life. Buildings are a big part of the problem, but they also represent great opportunities to improve our world. Zero net energy buildings are an important step in moving us toward a more sustainable future. Creating ZNE buildings is not the only thing we can do, but it is something that each of us can do immediately.

This book is about our future and what we can do about it. I will be gone by 2050 and forgotten by 2100, but the Earth will still be here and our descendants will be struggling to make a life for themselves. We have a responsibility to be good stewards and leave the best possible planet for our children and grandchildren to enjoy.

Acknowledgments

The following experts have shared their knowledge, stories, and insights with me for the sake of this book: Fahmida Ahmed, Gregg Ander, Chris Baker, Lindsay Baker, Tom Bauer, James Benya, Bob Berkebile, Keith Boswell, John Breshears, Cara Carmichael, Chris Chatto, Dimitri Contoyannis, Brian Court, Whitney Dorn, Jason Glazer, David Goldstein, Tony Hans, Lisa Heschong, Randall Higa, Cathy Higgins, Michael Holtz, Joy Hughes, Mark Hydeman, John Holtzclaw, Brad Jacobson, Todd Jones, Jim Kelsey, Erik Kolderup, Cliff Majersik, Jennifer Martin, Erin McConahey, Carey Nagle, Dan Nall, David Nelson, Carol Blevins Ormay, Bill Pennington, Kent Peterson, Shanti Pless, Snuller Price, Craig Randock, Cole Roberts, Mark Roddy, Michael Rosenberg, Paul Schwer, Scott Shell, Maziar Shirakh, Vern Smith, Ryan Stroupe, Geof Syphers, Steve Taylor, Paul Torcellini, Peter Turnbull, and Kevin Van Den Wymelenberg. The book is far richer as a result.

CHAPTER 1

Introduction:
We Have But One Earth

Buckminster Fuller, the futurist and inventor, referred to Planet Earth as a spaceship, with the sun as its energy source.[1] Our spaceship is far more advanced than the NASA shuttles, yet it is finite and delicate. It's our home and we need to take care of it. As Fuller said, "We are all astronauts."

The sun is responsible for all energy on Earth. Our reserves of oil and gas originate from plant materials grown from sun energy hundreds of millions of years ago. These fossil energy reserves are like wealth the Earth has saved for us. In the last 150 years, we have spent over half of this endowment. This is like working and saving for our entire career and then spending half of our lifetime savings in 15 minutes.[2] This is clearly not sustainable; our savings will quickly (in geologic time) run out and we will have to start living within the limits of the energy income that is provided by the sun and quit gorging on the reserves built up over eons. But the more pressing problem is climate change. We have to leave most of the remaining reserves of coal, gas, and oil in the ground if we are to keep global warming within the 2°C (3.6°F) limit agreed to by most of the world's governments at Paris in December 2015.[3] Climate change trumps peak oil.

The Threat of Climate Change

All of us share the Earth's atmosphere. Carbon dioxide (CO_2) emissions in China show up in the readings atop Mauna Loa, and emissions from

1

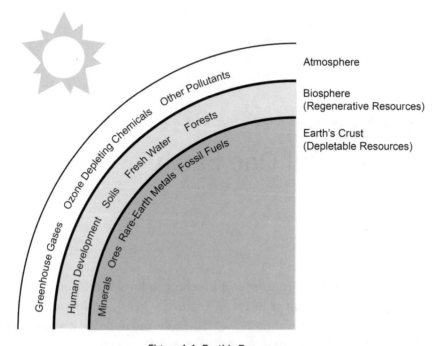

Figure 1-1: Earth's Resources
This conceptual diagram shows the biosphere that supports life and the atmosphere above.

a coal-fired power plant in Ohio affect CO_2 readings in China. If we are to address the problem of greenhouse-gas emissions and climate change, it must be done at the global scale. This does not mean that individual countries can't approach the problem differently and implement different solutions, but if we don't all work together, there will be little progress.

We have a special obligation in the United States to reduce CO_2 emissions and address climate change, since we use much more energy per person than the rest of the world. With only 4.5 percent of the population,[4] we consume about 19 percent of the world's energy.[5]

Buildings are one of the largest energy users in the United States. Approximately 8.05 quads,[6] or 28 percent of all natural gas consumption, is used directly in buildings and most of this is used for hot water and space heating.[7] Approximately 75 percent of all electricity (9.4 quads) is used directly in buildings for a variety of purposes including air-

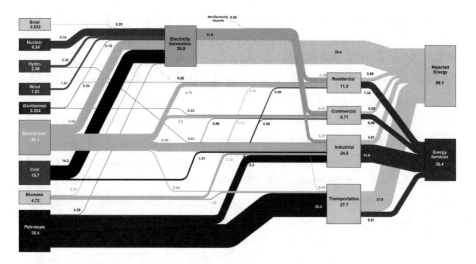

Figure 1-2: US Energy Use in 2015—97.5 Quads

Values shown are quads, which are 10^15 Btu. Data is based on DOE/EIA-0035(2015-03), March 2015. Data were compiled by Lawrence Livermore National Laboratory, which did the work under the auspices of the US Department of Energy. Distributed electricity represents only retail electricity sales and does not include self-generation. EIA reports consumption of renewable resources (i.e., hydro, wind, geothermal, and solar) for electricity in Btu-equivalent values by assuming a typical fossil-fuel-plant "heat rate." The efficiency of electricity production is calculated as the total retail electricity delivered divided by the primary energy input into electricity generation. End-use efficiency is estimated as 65 percent for the residential and commercial sectors, 80 percent for the industrial sector, and 21 percent for the transportation sector. Totals may not equal sum of components due to independent rounding. (Source: Lawrence Livermore National Laboratory-MI-410527.)

conditioning, lights, and computers.[8] The primary energy used to generate the electricity used in buildings is about three times greater that the energy that actually makes its way to the buildings, since so much is lost at the power plant and through the electricity distribution network.

In total, buildings used 39 percent of primary energy in 2015.[9] This is mostly electricity and natural gas but also includes smaller contributions of petroleum and biomass. This is a lot of energy, and there are certainly many opportunities to reduce building energy use through smarter design, efficiency, on-site renewable energy, and operation, as discussed later in the book.

US energy consumption in 2014 resulted in 5.4 gigatonnes of CO_2 being released to the atmosphere, about 15 percent of total global emissions.[10] Generating electricity resulted in 2.04 gigatonnes of emissions, or 38 percent of the US total. Buildings in the United States accounted for 39 percent of all CO_2 emissions in 2014.[11] Transportation needs represent the second-largest share of CO_2 emissions at 34 percent, and the location of our buildings within the urban fabric strongly influences this component of energy use (more on this in chapter 8). Industrial operations are next and represent about 18 percent. This includes emissions not only from energy consumption but from other industrial processes such as making cement.[12]

Carbon emissions and energy use track each other very closely. Buildings directly use 39 percent of primary energy and are directly responsible for 39 percent of carbon emissions. In general, if you reduce energy use by 10 percent you thereby reduce carbon emissions by about the same amount. On the other hand, if you increase energy use you increase carbon emissions by the same percentage change.

Buildings represent enormous opportunities to save energy and reduce environmental impact. The green building movement has been under way for almost three decades, starting with the American Institute of Architects' Committee on the Environment in 1990 and the formation of the US Green Building Council in 1993.[13] Energy efficiency is the single most important element of green buildings, but green buildings are about much more than energy efficiency. Green buildings also manage water movement and usage, are sited to avoid sensitive environmental areas like marshes and floodplains, and are efficiently constructed of materials that are sustainably produced or recycled. Green buildings also provide a healthy, comfortable, and productive interior environment that avoids the use of toxic material, meets high standards of air quality and thermal comfort, and provides occupants with abundant daylighting and views of the out-of-doors. Recognition programs such as LEED, Green Globes, and BREAM offer certificates for green buildings that meet their standards.

This book focuses on energy efficiency and renewable energy while respecting the broader goals of green buildings. It also raises the bar for energy efficiency and on-site renewable energy. A zero net energy

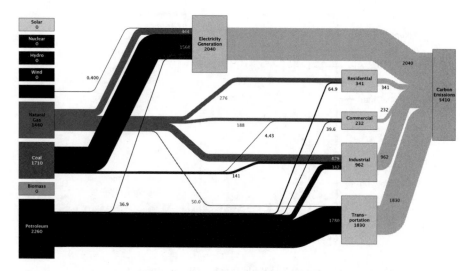

Figure 1-3: US Carbon Emissions 2014—5,410 Million Metric Tons
Values shown are millions of metric tons. Data is based on DOE/EIA-0035(2015-03), March 2015. Data were compiled by Lawrence Livermore National Laboratory, which did the work under the auspices of the US Department of Energy. Carbon emissions are attributed to their physical source and are not allocated to end use for electricity consumption in the residential, commercial, industrial, and transportation sectors. Petroleum consumption in the electric power sector includes the nonrenewable portion of municipal solid waste. Combustion of biologically derived fuels is assumed to have zero net carbon emissions—the life-cycle emissions associated with producing biofuels are included in commercial and industrial emissions. Totals may not equal sum of components due to independent rounding errors. (Source: Lawrence Livermore National Laboratory-MI-410527.)

(ZNE) building is one that uses no more energy on an annual basis than it produces. As can be seen in figure 1-4, the sum of all the energy delivered across the property line must be less than or equal to the sum of all the energy that is exported from the site. Energy transfers that happen inside the property line are not significant. The only thing that matters is what comes in and what goes out. The US Department of Energy (DOE) common definition of ZNE buildings allows the use of fossil fuels, but the production of electricity must be greater than the consumption of electricity by a margin adequate enough to make up for the use of gas, oil or any other non-electric energy that is delivered to the building.[14] ZNE buildings go by other names as well: zero energy

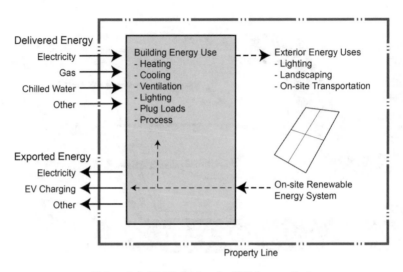

Figure 1-4: Site Boundary for ZNE Accounting

The solid arrows on the left represent the components of energy use that are considered by ZNE accounting. The dashed lines inside the property line are energy flows that are not considered in the accounting. (Source: Charles Eley, with concepts derived from DOE Common Definition of Zero-Energy Buildings.)

buildings (ZEB)[15] and net-zero energy (NZE) buildings. Recognition programs for ZNE buildings are just beginning to emerge. The International Living Building Future and the New Buildings Institute have ZNE recognition programs.

We already have the knowledge and technology to design and construct our buildings to be zero net energy. Zero net energy buildings represent an excellent opportunity to reduce our energy use and help mitigate the impact of climate change. ZNE buildings are not a complete solution to climate change, but they are a good place to start: they represent something that is immediately achievable. This book is about how we can have an impact as we design, build, and use our buildings.

The Architecture 2030 Challenge calls for all new buildings to be ZNE by the year 2030. This policy has been adopted by the American Institute of Architects, the US Conference of Mayors, the American Society of Heating, Refrigeration, and Air-Conditioning Engineers (ASHRAE), the Congress for the New Urbanism, the American Solar Energy Society, the Society of Building Science Educators, and various other professional organizations. It has been adopted as policy in California with the goal that ZNE commercial buildings will be required by code by 2030 and residential buildings by 2020. The Energy Independence and Security Act requires that all federal buildings meet the challenge. More than three-fourths of the twenty largest architectural and engineering firms have adopted the challenge.

ZNE buildings are an energizing concept and one that is broadly accepted by professionals and laypersons alike, yet there is little information on what is required to actually design and construct a ZNE building. Is the goal feasible? Is our construction industry up to the challenge? Do we have the wherewithal and the technologies to meet the challenge? What will ZNE buildings look like? How much will they cost?

This book begins to answer these questions by laying out the principles for ZNE design and construction. The solutions offered are easy to implement. They do not require that we develop breakthrough technologies or new knowledge: the tools and technologies we need exist right now. Pioneering architects, engineers, and building owners have already achieved the goal of zero net energy in many of their buildings. We know how to do it. Leading designers, builders, and owners have shown us the way. However, we need the mainstream to take up the cause. It is not enough to have a few isolated examples; ZNE buildings must become the norm if we are to curb climate change and address other environmental problems.

While this book is written primarily for architects, engineers, energy consultants, green building advisors, and miscellaneous design and construction professionals, others will find the material useful. I have tried to present the information in simple terms with a minimum of technical jargon. Such technical information as is necessary is presented in graphic form or in sidebars.

- Chapter 2 shows how we can design our buildings to be smarter, use far less energy, and improve environmental quality, all at the same time.
- Chapter 3 recounts the remarkable development of renewable-energy

systems in recent years; efficiency and reliability have improved and costs have declined.

- Chapter 4 explains the principles of energy modeling and how it may be used to compare design options, assess the potential for achieving ZNE, and understand complex building interactions.
- Chapter 5 details how to organize the building-project delivery system for success, to monitor energy performance, and to engage the building occupants.
- Chapter 6 reviews the various metrics for ZNE accounting and evaluates off-site options when on-site ZNE is not possible.
- Chapter 7 suggests some public policies and programs to extend ZNE from showcase examples to mainstream buildings.
- The final chapter paints a vision of an energy future that goes beyond ZNE, minimizes the impact of climate change, and provides a livable world for our grandchildren.
- An appendix has examples of low-energy and ZNE buildings that are referenced throughout the book.

CHAPTER 2

Smart Building Design: Contextual Design, Energy Efficiency, and Curtailment

Our buildings use a lot more energy than they need to. Before making investments in renewable-energy systems, it is almost always more cost-effective to design our buildings to use as little energy as possible. This can be achieved in a number of ways. Through smart building design, we can harvest daylight, cool with outside air, heat with the sun, and take advantage of other natural processes that require very little additional energy. Better insulation reduces heat losses in the winter and gains in the summer. High-performance windows enable us to enjoy views and to harvest daylighting with minimal solar gain. By improving the energy efficiency of boilers, air conditioners, and fans, we can enjoy the same comfort conditions, but with less energy. We can also reduce energy use through curtailment, or what some call conservation. With curtailment, we find a way to get by with less. Maybe we don't really have to continually air-condition parts of the building that are rarely used. Contextual design, efficiency, and curtailment are closely related, and sometimes the lines between them become quite muddled.

In this chapter, I illustrate the fundamental principles of energy-efficient design through the stories and examples of architects, engineers, and owners who have found ways to design, build, and operate exceptional buildings. They share with us what has worked for them, ways of addressing common barriers, and techniques for achieving success.

Long Life, Loose Fit

The American Institute of Architects (AIA) Committee on the Environment (COTE) has been selecting its top ten green buildings every year for more than a decade, and the program has celebrated numerous exceptional buildings. As the program has developed, the committee has steadily refined the criteria for what constitutes a green building. One of the most important criteria is what the committee calls "Long Life, Loose Fit." If buildings are designed to last a long time and remain adaptable to different uses in the future, we will need to build fewer new buildings when we can more easily modify or adapt the old ones. This reduces embodied energy, which is the energy that is used to mine and process materials, manufacture building products, deliver them to the building site, and assembly them into the building.

Building structures, by their very nature, are permanent. Even temporary structures last much longer than intended. Building 20 on the MIT campus was built in 1943 by the military to house an emergency war effort to develop radar. It was never intended to be a permanent building, but it lasted for fifty-five years, providing space for innovations in radar, acoustics, linguistics, and computer science. When it was finally demolished in 1998, it was dubbed the "Magic Incubator" and was celebrated in commemoration of its former occupants and their achievements.

Building 20 was by all accounts an ugly building, clad with drab asbestos shingles, and was a poor example of energy efficiency: it was cold in the winter, hot in the summer. But its design and construction provide a great example of how a building can accommodate change. The three-story building stretched along Vassar Street, with four wings extending to the southeast. Circulation was provided by a central corridor that provided flexible space for building services. It was constructed of heavy wood timbers (because of the steel shortage during the war), which would support heavy equipment and a multitude of activities. A continuous band of operable windows around the perimeter provided daylight and natural ventilation. Because it was considered a temporary structure, the MIT building-management staff was less than vigilant, and

Figure 2-1: Building 20 on Campus of the Massachusetts Institute of Technology
Building 20 is in the center of this photograph. This is an example of a building that was successfully adapted for multiple purposes over its fifty-five-year life. (© The MIT Museum, CC-20-407.)

tenants were free to knock down walls, build new ones, and basically modify the building to accommodate their needs. It was anything but a classy address, but it gave tenants the freedom to modify it as they saw fit. This freedom was an important factor in the multitude of innovations that had their birth there. Building 20 was the epitome of "loose fit." While it was never intended to have a "long life," it actually did.

Too often, we design our buildings to serve the needs of the first occupant, who may only use the building for five to ten years. Even worse, our buildings are sometimes so tightly tailored to that first use that it is very difficult for them to be adapted subsequently for other uses. Yogi Berra said, "It's tough to make predictions, especially about the future," but the construction of a building unavoidably represents a prediction of the future. In his wonderful book *How Buildings Learn*, Stewart Brand suggests that to achieve greater flexibility we should conduct scenario analysis at the programming phase, whereby we look not only at needs of the first occupant, but also the needs of possible future occupants as well as possible changes in technology, regulations, and economic competition that would affect future building use.[1]

We can't possibly anticipate exactly how our buildings will be used in the future. Nevertheless, we should expect that the first uses will not be permanent and attempt to provide as much flexibility as we can for future adaptation. When the design team for the Rocky Mountain Institute was planning their new Innovation Center (see appendix), they kept office space flexible and adaptable to evolving work styles and technologies. They even installed some empty conduit to allow for inexpensive adaptation to future information technologies and DC wiring. Modular heating and cooling systems expand easily. Furthermore, durable finishes on both the interior and exterior will weather well and last for a century or more.

Urban warehouses and industrial space are also good examples of enduring buildings. We have seen how these heavy-timber structures with high ceilings, large floor plates, and generous windows have been remodeled to function as office space, residential lofts, schools, and retail space. Building services (heating, ventilation, and air-conditioning — "HVAC" — as well as lighting) have been replaced along with windows, but the basic structure and building envelopes have lasted and have proved to be adaptable.

High-rise office buildings also offer flexibility, but in a more limited way. Most often, office towers are designed with an inflexible core that houses restrooms, elevators, and service shafts, but the core is surrounded by a donut of flexible space. The size of the floor plate is determined by use but usually ranges between about 25,000 and 35,000 square feet.[2] This provides an optimal mix of core services and surrounding tenant space.

Form and Configuration

An old maxim in architecture is that the most important decisions are made early in the design process, when the owner and design team decide where a new building will be located, how it will be positioned on the site, what the number of floors and the floor-to-floor height will be, how the major uses will be configured, and what the footprint will be. These decisions will have a century-long impact on future opportunities for daylighting, natural ventilation, lighting design, and HVAC, yet are often made with little forethought.

Our most successful energy-efficiency buildings are those where form and configuration are considered early in the design process. When the National Renewable Energy Laboratory (NREL) decided to construct a new Research Support Facility in Golden, Colorado (initial project completion, 2010), they wanted the new building to set an example for sustainability and energy efficiency (see the examples in the appendix). That is their business—and if they can't do it, how can they promote the concept to others? Paul Torcellini, a scientist at NREL, reports that their goal was to achieve a zero net energy building, and to do so they determined that the building would need to have a site energy utilization index (EUI) of less than 35 kBtu/ft²·yr, without consideration of renewables.[3] The average EUI for office buildings in the Denver area is over 60 kBtu/ft²·yr or more, so this represents a 42 percent reduction from the norm.[4] NREL determined that this level of energy efficiency would enable zero net energy with the installation of photovoltaic (PV) panels located on the roof and parking areas.

To achieve their goals, NREL wrote a tight performance specification for the building and invited proposals from design-build teams. They did not develop a preliminary design or "bridge documents," which are often done with design-build project delivery, but left the design of the build-

Energy Utilization Index (EUI)

EUI is a common way to express the energy use of a building. With EUI, all of the annual energy inputs to the building are added up and converted to common energy units like Btu or kWh. The total energy use is then divided by the area of the building and the result is kBtu/ft²·yr in the United States or kWh/m²·yr in other parts of the world. A low EUI is needed to achieve ZNE. (See table 2-7 for target values.)

ing completely up to the design-build teams. They specified the energy performance requirement along with many other requirements, and they challenged the design-build team to come up with a design that met their requirements, including a low EUI. Payment of the design fees was contingent on meeting these requirements.

Michael Holtz of the Architectural Energy Corporation reports that after numerous studies, the design team settled on a series of slender three- and four-story buildings extending in an east–west direction.[5] The buildings have a depth from north to south of only 60 feet, so everyone in the building is no more than 30 feet from a window and the benefits of natural ventilation and daylighting. The buildings are separated by about 100 feet so they don't shade each other, and they are linked together with walkways that provide services and points of entry. The basic form and configuration of each building enable it to incorporate natural ventilation, daylighting, and various other energy-efficiency measures. The building form also permitted conventional construction techniques and materials at typical construction costs for the area.

Bob Berkebile's firm, BNIM, used a similar concept when they designed the Iowa Utility Board building in Des Moines (see appendix). The IUB building is much smaller at just under 45,000 square feet and is just two stories, but again, as with the NREL facility, stretching the building in an east–west direction and limiting the building depth from north to south enabled the design team to provide daylight and natural ventilation to the majority of the occupants. Carey Nagle, the project architect, reports that building orientation and configuration was one of the foundational strategies and a principle for keeping the project simple and replicable. The RMI Innovation Center in Basalt, Colorado, is yet another example that uses form and configuration to maximize daylight and natural ventilation (see appendix).

The NREL, Iowa, and RMI sites are large, and the designers had the freedom to consider lots of different building configurations and settle on one that met their tough performance requirements. Many designers, especially for projects in dense urban areas, don't have this much freedom, since the size and configuration of the building is more constrained by the site. However, when opportunities present themselves, the form and configuration of the building should be the first consideration. Future opportunities for energy efficiency, especially related to daylighting and natural ventilation, will either be possible or not depending on these early decisions. The narrow building profile stretching east and west worked well for these buildings, but there are many other solutions that may be more suitable for other sites and other climates. The important thing is for the design team to spend some quality time early in the design process to explore the options that work best. Energy efficiency depends on it both initially and in the future as the building is remodeled and adapted for future occupants.

The Building Envelope

The building envelope consists of the walls, roofs, floors, windows, and doors that separate indoor space from the out-of-doors. The building envelope has a long life and should be given the greatest priority. While lighting systems last only five to fifteen years before they are replaced, and HVAC systems last from ten to twenty-five years, the building envelope will endure for fifty years or more and affect the energy use and design of lighting and HVAC systems for the entire life of the building. When the building envelope is well designed, it enables efficient daylighting systems and HVAC systems that only work in buildings with low thermal loads. The opposite is also true. The Seagram's Tower in Manhattan, designed by Mies van der Rohe, was constructed in 1958 and will likely last for at least another sixty years. While it represents a milestone in architectural history, its dark glass skin on all orientations marks it among the least energy-efficient buildings in New York.[6] Other landmarks such as the Chrysler Building and the Empire State Building are eighty-five years old and will likely last much longer, especially since they have been recently upgraded to be energy-efficient. The Flatiron Building was constructed in 1902 and is coming up on its 115th birthday.

The envelope does not directly use energy, but has an enormous impact on how much energy is needed for lighting, heating, cooling, and ventilation. The ideal building envelope modulates the flow of heat, air, and light to and from the building. When outdoor conditions are perfect, the ideal building envelope opens up and "breathes" in light and air. But when outdoor conditions are harsh, the ideal building envelope "buttons up" and forms a barrier against heat flow, airflow, and excessive sunlight. Think of a wildflower that opens its pedals to the sun during the day but closes up at night to protect itself from winds and cold temperatures.

The building envelopes of most commercial buildings do a fair job of "buttoning up," but not "opening up." Conventional practice and building codes encourage designers to insulate and seal the building envelope, but rarely do commercial buildings have the capability to naturally release internal heat or to breathe in fresh air when the conditions are right. This function is too often left to the HVAC system, which does the job effectively but at the price of high energy use and a loss of resiliency during emergencies. When there is a sustained power outage, a building that relies solely on the HVAC system and electric lighting can be practically unusable.

Windows that open and close automatically are expensive, but there are other solutions. A compact weather station is installed at the Iowa Utilities Board building (see appendix) that measures outdoor temperature, wind speed, humidity, and more. Data from the weather station is shared with the building's energy-management system. The building operators have determined that conditions are suitable for natural ventilation when the temperature is between 62°F and 79°F, the humidity is below 50 percent, and winds are less than 10 miles per hour. When these conditions exist, the energy-management system automatically sends an e-mail to the building occupants advising them that they should open their windows. When it is too hot, too cold, too humid, or too windy, an e-mail is sent advising the occupants to close their windows. For security, the operable windows have sensors that indicates if a window is open or closed. The energy-management system uses this signal to disable the heat pump serving an area where the windows are open. When the windows are closed, the heat pump is enabled. Dr. Ran Liu of the Iowa Energy Center has verified through monitoring that the e-mail system works very well indeed.[7]

The Y2E2 Building on the Stanford campus is another example of a building that breathes, but the concept is different. When the outside temperature is below 82°F, openings at the top of a central atrium automatically open (humidity and wind are not an issue in Palo Alto) and occupants are sent an e-mail advising that they open their windows. For temperatures above 82°F, the atrium windows are closed and an e-mail advises occupants to close their windows. Another strategy for the Stanford building is to cool down the mass of the building at night when the temperatures are low. For night cooling, the windows in the top of the atrium open as well as other actuator-controlled windows in common areas. Cole Roberts of Arup North American Ltd., the engineers for the building, refers to the atrium as "the lungs of the building."

The Bullitt Center in Seattle automates everything (see appendix). Exterior shades open and close based on an astronomical time clock.

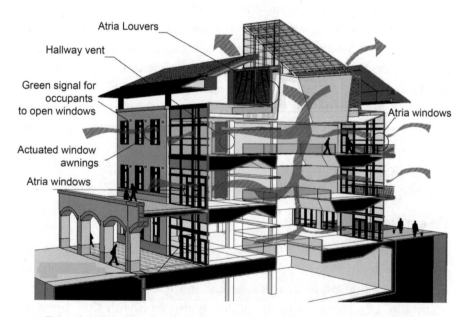

Figure 2-2: Ventilation Strategies at the Y2E2 Building on the Stanford Campus
This diagram shows natural airflows when the outdoor temperature is below 82°F. Similar airflows occur at night to lower the temperature of the building and remove heat from thermal mass. (Source: Bora Architects, printed with permission.)

Windows open and close automatically to provide both natural ventilation and nighttime cooling (see appendix).

CLIMATE ZONES

To help explain the dependency of building energy use on climate, the US Department of Energy (DOE) and ASHRAE developed climate zones for the United States, and these have been extended to the entire planet. Thermal zones are numbered between 1 and 8, with the southern tip of Florida being thermal zone 1 and the upper stretches of North Dakota, Minnesota, and Wisconsin being thermal zone 7. Northern Alaska is in thermal zone 8, the coldest of the zones. Other states are somewhere in between. Recently, DOE and ASHRAE have added a climate zone 0 (zero) to better characterize really hot places like parts of Saudi Arabia (increasing the number of climate zones to nine).

Further, there are three moisture zones: A, B, and C. Zone A is the moist or humid zone and includes the eastern and midwestern states. Zone B (the dry zone) extends from West Texas up through Colorado, Wyoming, and Montana, and it includes states all the way to the Pacific Ocean. Zone C is a narrow band along the Pacific coast, extending from southern California through Oregon and Washington, but only includes areas close enough to be influenced by the chilly Pacific Ocean. For some of the analysis in this book, the climate zones have been aggregated into seven regions, as shown on figure 2-3. It is worth noting that climate change is causing some of the boundaries between the zones to shift; for instance, Dallas, Texas, recently moved from Zone 3a to Zone 2a.

FENESTRATION

Windows, skylights, and doors are the key elements for buildings that breathe. When designed properly, they can be opened to bring in daylight and outside air, and to let heat and moisture escape. They are generally the only elements of the building envelope with this capability. Their numbers, size, placement, and construction are critical to achieving the low EUIs needed to achieve ZNE, but energy is not the only consideration in window design. Windows provide views to the out-of-doors

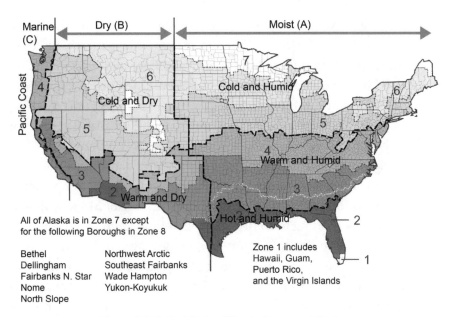

Figure 2-3: United States Climate Zones and Regions

This map was developed by the United States Department of Energy and ASHRAE. The consolidated seven climate regions were created by the author.

and they brighten spaces in ways that lift our spirits. Studies show that students learn better, patients recover more quickly, and workers are more productive in spaces that have views and daylighting.[8] On the negative side, windows represent 60 percent or so of the total heat loss on cold days and, on hot days, are a source of much of the heat gain that creates air-conditioning loads.[9] Choosing the right windows and placing them properly in the building is both critical and tricky, since windows provide so many useful services (daylighting, ventilation, views), while at the same time they create heating and cooling loads that must be addressed by HVAC systems.

The design of fenestration is the most important and most challenging part of smart building envelope design, since it can have both positive and negative effects on views, daylighting, ventilation, infiltration, heating loads, and cooling loads. The best window location for views rarely aligns with the best window location for daylighting. View windows need

19

to be at eye level, while the best windows for daylighting are positioned as high as possible in the room. Windows that provide natural ventilation, on the other hand, should be located near the floor and near the ceiling and should be separated by as much elevation difference as possible so that cool air can enter at the bottom and warm air can exit at the top—i.e., the stack effect. Separate windows for views, daylighting, and ventilation are usually warranted, since their requirements are so different.

Cooling loads can be minimized if windows face either north or south. North and south orientations are also best for daylighting. North-facing windows receive little direct sun (in the Northern Hemisphere) and require little shading to control glare, except in latitudes closer to the equator, yet they provide soft, diffuse daylight preferred, for example, by fine-art painters. Solar gain and glare can be controlled for south-facing windows with simple exterior shading devices like overhangs and/or side fins. East- and west-facing windows are more troublesome and should be minimized. The sun is low in the sky when it rises in the east and sets in the west, making it very difficult to control solar gains, which create cooling loads and glare for building occupants. Orientation is the most fundamental way to control solar gain through windows, and, of course, the opportunities for proper window orientation are enabled or prevented by the basic form and configuration of the building.

Fixed shading devices like overhangs and side fins are effective, but naturally there are times when they are not optimal. Both the Bullitt Center and the RMI Innovation Center use automatically controlled exterior blinds that can be raised, lowered, opened, or closed. They work like big venetian blinds on the outside of the building but are much sturdier and hold up to the elements. The devices are controlled by an astronomical time clock that knows at all times the position of the sun relative to each window.

We need to scrap the notion of buildings with the same window treatment on each façade. One of the most predictable things in our unpredictable world is the position of the sun in the sky on any given day and at any given time. Our buildings should use this information to their advantage and adjust window area and treatment accordingly.

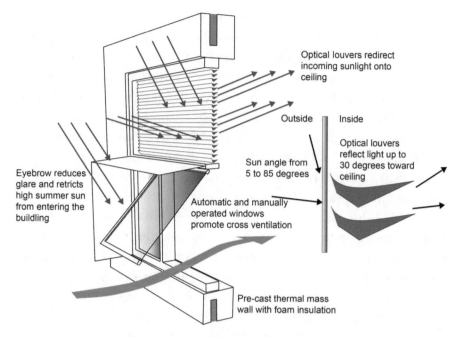

Figure 2-4: Solar Control, Daylighting, and Ventilation at the NREL RSF
The south-facing windows at the NREL RSF are a good example of how to minimize heat gain while maintaining views and maximizing daylight. Light louvers in the upper portion of the windows deflect direct light to the ceilings. An eyebrow around the view portion of the window provides shading while maintaining views and natural ventilation.

Window technology has made amazing advances in the last couple of decades. The thermal resistance of windows has improved, as have the solar optic properties. Modern state-of-the-art windows have low U-factors, reducing heat loss. A low U-factor (or high thermal resistance) is achieved through multiple panes of glass, but also through low-emissivity

U-Factor

The U-factor is the amount of heat lost during an hour through a square foot of fenestration when the temperature difference between the inside and the outside is 1°F. The units are Btu/h·ft^2 in the United States and W/m^2 in other parts of the world.

(or "low-e") coatings that reduce radiation transfer between a warm pane and a cooler pane. This is also accomplished through thermally improved spacers that separate the panes of glazing. Some advanced windows use Mylar or other suspended films to provide additional air gaps with less weight. Advances have also been made in the design of window frames to reduce heat loss. The interior and exterior portions of metal window frames and mullions are commonly separated by a nonmetallic bond that significantly reduces thermal bridging. Modern windows have heat loss of less than a third of typical single-glazed windows, and advanced technologies can reduce heat loss even more.

The RMI Innovation Center, located in Basalt, Colorado (one of the coldest climates in the United States), uses high-performance quadruple-glazed windows that have a center-of-glass U-factor of less than 0.08 (R-value is greater than R-13).[10] As a result, special heating systems at the perimeter of the building could be eliminated, which reduced construction costs. In the milder Seattle climate, perimeter heating systems were similarly eliminated at the Bullitt Center through the use of triple-glazed windows.

The solar optic properties of windows have also made astonishing improvements through both tints that are added to glass when it is in a molten state and special low-e coatings that are added to one or more surfaces of the finished glass. As a result, windows can filter out most of the harmful ultraviolet light (which can damage fabrics) and block much of the infrared radiation, while allowing most of the visible light to pass through the window. The benefits of view and daylighting are related only to the visible light and are unaffected if the ultraviolet (UV) and infrared light are removed. Glazing with these properties is called *spectrally selective*; an ideal window would be completely transparent to visible light and completely opaque to sunlight outside the visible portion of the spectrum (that is, ultraviolet and infrared light). No window is perfect, but some windows do a pretty good job.

Traditional tints are bronze or gray, which absorb energy from the sun and cause the surface of the glass to heat up, creating uncomfortable conditions for building occupants who work next to the windows. A larger problem is that they block a disproportionate amount of visible light while doing less to reduce UV and infrared; such glazing does the exact opposite of what is needed. Higher-performance tints are typically blue or green, which are more transparent to sunlight in the visible portion of the spectrum and less transparent to sunlight in the UV and infrared spectrums.

Many of the performance improvements with regard to both thermal and solar properties are due to low-e coatings. Generically, there are two types of coatings: hard and soft. Hard coatings are fused into the surface of the glass and are more durable, but soft coatings offer better performance. Soft coatings are applied with a sophisticated sputter technology, whereby the glass is scrubbed, cleaned, and dried in a clean-room environment similar to that used in the production of computer chips. The glass then passes through a series of chambers where microscopically thin coatings are applied, one on top of the other, via a "sputtering" process. Some advanced coatings have as many of twelve such applications.[11] The combination of these coatings can tune glass to block some wavelengths while being transparent to others.

Both hard and soft coatings also significantly reduce emissivity, which is the ability of a surface to emit radiation. In double- or multi-layered glazing assemblies, much of the heat transfer is radiation from the warmer pane to the cooler pane. Uncoated glass has an emissivity of about 84 percent, but some of the best low-e glasses have an emissivity below 4 percent, which is more than twenty times lower.

Soft coatings are typically applied to the second or third surface of double glass (you start counting surfaces from the outside, so double glass has four surfaces, triple has six, etc.). Coatings on the second or third surfaces are protected from abrasion and other physical damage. In climates that predominately require heating, the best position for the low-e coating is the third surface, but when cooling is a larger issue, the second surface generally works better.

Figuring the performance of a window or skylight can be complicated, because there are so many factors: the number of panes, the presence of spacers, coatings, and tints, and the type of frames. The National

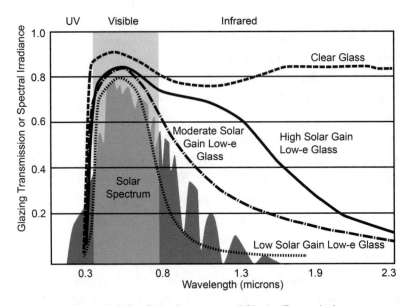

Figure 2-5: The Solar Spectrum and Glazing Transmission

Glazing transmission data is taken from www.commercialwindows.org and www.efficientwin dows.org; the information was consolidated into one graph by the author. ("Low-e" means that the glass has a low-emissivity coating.)

Fenestration Rating Council (NFRC) was created (originally with support from the California Energy Commission) to provide consistent performance data on windows and to keep the sales staffs of window and glass manufacturers honest. The NFRC labels glazing and pre-manufactured windows to indicate the U-factor, the solar heat-gain coefficient (SHGC), and the visible transmission (VT). Rated values are generated through a process of both physical testing and modeling.

OPAQUE ELEMENTS

Walls, roofs, floors, and other opaque elements of the building envelope don't provide views, daylight, or ventilation, so the design goals are simpler and more straightforward: reduce heat gain and loss. While the goal is simpler, the design of opaque envelope components requires careful attention to detail and is achieved through a combination of insulation, moisture control, air barriers, exterior color, and

Table 2-1 — Glazing Technologies

Technology		Description
Number of Panes		The number of panes in the glazing assembly. Each additional pane creates an insulating air gap.
Spacers		Spacers separate multiple panes of glass and are traditionally made of aluminum channels or tubes and contain a desiccant to absorb any moisture trapped in the cavity. Advanced spacers are made of thermoplastic or foam and reduce heat transmission around the perimeter of the glazing.
Coatings	Hard	Hard coatings are applied through a chemical vapor-deposition process at a high temperature while the glass is being manufactured. Coatings can be used to achieve a reflective coating, a low-emissivity coating, or both.
	Soft	Soft coatings are applied off-line after the glass has been cut to size with a magnetron sputter-vacuum-deposition process. Multiple coatings are typically applied, both to achieve a low emissivity and to filter out certain wavelengths of light.
Suspended Films		Suspended polymer films can substitute for a third or fourth pane of glass. They can also be soft-coated in a manner similar to glass. Films must be durable, since they are exposed to ultraviolet and short-wave visible radiation.
Gas Fills		Air, mostly nitrogen and oxygen, is the traditional and least expensive gap fill. Argon has a conductivity 30 percent lower than air and is commonly used to improve performance. Krypton and xenon perform even better, but are less common because of their high cost.
Dynamic Glazing		Dynamic glazing has the capability to change its solar optic properties in response to sunlight, temperature, or an electric signal. Photochromic glazing works like eyeglasses and becomes darker when directly illuminated by sunlight. Thermochromic glazing changes its solar optic properties at different temperatures. The most interesting technology is electrochromic glazing, which can go from light to dark in response to an electric signal. Electrochromic glazing is now offered commercially by a number of manufacturers.
Aerogels		Aerogels, also known as "solid air," are the result of NASA research and are the lowest-density solid known. Aerogels are used instead of air or argon in the air gap. They are typically only used in skylights, since they are light-diffusing.

Table 2-1 — continued

Technology	Description
Solar Cell Glazing	Solar cell glazing combines glazing with photovoltaic electric production. Typical products use thin-film PV technology, but some have conventional monocrystalline or polycrystalline solar cells bonded to glass. Efficient solar cell glazing has a low transmission because light is captured to make electricity. This reduces its effectiveness for daylighting and views. It is most commonly used in spandrel panels.

Table 2-2 — Window Requirements from ASHRAE Standard 90.1-2013

These are typical criteria for nonresidential buildings. The requirements are less stringent for semi-heated buildings and more stringent for residential buildings that are heated and cooled on a continuous basis. Climate zones are shown in figure 2-3. Three criteria are given: the U-factor limits heat loss, SHGC limits solar heat gain, and the ratio of VT/SHGC assures that the window provides useful daylighting.

Climate Zone	Maximum Window U-Factor			Solar Optic Properties	
	Non-Metal Framing	Metal Framing	Metal Framing (Operable)	Maximum Solar Heat Gain Coefficient (SHGC)	Minimum Ratio of VT/SHGC
1	0.50	0.57	0.65	0.25	
2	0.40				
3	0.35	0.50	0.60		
4				0.40	1.10
5		0.42	0.50		
6	0.32				
7		0.38	0.40	0.45	
8					

special consideration to corners and joints, which can be the source of thermal bridges.

Insulation is perhaps the most fundamental requirement of building codes, and the most recent codes do a pretty good job of specifying cost-effective levels. Modern codes like ASHRAE 90.1 and California's Title 24 call for different insulation levels for different classes of construction. Table 2-3 shows the insulation levels required by ASHRAE Standard 90.1-2013 for typical roofs, walls, and floors. This is a simplification of the standard and leaves out the separate requirements for metal buildings and heavy concrete or masonry construction. For steel-framed and wood-framed walls, there are two insulation requirements: the insulation that is installed between the framing members (within the cavity) and the insulation that is installed in a continuous manner (uninterrupted by the framing members). For most climates, both cavity and continuous insulation are required for walls. Construction methods other than those shown in table 2-3 may be used if they result in an equal or lower U-factor.

Thermal bridges are elements of building construction where metal,

Table 2-3 — Insulation Levels from ASHRAE Standard 90.1-2013

These are typical R-values for nonresidential buildings. Less insulation is required for semi-heated buildings and more insulation is required for residential buildings that are heated and cooled on a continuous basis. Separate requirements are also given for metal buildings and heavy concrete construction, which are not included here for the sake of simplicity. "NR" means "no requirement." The climate zones are shown in figure 2-3.

	Roofs		Steel-Framed Walls		Wood-Framed Walls		Steel- or Wood-Framed Floors
Climate Zone	Insulation over Deck	Attic	Cavity Insulation	Continuous Insulation	Cavity Insulation	Continuous Insulation	
1	R-20			NR			NR
2	R-25	R-38		R3.8		NR	
3				R5			
4				R7.5		R3.8	
5	R-30	R-49	R-13+	R10	R-13+		R-30
6				R12.5		R7.5	
7	R-35	R-60					R-38
8				R18.8		R18.8	

concrete, or other highly conductive materials penetrate the thermal barrier (insulation). Common examples are structural concrete slabs that penetrate exterior walls to support a balcony, or structural steel supports for pre-cast concrete facades or curtain walls. The framing members in steel walls are thermal bridges, which is why most standards require continuous insulation for this type of construction. When possible, thermal bridges should be avoided through building design. When they are unavoidable, their impact should be mitigated as much as possible by using continuous insulation on the exterior of the building or through other techniques.

Advanced building envelopes typically include a continuous air barrier to control air leaks and to resist positive and negative pressures caused by wind, stack effects, or mechanical ventilation. An air barrier can be located on the exterior, the interior, or anywhere in the construction assembly, but a common solution for commercial buildings is to use a self-adhering membrane applied over waterproof exterior sheathing. Continuous air barriers are required by most modern energy codes.[12]

Designers must also pay attention to moisture migration. Water moves from moist to dry. In cold climates, the interior of the building will have more moisture than the outdoors, and moisture will attempt to migrate from the interior of the building to the outdoors. For air-conditioned buildings in humid climates, the opposite is true: moisture will attempt to migrate from the moist exterior to the air-conditioned interior. When moist air is cooled, the water condenses, and so a moisture barrier is needed to prevent condensation from occurring in the middle of a wall or roof cavity, which can damage the structure, degrade the insulation, and in some cases result in mold and air-quality problems.

The color and surface properties of walls and especially roofs is important, especially in hot climates. Light-colored roofs with a high reflectance and high emittance should be used in hot and warm areas. The light color reflects solar radiation and lowers the temperature of the roof, which in turn reduces heat gain. The high emittance allows heat buildup to escape through radiation when the roof gets hot. Light-colored roofing products are labeled by the Cool Roof Rating Council.

- ASHRAE Standard 90.1-2013 or the latest version.
- Windows for High-Performance Commercial Buildings: www.com mercialwindows.org. This website was developed by the Windows and Daylighting Group at LBNL and the Center for Sustainable Research at the University of Minnesota.
- Efficient Windows Collaborative: www.efficientwindows.org. This website was developed by the same parties as above, but focuses more on residential windows.
- Thermal Bridging: https://en.wikipedia.org/wiki/Thermal_bridge#.
- Understanding Air Barriers: http://buildingscience.com/documents /digests/bsd-104-understanding-air-barriers.
- Cool Roof Rating Council: www.coolroofs.org.
- National Fenestration Rating Council: www.nfrc.org.

Lighting Systems and Visual Comfort

We need quality light to do our work and live our lives, whether it is at a computer, an assembly line, a kitchen, or a lounge. Visual comfort means having enough light, but not too much. The space around us should feel cheery and inviting, not drab and gloomy. Light should be balanced; not too warm, not too cool. We should be able to enjoy views to the out-of-doors, but the windows we look through should not be a source of uncomfortable glare or unnecessary heat gain. Skylights and roof apertures should diffuse and filter the light that passes through and not create hot spots.

The systems that provide quality illumination are extremely important in order to reach the low EUIs needed to achieve ZNE. Electric lighting is the largest component of energy use in most commercial buildings. Not only does electric lighting directly use energy, it also creates heat that must be removed by cooling systems. In typical commercial buildings, electric lighting directly accounts for about 25 percent of energy use — about the same as heating, cooling, and ventilation combined.[13] The numbers are even higher for some building types like retail stores, or in temperate climates where HVAC energy is lower.

Daylighting is the most efficient of all lighting systems. It requires no energy and when utilized properly, adds little heat gain. It's also resilient during power outages or emergencies. However, providing good daylight and visual comfort in our buildings can be one of the more challenging aspects of design, requiring careful coordination among the architect, lighting designer, and the interior architect.

Quality daylighting begins with the design of the building envelope. Windows need to be carefully positioned in the building, glazing materials need to be selected with the right solar optic properties (SHGC and VT), and they need to be shaded with overhangs or other devices to block direct sunlight when this can be a source of glare. Interior spaces need to be carefully laid out so that work stations are positioned to receive the right amount of light and workers are not looking toward sources of glare. The materials and colors selected for walls, ceilings, and floors

Figure 2-6: Office Daylighting

This image shows a typical office space at the NREL Research Support Facility. Daylight is reflected onto the ceiling and trusses by LightLouver devices located in the upper part of each window. See figure 2-4 for details. (Source: Dennis Schroeder, NREL.)

need to have a light color, both to reduce gloom and to reflect light deeper into the space. The height of partitions needs to be limited so as not to block daylight. Finally, the electric lighting system needs to be designed to provide light at night and to supplement daylight in areas too far from windows or skylights. The electric lighting system should use efficient lamps and luminaries, and should incorporate controls so that the electric lighting is used only when needed, i.e., when the space is occupied and there is inadequate daylight.

HISTORICAL PERSPECTIVES

Until 1879, when Thomas Edison found a way to make electric light commercially practical, indoor lighting was provided by fire—e.g., with natural gas, kerosene lamps, and candles. Edison's first electric lamp was not all that practical, since it only lasted for thirteen hours, but it paved the

---

Lighting Terms

Efficacy. Lighting efficacy is the ratio of the total light produced to watts of power needed to produce the light (lumens per watt). Like miles per gallon for automobiles, the higher the number, the more efficient the system. A standard incandescent lamp produces only about 10–15 lumens per watt, but modern fluorescent and LED technologies are ten to twenty times more efficient.

Color Temperature. Color temperature is an indication of how warm or cool a particular lighting source is. Incandescent lamps have a warm color temperature of less than 3,000°K. Color temperatures over 5,000°K are cool. Most fluorescent lamps have a color temperature of about 3,500°K.

Glare. Glare is visual discomfort or difficult in seeing as result of a bright light source. Direct sunlight through windows or reflections through windows are common sources of glare.

Color Rendering Index (CRI). CRI is the ability of a light source to reveal the colors of various objects faithfully in comparison with an ideal or natural light source. The point of reference is a quality incandescent lamp, which is defined to have a CRI of 100. High-quality fluorescent lamps have CRIs greater than 80. High-pressure sodium and mercury vapor lamps have the worst CRIs, at less than 25.

way for a whole new way of producing illumination. Edison's first lamp was what we call an incandescent lamp because light is created by passing electricity through a carbon wire (called a *filament*). When sufficient electricity passes through the wire, it gets hot and begins to glow—to incandesce.[14] To keep the filament from burning up, it is encased in a glass bulb to deprive it of oxygen, and this is why we call them "lightbulbs." Incandescent lamps produce more heat than light and are not very efficient by modern standards.

Nevertheless, incandescent technology was the primary electric lighting source in just about all our buildings until General Electric made the fluorescent lamp commercially available in 1938. The fluorescent lamp produced a lot more light and did it with a lot less energy. The efficacy of early fluorescent lamps (including the power of their ballasts) was in the range of 40 lumens per watt—three to four times more efficient than incandescent lamps. Today, the efficacy of the best fluorescent lamps is greater than 100 lumens per watt.

Before World War II, daylighting was still the primary source of illumination. Most offices and work environments were designed so that everyone was fairly close to a window or a skylight, since inefficient incandescent lamps did not produce much light and were expensive to operate. Offices also had tall ceilings and windows. This configuration worked well for daylighting as well as natural ventilation. Before the fluorescent lamp and air-conditioning, both of which became widespread in the 1940s, architects and lighting designers better understood the principles of daylighting and used those principles in just about all buildings.

Pay attention to buildings constructed before World War II. You will notice that most of them have courtyards, light wells, and other features to enable most of the interior space to be close to windows and the services provided by windows—light and air. These older buildings tend to have a lot of exterior perimeter in relation to the floor space they enclose. Most modern buildings, especially high-rise towers, are just the opposite. The floor plate is square or rectangular and quite large. As a result, a much smaller percentage of floor space is close enough to windows to

Figure 2-7: Example of Pre–World War II Office Building with High Perimeter for Daylighting
The Russ Building in San Francisco was built in 1927 and stood for thirty years as the tallest building west of Chicago. The building has narrow floor plates and high windows so that most spaces enjoy the benefits of daylight and natural ventilation. It's still a prestigious address. (Source: Charles Eley.)

enjoy the benefits of the free light and air. As discussed earlier, many ZNE buildings are returning to the principles of narrow buildings with more interior space close to windows.

By the mid-1950s everything had changed, not only with regard to building shape but also lighting design. The office spaces in the popular TV series *Mad Men* are a good example: fluorescent lighting fixtures are placed quite close together, and each fixture had four fluorescent tubes. Don Draper's office was vastly overlighted and used far more electricity than was necessary. Lighting design in this era was less about providing illumination and more about fitting in as many fixtures as could be accommodated. My first job as an architectural apprentice was positioning two-foot-by-four-foot lighting fixtures in reflected ceiling plans. The goal of my job had less to do with providing light and more to do with arranging lighting fixtures in a pleasing way that did not conflict with air vents and other ceiling accessories.

Office lighting designs in this era used something on the order of four to five watts of electric power per square foot of floor area. There was little or no consideration of daylighting, since it was a lot easier to just fill the ceiling with light fixtures. For a while there was even a trend for luminous ceilings with continuous wall-to-wall lighting fixtures. Controls were an afterthought. Often the only way to turn the lights off in a 1950s-era office or commercial building was to locate the electric panel and trip the circuit breakers. Even worse, the lights in some buildings were considered to be part of the heating system, so they were left on all night so that the building did not cool down too much.

This wasteful design mentality continued through the 1960s and persisted until 1973, when the shock of the OPEC oil embargo provided the first wake-up call on our wasteful energy practices. The transition to greater efficiency was a slow process, but following the long gas lines and high fuel prices, we began to make progress toward more-efficient lighting systems. We still have a long way to go, but the best lighting systems in our modern offices and work environments use only 10 percent or so of the energy that was typically used for lighting in the 1950s and 1960s. They are also more visually comfortable and even look better.

LIGHTING TECHNOLOGY

Efficient electric lighting systems begin with high-efficacy lamps and ballasts. Modern fluorescent lamps have a smaller diameter, measuring only an inch or in some cases five-eighths of an inch. The best of these lamps produce something on the order of 110 lumens per watt—at least ten times more efficient than standard incandescent lamps. These linear light sources are appropriate for a wide range of lighting applications, from offices and meeting rooms to warehouses and retail stores. Fluorescent lamps used to have poor coloring, i.e., reds and other warm colors were not as vivid and skin colors looked pale and lifeless. They also

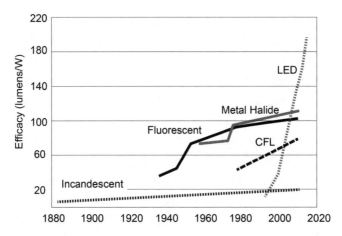

Figure 2-8: Efficacy Improvement of Various Lighting Technologies

The efficacy of most lighting technologies has steadily improved over time. The fluorescent lamp had an efficacy of only 38 lm/W when it was first introduced, but modern fluorescent lamps are now well over 100 lm/W. Light-emitting diodes (LEDs), first introduced in the 1990s, are the most recent fluorescent lighting technology. The original LEDs had a low efficacy, but modern products are over 150 lm/W and LEDs are expected to exceed 200 lm/W in the near future. (Source: LED Academy, http://www.ledacademy.net/5-1-high-efficacy/.)

had a tendency to flicker. However, fluorescent technology has improved significantly and is available in a range of color temperatures; modern high-frequency ballasts have virtually eliminated flicker. Fluorescent lamps are still the workhorses in most commercial buildings, but, as we will see, they are being replaced by modern LED lamps.

A different variety of fluorescent lamp is the compact fluorescent lamp, or CFL. CFLs are still tubes but instead of being linear, they often have a curly shape that emulates the standard incandescent lightbulb. Some of these have integral ballasts and are designed to be direct replacements for screw-in incandescent lamps. Others fit in special housings with separate ballasts. CFLs are far more efficient than the incandescent lamps they are designed to replace, but are not nearly as efficient as the four-foot-long tubes described in the previous paragraph. Their efficacy is in the range of 40–80 lumens per watt, about halfway between incandescent lamps and the best long-tube fluorescent lamps.

The latest and most promising lamp technology is light-emitting diodes (LED). These are solid-state lighting systems that are manufactured using a process similar to that of computer chips. LED lamps are very directional, which makes them good for applications where lighting fixtures need to be located some distance from the visual task. Examples are streetlights and indoor fixtures for gymnasiums or high-bay manufacturing and warehousing. LEDs are also making headway into other applications. There are LED replacements for fluorescent tubes and compact varieties that can screw into incandescent sockets.

CMTA Engineering in Louisville, Kentucky, has designed a number of ZNE buildings, mostly schools. Tony Hans, a principal there, reports that they use only LED lighting in their buildings and that the installed power for their schools is between 0.4 and 0.5 watts per square foot—about one-tenth of that used in Don Draper's office. Tony reports that lighting power is so low that daylighting has far less importance in reducing energy use, but is still used because of its other advantages.

One of the most exciting applications for LEDs is replacements for display lighting in retail stores and galleries. Merchants like a lot of light on items that are for sale; as they say, "light sells." The track lights that you see in most retail stores are mostly inefficient incandescent or halogen lamps. And not only are these inefficient, but additional air-conditioning is needed to remove all the heat they produce. LEDs have the potential to reduce the lighting used for this application by two or three orders of magnitude, and also to significantly reduce the heat produced by the lights, which means that stores will require less air-conditioning.

The Edge office building in Amsterdam is perhaps a picture of the future potential for LED lighting.[15] The LED luminaires in this building use so little energy that they can be powered through the Ethernet cables used for data communication. The alternating-current (AC) wiring to the lighting is eliminated and replaced by direct-current (DC) wiring that is part of the plug-and-play CAT5 or CAT6 cables (the kind you plug into your computer for Internet service). The ceiling panels are packed with sensors to measure motion, light, temperature, humidity, and more. This information is used to control lighting as well as HVAC and other systems. Every luminaire is addressable and can be turned off or dimmed by the sensors, but employees can use their smart phones to request more or less light.

DAYLIGHTING AND CONTROLS

The best way to reduce lighting energy is to not turn on the lights at all. This can be achieved when we return to the principles of daylighting and use the free energy of the sun. The best daylighted buildings have narrow floor plans so that more space is close to windows. The best solar orientations for daylighting are south-facing and north-facing windows. East-facing and west-facing windows are more difficult to shade with fixed devices, and the balance shifts away from useful daylighting and more toward unwanted solar gains and visible glare. Effective window design is finding the right balance between the desirable daylight and the undesirable heat gains. Both the NREL RSF and the Iowa Utilities Board building have a narrow building profile that extends in an east–west direction. Automatic exterior blinds like those used at RMI and the Bullitt Center can provide the necessary shading for awkward orientations, but at a cost.

Daylighted spaces should also have high ceilings. Daylight will reach into the space a distance of about 1.5 times the distance from the floor to the top of the window, so it is important to position the windows as high in the space as possible. With special devices like light shelves or reflective louvers, useful daylight can reach as far as thirty feet. The NREL Research Support Building uses a LightLouver™ device in the top portion of the south-facing windows to reflect daylight onto the ceiling and bounce it deep into the space. (See figs. 2-4 and 2-6.)

No energy is saved if you don't turn off the electric lights when daylighting is available. *Controls* are just a fancy way to say "light switches." Controls can be manual or automatic. Occupant sensors are a type of automatic control with sensors that determine if a room is occupied; after five or ten minutes of "vacancy," a switch automatically shuts off the lights. Occupant sensors are very common these days. Some are simple wall box replacements, but these only work well in small rooms. When the sensor is located in the ceiling, it can "see" more of the room and is more effective in determining "vacancy" and avoiding false positives. One of the annoying characteristics of poorly placed occupant sensors is that they sometimes turn off the lights when an occupant is sitting quietly, but modern technology includes both ultrasonic and passive infrared sensors that minimize this problem.

Time clocks are another useful automatic control. These can be programmed to turn off the lights automatically at a specified time, usually with the ability for local override if someone is working late. Time clocks are also available as wall box replacements, but in larger commercial buildings most time clocks are centrally located to make it easier for building managers to keep their time schedules current with the needs of occupants.

Photo switches use light sensors to determine if enough illumination is being provided by daylight. The electric lights are then either turned off or dimmed in response. All of the controls and switches can be integrated into a building energy management system (EMS) that enables building operators and managers to keep the programs up to date and to monitor energy performance (see ch. 5 for more information).

A modern building with integrated lighting controls is an intelligent building. Lights come on when they are needed and automatically shut off when they are not. Lighting power responds to available daylight; when daylighting is adequate, the electric lights are automatically shut off. On cloudy days, some of the lights come on to supplement the daylighting. Occupant sensors shut off lights when spaces are not being used, and in the most advanced systems, this information is conveyed to a building-level energy management system that learns from the signals it receives and tunes the building time clocks.

The lighting industry has made great strides in the last forty years to improve both the quality and the energy efficiency of lighting systems. However, few new buildings take full advantage of daylighting, efficient sources, and controls, and most existing buildings still use substandard and inefficient systems. The energy that can be saved in a short period of time from improving these old systems will more than pay for the initial investment. As a result, a new form of business, the energy service company (ESCO), has emerged to take advantage of these opportunities in existing buildings. ESCOs install new and efficient lighting systems (as well as other improvements) at no cost to the owner, and they recover their investment from future energy savings.

LIGHTING POWER DENSITIES

Energy standards limit the amount of installed lighting power that can be used in buildings. Figure 2-9 shows how these numbers have declined over the years as new technology has been developed. The lighting power allowed in the most recent standard is less than half the power allowed in the original standards. Figure 2-9 shows the requirements for just a few of the building types addressed by standards; these requirements are expressed either for the whole building or for individual spaces within the building.

FOR MORE INFORMATION

• Daylight Pattern Guide, New Buildings Institute, http://www.ad vancedbuildings.net/daylighting-pattern-guide

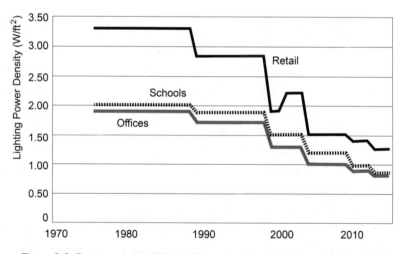

Figure 2-9: Representative Lighting Power Density Limits from Standard 90.1

This data was compiled by the author for various versions of ASHRAE Standard 90.1 since it was introduced in 1975.

- Advanced Lighting Guidelines, New Buildings Institute, https://alg online.org/
- California Lighting Technology Center, www.cltc.ucdavis.edu

Heating, Cooling, Ventilation, and Thermal Comfort

Most people are thermally comfortable when the air temperature is in the range of 68–78°F. But, when mechanical cooling is unavailable, people adapt to warmer conditions in the summer and cooler conditions in the winter, i.e., the comfort envelope drifts toward higher temperatures in the summer and drops toward lower temperatures in the winter. The temperature comfort range also moves around depending on humidity, the temperature of the surrounding surfaces (mean radiant temperature or MRT), and the velocity of air moving across the space. When you are sitting next to a cold window, the surrounding air temperature needs to be warmer to make up for the radiant losses from your body to that cold surface. When you are sitting next to a warm surface, the air temperature needs to be cooler. When there is a gentle air movement across our bodies, we are comfortable at a higher temperature. With higher humidity, the temperature range for comfort is cooler. Comfort also depends on how active we are (our metabolic rate) and what we are wearing (our clothing level).

Researchers have developed models that take all these factors into account and predict the likelihood that people will be comfortable for a given set of conditions. One of the more valuable tools is the Thermal Comfort Tool developed by the UC Berkeley Center for the Built Environment.[16] For given conditions of air temperature, mean radiant temperature, humidity level, air speed, metabolic rate, and clothing level, the tool will give the predicted mean vote (PMV), which is a scale between −3 (cold) and +3 (hot) with zero being neutral (neither hot nor cold). The tool also gives the predicted percent dissatisfied (PPD), which is, of course, related to the PMV. (See fig. 2-10.) It is important to understand that thermal comfort is a state of mind. When one person is comfortable, another in the same space might be cold and yet another might be hot. The common threshold is to design for a PPD of 20 percent, i.e., 80 percent of people are comfortable. This translates to a PMV between +1 and −1.

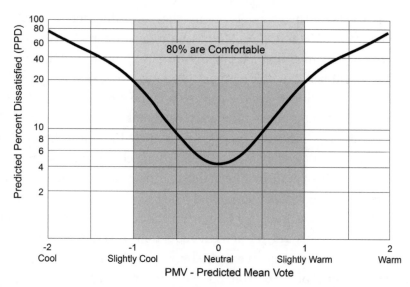

Figure 2-10: Predicted Mean Vote (PMV) and Predicted Percent Dissatisfied (PPD)
The horizontal scale is the predicted mean vote (PMV). The shaded area indicates the range of human satisfaction. The vertical scale is logarithmic and shows the predicted percentage of dissatisfied (PPD). The heavy line shows the relationship between PMV and PPD.

When it is too cold we add heat to the building, and when it is too hot we remove heat. When the air is too dry we add moisture, and when it is too humid we remove moisture. We also need to provide outside air to the building, either through operable windows or through mechanical fans, so that the indoor air is not too contaminated by carbon dioxide (CO_2) or other pollutants that are produced by both people and the building furnishings. When the outside air is itself contaminated, it needs to be filtered or treated before it is brought into the building. These are the functions of the heating, ventilating, and air-conditioning (HVAC) systems in buildings.

For most buildings, engineers try to keep the temperature of the entire building within an acceptable range of comfort, but the designers of the Rocky Mountain Institute Innovation Center in Basalt, Colorado, took a different approach (see appendix). Since comfort conditions for every person are different, the designers let the temperature of the building naturally drift toward being warm on sunny days and cool at night and on cold, cloudy days. Their models predict that the indoor temperature will range between 64°F and 82°F. (The building just opened at the time of this writing, and they don't yet know for sure how wide the temperature swing will be.) A wider temperature range reduces energy use and improves the effectiveness of the passive solar heating systems.[17] To compensate for the temperature drifts, each occupant has their own personal comfort system, which includes a Hyperchair with built-in heating and cooling elements as well as five-volt USB-powered fans for use on warm days.[18] The chair operates on rechargeable batteries and automatically turns off when the desk is unoccupied. The personal comfort system was developed by the UC Berkeley Center for the Built Environment, which predicts it can result in a 30 percent reduction in HVAC electricity use and a 39 percent reduction in gas use for a typical California office.[19] The idea is to heat or cool the person, not the whole building. Comfort at RMI is also enhanced by super-efficient quadruple-glazed windows that have an interior surface temperature much warmer than typical windows and closer to the indoor air temperature.

The HVAC system is at least as important as lighting in terms of energy efficiency, and is even more important in many climates.[20] In contrast to lighting energy, the pattern of HVAC energy is much more dependent on climate. Naturally, cold northern climates have a much larger heating load and warmer southern climates have a much larger cooling load. Humidity also varies with climate; the western United States is mostly dry while the eastern United States is mostly humid, especially in the summer.

CONVENTIONAL SYSTEMS

Thermal loads in commercial buildings can vary significantly depending on their orientation and the available energy services.[21] The variation is temporal, but also spatial. East-facing spaces can require cooling in the morning, when they are exposed to sun, and require heating later in the day, when the sun passes to the other side of the building. Some spaces in the building may require heating even as other spaces require cooling.

Nevertheless, it is typical for all spaces in commercial buildings to be served by the same HVAC system, despite each space having a different thermal load. In the 1960s and 1970s, it was common practice to solve this problem by delivering a constant volume of cool air to all spaces in the building and then warm the air back up with electric-resistance heaters when a space required heating or less cooling. First cooling the air and then warming it up before it is delivered to the space is terribly inefficient and indeed seems preposterous, yet this was common practice for decades. These inefficient constant-volume reheat systems (CVRH) systems have mostly been phased out, but some are still used in hospitals and laboratories, where it is important to maintain air-pressure differentials between rooms in order to control the migration of contaminants.

The most common system used in large buildings today is the variable air-volume (VAV) system, which is like a CVRH system but works by first reducing the volume of air sent to a space to the minimum before the air is warmed up. The minimal volume of air is either the least amount required to cool the space or the least amount required for outside air ventilation, whichever is greater. Cooling air and then warming it back up still occurs, but the energy impact is reduced. Also, reheating at the space level is typically accomplished with more-efficient hot-water coils instead of electric resistance. The volume of air sent to a space can't be completely shut off because the space requires a minimum amount of outside air ventilation. VAV systems can be quite efficient when well designed and when efficient chillers, boilers, cooling towers, and fans are used.[22] They are still the favored system of many leading HVAC designers.

A major advantage of VAV and other conventional air-delivery systems is that they can shut down mechanical cooling and operate with 100 percent outside air when outdoor conditions are suitable. All the return air is exhausted and replaced by all outside air; no air is recirculated. Controls that enable this pattern of operation are known as *economizers*. Simple economizers monitor the temperature (and sometimes humidity) of outside air, and when it is cool enough (and dry enough) to provide cooling, the system shifts to economizer mode and the mechanical cooling is disabled or scaled back. Integrated economizers can operate when the outside air is cooler than the return air (a much wider temperature range); the mechanical equipment is still operated but not at full capacity. Economizers are not as effective in humid climates because removing moisture from the outside air is energy-intensive.

Blowing air around a building is still the most common means of providing heating and cooling, but other, more-efficient options are emerging. A one-inch water pipe can move the same amount of heat as a sixty-inch air duct.[23] For this reason, many of the emerging low-energy systems use water or other fluids instead of air to transfer heat. These include localized fan coils, water-source heat pumps, variable refrigerant flow systems, active and passive chilled beams, and radiant floors (both heated and cooled). These advanced systems are often used in combination with a dedicated outside air system (DOAS) to provide fresh ventilation air.

PASSIVE HEATING AND COOLING

The most efficient way to maintain thermal comfort in our buildings is with passive solar design, with mechanical heating or cooling used only for backup. Windows are positioned facing south and shaded with overhangs to block the summer sun but let the winter sun pass through. Exposed thermal mass is warmed by the sun and provides inertia to help maintain thermal comfort after sunset. Operable windows are opened when it gets too hot and the building is cooled by natural ventilation. Passive solar works pretty well in residences and other buildings where heating is dominant, but there are two major challenges in applying passive solar to most commercial buildings. First, cooling loads (not heating) are dominant in most commercial buildings even in northern climates, and passive cooling strategies are limited. Second, most passive solar heating strategies depend on direct sunlight entering the building, and this can be a source of glare and visual discomfort in work environments, thus conflicting with good daylighting. Passive solar in commercial buildings still works in spaces like corridors, atriums, and lounges where direct sunlight is desirable and visual tasks are less critical, but its application is limited.

However, the RMI Innovation Center has been able to combine passive solar and daylighting (see appendix). Glare is managed by maintaining a walkway on the south perimeter of the building, so that no one is sitting right next to a window. An interior light shelf provides shade for nearby workstations, and manually operated blinds provide additional glare control. The circulation areas at the south wall and in the interior have a polished concrete surface so that the thermal mass can better absorb the sun's energy during the day and release it at night. RMI also uses a high-tech phase-change material within the light shelves and just behind the drywall of interior walls. This is attached to the framing members, similar to batt insulation.[24] The phase-change materials are intended primarily for cooling, so at night, ventilation air cools the material and causes it to "freeze" at about 77°F. The light shelf and walls maintain this temperature during the following day until the phase-change material melts. Only then does its temperature rise. Under heating conditions, the material works in reverse. The material looks a little like bubble wrap, with each cell filled with the phase-change material. Typical thermal mass consists of heavy concrete or masonry, but phase-change materials can do the same job in a much lighter configuration.

The RMI Innovation Center also relies on natural ventilation for cooling, as do many other energy-efficient buildings such as the Bullitt Center, the Iowa Utilities Board building, the NREL RSF, and the Stanford Y2E2 Building. One of the challenges is to make sure that the HVAC systems don't try to heat and cool the outdoors when the windows are open. A common strategy is to use the security switches commonly installed on operable windows and to link these with the energy-management system so that the heating and/or cooling is disabled when the windows are open. The Iowa Utilities Board building and the Y2E2 Building both lock out the HVAC system when the windows in a space are open.

Nighttime heat flushing is a design strategy that is related to natural ventilation. Windows are opened at night when the outdoor air temperature is low. The cool air removes heat from the walls, roofs, floors, and furniture within the building. If these elements have enough thermal mass, they will provide enough inertia to stay cool through the following

Table 2-4 — Heating and Cooling Technologies

Function	Fuel	Equipment Type	Description
Heating	Electricity	Electric-Resistance	Electric-resistance heating is the least efficient form of electric heat and should be avoided in most instances. A high-quality form of energy (electricity) is converted to a low-quality form of energy (heat). Electric-resistance heat is used for baseboards around the perimeter of buildings, or as the heating element of a furnace or boiler.
		Air-Source Heat Pumps	Air-source heat pumps work like direct-expansion air conditioners but in reverse. They "pump" heat from the outdoors to the indoors. The efficiency of air-source heat pumps declines when the outside air temperature is low, which is when a building will typically need the most heat.
		Water-Source Heat Pumps	Water-source heat pumps also use the refrigeration cycle to "pump" heat, but the source of the heat is water rather than air. The advantage of water is that it can usually be maintained at a warmer temperature, which improves the efficiency of the equipment. When the condensing water is cooled (or warmed) by the ground, the system is referred to as a ground-source or geothermal heat pump.
	Gas	Furnace	Gas is burned to produce heat that in turn is used to warm air. Most furnaces operate in conjunction with fans that blow air through a heat exchanger. Furnaces are classified as condensing and non-condensing. *Condensing* means that some of the flue gases reach a low temperature and become liquid. Non-condensing furnaces have efficiencies up to about 85 percent while condensing furnaces have efficiencies of about 95 percent.
		Boiler	Gas is burned to produce heat that in turn is used to make hot water or steam. Most modern boilers are the condensing type and operate at efficiencies greater than 95 percent. Pumps deliver the hot water to convection baseboards, radiant panels, or heating coils.

Table 2-4 — continued

Function	Fuel	Equipment Type	Description
Cooling	Electricity	Direct-Expansion	Direct-expansion (DX) air-conditioning is the most common system for room air conditioners, split systems, and rooftop air conditioners. A refrigerant is compressed at the condenser, where heat is rejected. The refrigerant leaves the condenser as a liquid. As it passes through an expansion valve in the evaporator, it changes state from a liquid to a gas and becomes cool. Air is blown over evaporator coils and delivered to the building.
		Chilled Water	Chillers also use the refrigeration cycle to chill water instead of air. The chilled water is then pumped to cooling coils, chilled beams, or radiant surfaces. Chillers can be water cooled, in which case they are connected to a cooling tower or other supply of water, or they may be air cooled. Larger chillers are commonly water cooled. Chillers are classified by the technology used to compress the refrigerant. Older chillers used reciprocating pistons as in a car engine, but these are less common today. Screw chillers are common up to about 500 tons, but larger chillers are centrifugal.
	Gas	Engine-Driven Chillers	These chillers can use any of the technologies described above, but the electric motor is replaced with a gas engine. These are less common.
		Absorption Chillers	Absorption chillers use a thermal process to make chilled water. They are used where natural gas or some other form of heat is abundant or the cost of electricity is very high.

day as outdoor temperatures rise and heat is produced within the building by people and computers. Nighttime flushing is more effective for buildings with significant thermal mass, which is why the designers of the RMI Innovation Center incorporated phase-change materials. Nighttime flushing, coupled with high thermal mass, is a strategy for many other energy-efficient buildings, including the Bullitt Center, NREL, and the Iowa Utilities Board building. The strategy is most effective in climates where there is a big temperature difference between night and day.

GROUND-SOURCE HEAT PUMPS

The Bullitt Center, the Iowa Utilities Board building, Richardsville Elementary School, and many other ZNE buildings use ground-source heat pumps, also called geothermal heat pumps. Ground-source heat pumps are a favorite of Tony Hans of CMTA Engineers, which has designed a number of ZNE buildings. Heat pumps use the refrigeration cycle to "pump" heat from a source to a sink. The efficiency of the process is vastly improved when the temperature difference between the source and the sink is low. For conventional heat pumps, both the source and the sink are air, and on cold days the temperature difference between the inside air and the outside air can be 60°F or more; at these extremes, a conventional heat pump has very little capacity and is supplemented by less efficient electric-resistance heat. By contrast, a ground-source heat pump uses the earth as the source in heating mode and as the sink in cooling mode. Wells are drilled into the earth a depth of 300–600 feet, and a piping loop is dropped into each hole and grouted for good heat transfer. A manifold couples the piping loops near the surface. The result is near-constant water temperature to serve as the sink (cooling mode) or source (heating mode). Heat can be "pumped" back and forth from the building to the more stable water temperature. The Bullitt Center uses water-to-water heat pumps that are used to warm or cool the concrete slabs that separate the floors of the building. The Iowa Utilities Board building and Richardsville Elementary use the more conventional water-to-air heat pump in which air is passed over a direct-expansion coil and blown into the space that is to be heated or cooled.

Ground-source heat pumps work best in climates where there is an annual balance between heating and cooling. If the system is used in applications where there is only a cooling load, the ground around the wells can warm up over time, reducing the efficiency of the system. Similarly, if they are used in applications where there is only a heating load, the ground around the wells will cool, again reducing efficiency.

Typical GSHP systems are closed-loop, but an open-loop variation called an aquifer thermal storage system (ATES) is used in the Netherlands and other parts of Europe. The Edge ZNE building in Amsterdam uses a system like this.[25] In its basic form, an ATES system consists of two wells that provide seasonal thermal storage. One well is used for heat storage, and the other for cold storage. During winter, (warm) groundwater is extracted from the heat storage well and injected in the cold storage well. During summer, the flow direction is reversed such that (cold) groundwater is extracted from the cold storage well and injected in the heat storage well. Heating and cooling are provided by heat exchangers and supplemented by water-to-water heat pumps. These systems require a careful analysis of natural water flow within the aquifer and of other soil conditions. Such systems are only applicable when there is a suitable aquifer and codes permit an open system.[26]

RADIANT FLOORS

The Bullitt Center uses radiant floors for both heating and cooling, but this is supplemented by natural ventilation, nighttime flushing, and high-performance windows with automatic exterior shading. A continuous loop of PEX tubing is laid out on the floor for each thermal zone before the concrete slab is poured. Water is then pumped through the tubing to either heat or cool the slab. Radiant slabs, which provide a very comfortable form of heat, have been used for years and their popularity is resurging. They work most effectively with hard surfaces like those used at the Bullitt Center, and are far less effective when the floor is covered with carpet, which provides a layer of insulation. Radiant slabs are slow to respond to changing loads or temperature requirements, but Paul Schwer of PAE engineers notes that this has not been a problem at the Bullitt Center because the building envelope is so tight and well insulated.

Cooling with radiant slabs can be tricky, especially in humid climates. Dan Nall, an engineer who has designed a number of buildings he calls "thermally active," recommends that the temperature of the floor not be cooled below about 68°F to avoid condensation, which can cause slipping and become a serious safety hazard. Furthermore, radiant slab cooling has a very limited capacity and only works for buildings where both internal and external loads are very low. The technology is effective at the Bullitt Center because solar gains are controlled with exterior blinds, triple glazing, and lots of insulation.

CHILLED CEILINGS AND BEAMS

Another low-energy system, chilled beams, are used in the Packard Foundation building and the Stanford Y2E2 Building. Chilled beams can be active or passive. With passive chilled beams, chilled water is passed through the "beam," which is integrated into the ceiling like a light fixture. As the air around the beam is cooled, it becomes denser and descends to the floor. The cool air is replaced by warmer air moving up from below, and the result is a constant flow of convection cooling. There is also a radiant-cooling component, since the surface of the chilled beam is cooler than the room air. An active chilled beam has a small fan that assists with air movement; these work better in a cooling mode. A variation is a chilled ceiling, in which the pipes are located behind metal ceiling plates. Chilled ceilings rely more on radiant cooling, since the effectiveness of convection is much less.

Like radiant floors, chilled beams and ceilings have a limited cooling and heating capacity and are only effective in buildings that have very low internal and external loads. In humid climates, temperature and humidity must be carefully controlled to avoid condensation, i.e., interior rain.

EVAPORATIVE COOLING

When you add moisture to dry air, it lowers the temperature but increases humidity. The ZNE offices for DPR Construction in Phoenix take advantage of this ancient principle to reduce energy use and achieve ZNE (see appendix). Evaporative cooling does not work everywhere, but the Phoenix area has the ideal climate—warm and dry. The Phoenix project wraps an old concept in catchy new terms. A *shower tower* is where incoming outdoor air passes through a mist of water to reduce its temperature. A *solar chimney* on the other side of the building is used to induce ventilation through the building.

DEDICATED OUTSIDE-AIR SYSTEMS

Warming up or cooling down the outside air that is brought into the building uses a significant amount of energy. Most of the low-energy systems described above provide heating and/or cooling but do not deliver a positive supply of outside air to the space. For this reason they are often coupled with a dedicated outside-air system (DOAS) that provides this function. The sole purpose of the DOAS is to bring outside-air ventilation into the building; in some cases this is also used to reduce humidity. A big advantage of having a separate system for outside-air ventilation is that this makes it easier to recover heat and even moisture through heat wheels and other heat-recovery devices.

The Bullitt Center uses a very simple heat-recovery wheel. Warm air being exhausted from the building passes through one side of the wheel, which has a honeycombed pattern of air passages. Cool outside air is brought through the other side of the wheel through the same honeycombed air passages. The wheel slowly rotates such that about 65 percent of the heat leaving the building is transferred to the air entering the building. Heat-recovery devices like this are major energy-efficiency features. Most other ZNE buildings, including the RMI Innovation Center, also have a DOAS with heat recovery.

DISPLACEMENT VENTILATION

Displacement ventilation systems use air to heat and cool spaces but are different from VAV and other more-conventional HVAC systems in that air is distributed mostly by gravity. Traditional systems deliver air through ceiling diffusers in order to condition the whole space. With displacement ventilation systems, air is delivered near the floor at a low velocity and at warmer temperature (63–65°F) as compared to a typical 55°F supply temperature for conventional systems. This higher supply temperature increases the range within which economizers can operate.

Such a system has other advantages as well. Displacement venti-

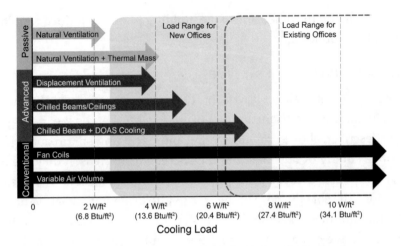

Figure 2-11: HVAC System Applicability for Various Cooling Loads

This information is derived from a presentation by Erin McConahey of Arup North American Ltd., delivered in October 2014 at the Pacific Energy Center. (Graphic developed by the author.)

lation does a better job of providing cooling where it is needed. The cool air "puddles" at the floor, since it is denser than the room air. This displaces warmer and more contaminated room air, which rises to the ceiling where it is collected and returned to the air handler, where it is filtered or exhausted. The cool air rises more quickly over people and other warm objects, providing a gentle, localized thermal plume of vertical airflow. This is an important benefit in classrooms and work environments because there is far less mixing of contaminants than with conventional systems. In fact, it becomes less likely that a child with a cold will infect the other students.

CAVEATS AND APPLICATIONS

Most low-energy systems only work in buildings that have very low peak cooling loads. The peak cooling load is the amount of heat that needs to be removed from a space on the hottest day. Natural ventilation only works when the loads are below about 2 W/ft²; the threshold can be increased to about 4 W/ft² if natural ventilation is coupled with nighttime cooling and significant thermal mass to provide heat storage, like the system used at the Bullitt Center and the RMI Innovation Center. Displacement ventilation only works when the cooling load in the space is below about 4 W/ft². Chilled beams or ceilings work up to about 4.5 W/ft² but higher if they are combined with a DOAS. Conventional systems like fan coils and variable-air-volume systems work with just about any load range if they are made large enough.

Achieving cooling loads low enough to enable these low-energy systems is a design challenge for the whole team. It begins with the design of the building envelope. Windows need to be designed to minimize solar heat gains through proper orientation, selection of glazing materials, and shading. The electric lighting system needs to be designed with low-energy lamps and ballasts and controlled to operate only when the space is occupied and not daylighted. Perhaps the biggest challenge is managing plug loads, since this requires the participation of the building tenants or occupants (see ch. 5 for more on this). In modern buildings, the heat produced by computers, monitors, and other office equipment can be the largest component of cooling load.

FOR MORE INFORMATION

- Advanced Variable Air Volume System Design Guide, California Energy Commission, October 2003, http://www.energy.ca.gov/2003 publications/CEC-500-2003-082/CEC-500-2003-082-A-11.pdf.
- Energy Design Resources: https://energydesignresources.com. This website has a number of design briefs and guides on various advanced HVAC systems.
- Advanced VAV System Design Guide: https://energydesignresources .com/resources/publications/design-guidelines/designguidelines-ad vanced-variable-air-volume-(vav)-systems.aspx
- Articles from the folks at Taylor Engineering: http://www.taylor-engi neering.com/articles

How Low Can We Go?

The buildings and examples discussed in this chapter show how designers have significantly reduced energy use to levels that can be easily offset by renewable-energy systems. These designers have taken advantage of the unique opportunities afforded by each site as well as the needs of their specific clients. This contextual information reveals more opportunities than if buildings are designed in the abstract.

Sometimes, though, a more abstract analysis is useful. The US Department of Energy, with support of the national laboratories, has taken a broader look at building energy efficiency based on energy modeling. A series of energy models have been developed to represent nonresidential building types (see ch. 4 for more information on energy models). Weights are assigned to each model and the climate where it is located in order to represent the relative share of construction activity for that building type in that climate. The models represent about 80 percent of building construction, except for low-rise residential.

The models were originally developed by the National Renewable Energy Laboratory (NREL) based on national surveys (CBECS 2003), but they have been subsequently modified by Pacific Northwest National Laboratory (PNNL) as part of its support of the ASHRAE code-development process. About sixteen models have been developed to represent different kinds of offices, restaurants, health care facilities, and other building types. Since these are models (and not real buildings), the energy-efficiency features can be easily modified to predict an EUI for typical existing buildings, buildings that comply with the latest energy efficiency standards, and buildings that pull out all the stops and use all available design strategies and technologies.

The data produced by the national laboratories and other researchers is quite detailed, so I have simplified it here by consolidating similar climates into climate regions and by combining similar building types. (See fig. 2-3 for a description of the consolidated climate regions.) Table 2-5 shows the site EUIs for typical buildings at the turn of the millennium. The site EUIs are quite high, compared to the examples of ZNE buildings described in the previous pages. Office EUIs range between 58 and 77 in the lower forty-eight states. Retail is even higher, ranging from 99 to 142 in the lower forty-eight states.

Table 2-6 shows the estimated site EUIs for the same buildings and

Table 2-5 — EUIs for Typical Buildings at the Turn of the Millennium
(site Btu/ft²·yr)

The underlying data for this analysis are drawn from National Renewable Energy Laboratory EnergyPlus simulations (see: http://energy.gov/sites/prod/files/2013/12/f5/ref bldgs_eui_tables_1-4_7-0.pdf). This data has been consolidated and adjusted to better align with the data presented in tables 2-6 and 2-7. The NREL simulations include estimates for older buildings built before 1980 and buildings built between 1980 and 2000. The data below represent a weighted average of 60 percent pre-1980 and 40 percent post-1980.

	Pacific Coast	Warm and Dry	Hot and Humid	Warm and Humid	Cold and Dry	Cold and Humid	Arctic
	(3c, 4c)	(2b, 3b, 4b)	(1a, 2a)	(3a, 4a)	(5b, 6b)	(5a, 6a, 7)	(8)
Warehouses	34	20	23	40	53	65	161
Offices	58	62	69	69	69	77	126
Retail	101	86	99	114	122	142	249
Schools	70	59	71	78	77	91	165
Apartments	62	42	52	69	73	86	153
Hotels	122	99	119	126	126	134	151
Health Care	232	202	232	242	218	238	281
Restaurants	558	497	522	569	598	660	965

climates, but in compliance with the energy-efficiency requirements of Standard 90.1-2013, the latest national energy standard at the time of this writing. The differences are remarkable. For most building types and climates, the latter EUIs are half of that of a typical turn-of-the-millennium building. The most recent standard requires double-glazed, low-e windows, lots of insulation, efficient lighting, and efficient equipment, and it even requires daylighting in specific instances—but, as we will discuss in chapter 7, only a few states are enforcing such stringent standards.

Table 2-7 is an estimate of how low the EUIs would be if all technology known and available today were applied to the building models. These estimates result from a multiyear ASHRAE research project conducted

Table 2-6 — EUIs for Buildings in Compliance with Standard 90.1-2013 (site Btu/ft²·yr)

Source: Jason Glazer, GARD Analytics, "ASHRAE 1651-RP, Development of Maximum Technically Achievable Energy Targets for Commercial Buildings, Ultra-Low Energy Use Building," December 31, 2015. These data are similar to data generated by PNNL, but are used here to provide better consistency with the data for maximum technical potential in table 2-7.

	Pacific Coast	Warm and Dry	Hot and Humid	Warm and Humid	Cold and Dry	Cold and Humid	Arctic
	(3c, 4c)	(2b, 3b, 4b)	(1a, 2a)	(3a, 4a)	(5b, 6b)	(5a, 6a, 7)	(8)
Warehouses	16	15	12	17	20	26	33
Offices	22	31	33	32	31	34	41
Retail	35	49	48	50	53	59	81
Schools	35	46	49	47	48	50	68
Apartments	35	48	48	51	53	61	76
Offices/Data Centers	62	69	71	70	72	77	88
Hotels	57	75	80	78	77	83	100
Health Care	101	108	117	116	111	120	140
Restaurants	360	431	414	471	513	574	759

by Jason Glazer of GARD Analytics.[27] Jason investigated more than thirty advanced energy-efficiency measures. These included simple things like added roof insulation, LED lighting operating at 200 lm/W, and quadruple glazing like that used at the RMI Innovation Center. He also looked at more-complex design strategies like displacement ventilation, underfloor air distribution, and other advanced HVAC systems and controls. He factored in the use of high-efficiency office equipment, including monitors, photocopiers, etc. However, the scope of his study did not include savings related to refrigeration and cooking equipment in restaurants or strategies for reducing the energy use in data centers, and as a result, the savings potential for these building types are underestimated. The reductions vary by building type and climate, but for the most part, the EUIs are half of

Table 2-7 — Estimated Maximum Technical Potential EUIs (site Btu/ft²·yr)

Source: Jason Glazer, GARD Analytics, "ASHRAE 1651-RP, Development of Maximum Technically Achievable Energy Targets for Commercial Buildings, Ultra-Low Energy Use Building," December 31, 2015.

	Pacific Coast	Warm and Dry	Hot and Humid	Warm and Humid	Cold and Dry	Cold and Humid	Arctic
	(3c, 4c)	(2b, 3b, 4b)	(1a, 2a)	(3a, 4a)	(5b, 6b)	(5a, 6a, 7)	(8)
Warehouses	6	6	5	6	7	8	7
Offices	8	10	11	11	11	11	12
Retail	13	18	18	17	18	19	27
Schools	16	21	23	22	21	23	26
Apartments	24	30	29	31	32	34	35
Offices/Data Centers	43	47	47	44	47	46	47
Hotels	40	49	49	51	51	54	58
Health Care	63	64	68	67	66	69	72
Restaurants	265	323	324	336	343	353	377

those that would result from enforcement of the latest energy standards, and only a quarter of those of typical turn-of-the-millennium buildings.

You will notice significant variation by building type and some variation by climate zone. Restaurants have by far the largest EUIs because of all the energy required for walk-in freezers and refrigerators, cooking equipment, dishwashing, and kitchen ventilation. The energy use for restaurants is more than ten times greater than for typical offices, schools, and retail stores. It is possible for restaurants to rely less on frozen, pre-packaged foods and switch to farm-to-table freshness, but this is a paradigm shift that is not factored into the savings estimates and was not within the scope of Jason's study.

Hospitals are also quite energy-intensive because of longer hours of operation as well as specialized medical equipment. EUIs for hospitals range between 63 and 72, depending on climate. Hotels are also very

Table 2-8 — Construction Weights by Building Type and Climate

Source: Mark Halverson et al., Pacific Northwest National Laboratory, "ANSI/ASHRAE/IES Standard 90.1-2013 Determination of Energy Savings: Quantitative Analysis," PNNL-23479, August 2014. These data have been consolidated by the author into the climate regions and building types used in this book.

	Pacific Coast	Warm and Dry	Hot and Humid	Warm and Humid	Cold and Dry	Cold and Humid	Arctic	Sum
	(3c, 4c)	(2b, 3b, 4b)	(1a, 2a)	(3a, 4a)	(5b, 6b)	(5a, 6a, 7)	(8)	
Warehouses	0.0059	0.0295	0.0294	0.0541	0.0074	0.0409	0.0000	0.1671
Offices	0.0053	0.0185	0.0209	0.0386	0.0073	0.0258	0.0001	0.1166
Retail	0.0083	0.0278	0.0357	0.0696	0.0110	0.0567	0.0002	0.2092
Schools	0.0049	0.0175	0.0268	0.0575	0.0079	0.0388	0.0002	0.1535
Apartments	0.0116	0.0179	0.0438	0.0568	0.0051	0.0276	0.0000	0.1629
Offices/Data Centers	0.0027	0.0035	0.0043	0.0158	0.0012	0.0059	0.0000	0.0333
Hotels	0.0029	0.0112	0.0103	0.0218	0.0038	0.0168	0.0001	0.0668
Health Care	0.0039	0.0082	0.0112	0.0248	0.0049	0.0251	0.0000	0.0782
Restaurants	0.0004	0.0017	0.0022	0.0043	0.0006	0.0034	0.0000	0.0125
Sum	0.0459	0.1358	0.1846	0.3431	0.0491	0.2409	0.0006	1.0000

energy-intensive compared to offices, schools, and retail, with EUIs ranging from 40 to 58. Hotels are "24/7" operations and also contain energy-intensive restaurants.

The ASHRAE reference building for large offices includes a large data center, which causes this building model to have an EUI that is four to five times greater than that for small- and medium-sized offices that do not have a data center. For this reason, I have identified this large office as its own building type to distinguish it from typical offices. One of the lessons from this research and also from the low-EUI building examples reviewed in this chapter is that as we reduce the energy for lighting, ventilation, heating, and cooling, the share of energy for process and equipment increases significantly. For the Bullitt Center, about 47 percent of the energy use is for office equipment and miscellaneous appliances.[28] This is a growing concern for ZNE buildings that will be addressed in greater detail in chapter 5.

As part of the analysis, PNNL and its contractors estimated the number of square feet of building-construction activity for each building model and climate zone. While restaurants and health care facilities are very energy-intensive, there are not that many of them. Likewise, the EUIs for the Arctic climate region are significantly higher than those for the other regions, but there is considerably less construction activity there. Figure 2-12 combines the construction weights, the climate regions,

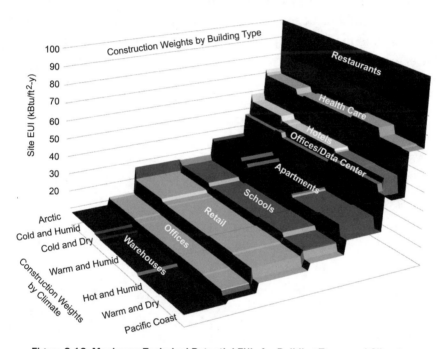

Figure 2-12: Maximum Technical Potential EUIs for Building Types and Climates, Weighted by Construction Activity

The horizontal surface area represents the relative share of construction activity by climate region in one direction and by building type in the other. The rectangle in the lower corner, for instance, represents the relative construction activity for warehouses in the Pacific Coast climate region. The format for this presentation is adapted from "The Technical Feasibility of Zero Net Energy Buildings in California," prepared by Arup North America Ltd. for PG&E and other California utilities, December 2012. The underlying data is from ASHRAE Research Project 1651.

the building types, and the maximum technical potential EUIs, all in one graph. It may be a little confusing at first but is very informative after you understand it. The horizontal area or footprint represents the total construction activity. The share of construction activity by climate zone is shown on the left side. The share of construction activity by building type is shown on the front axis. The area of the intersections is the relative volume of construction activity for a particular building type in a particular climate. The vertical axis is the site EUI.

What this graph shows is that the vast majority of building construction is capable of having an EUI less than about 30 kBtu/ft^2. In the next chapter we will look at solar potential and see that most buildings with an EUI in this range are capable of achieving ZNE with on-site renewable energy.

CHAPTER 3

Here Comes the Sun: The Future of Renewable-Energy Systems

It is not possible to completely eliminate energy demand in our buildings. Energy utilization indices (EUIs) will never go to zero through smart building design alone. We need to heat our buildings when it is cold and cool them when it is hot. We need to power our computers and other equipment. Lighting can be minimized through daylighting, but not eliminated altogether. We do need energy—just not as much as we are currently using. This chapter shows how we can produce what we need without using fossil fuels and without adding carbon dioxide (CO_2) to the atmosphere.

The Potential of Renewable Energy

The energy we receive from the sun is vast. In a little less than twenty-six minutes, the earth receives enough energy to power the global economy for a year.[1] An area about fifty miles by fifty miles square (roughly 2 percent of the state of Colorado) receives enough sun to continuously and cleanly power the United States economy at our current rate of energy use.[2] And this is before we do all we can to reduce our energy consumption. These are theoretical numbers and assume that the process of turning solar energy into electricity is 100 percent efficient. NREL has made a more realistic estimate that takes our current technology into account.[3] NREL estimates that to produce all the energy to power its economy, the

United States would need to take about 0.6 percent of the total United States land area, or about 2 percent of the land area now used for crop production. To look at it another way, we would need about 1,000 square feet of collector area for each person.

The annual sunlight that arrives at a building site is greater near the equator and less in northern (and southern) latitudes, but of course it is also affected by sky conditions. Figure 3-1 shows the variation in annual insolation (exposure to sunshine) in the United States. The southwestern portions of the country have the greatest solar potential, especially the desert areas of southern California, Nevada, Arizona, and New Mexico.

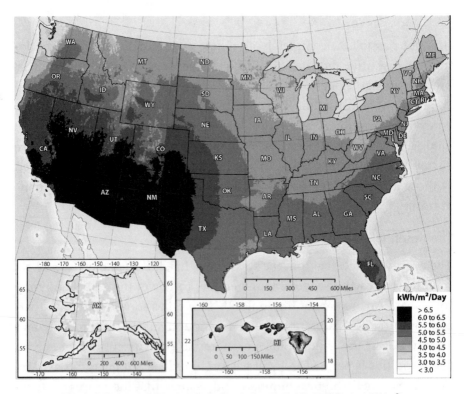

Figure 3-1: Annual Average Daily Insolation in the United States (W/m²)
This map displays the average daily solar exposure (insolation) on a surface facing south and tilted at an angle equal to the latitude of the location. (Source: National Renewable Energy Laboratory.)

These are areas where large, utility-scale solar power plants are now being constructed. The areas with the least annual insolation are the northern states around the Great Lakes and western Washington around Puget Sound. Alaska has the least insolation because it is so far north. Hawaii, of course, is bathed in sunlight. The data in figure 3-1 is expressed in average daily kilowatt-hour of energy per square meter of collector surface area facing south and tilted at an angle equal to the latitude of the location.

Direct energy from the sun is the purest form of renewable energy. It is extremely reliable and non-depletable, but variable. For any given spot on the planet, we have sun during the day but not at night. We receive more sun in the summer and less in the winter. We receive more energy on sunny days and less on cloudy days. Dealing with the variability of sunlight is a challenge, but it is not insurmountable. As we transition toward an economy powered by solar energy, our utility grids will be able to buy the excess energy we produce during the day and power our lights at night when the sun is down. In the short term, serving this energy storage function will actually benefit most utilities, since the times when insolation is most abundant align with times when the utility is experiencing its peak loads. In the long term, we will incorporate batteries and perhaps other forms of energy storage in our buildings.

Some buildings are already doing this. The RMI Innovation Center (see appendix) has a set of batteries with a capacity of 45 kWh (about half of the battery capacity of a Tesla automobile). Banks of these batteries can be used to even out the daily demand for power in small buildings. In the future, some of this storage function may be performed by our electric cars when they are plugged into the grid.[4]

Other forms of non-depletable renewable energy include wind energy, geothermal energy, and ocean tides and waves, but the sun is the driving force behind these forms of energy as well. Wind energy is a significant contributor to the energy grid here and in many other countries. In the United States, wind represents 5.7 percent of the installed electricity generating capacity at the national level, and in Iowa and South Dakota more than 25 percent of electricity generation is from wind.[5] Modern wind turbines are quite large and very different from the windmills used to pump

Figure 3-2: Modern Utility-Scale Wind Turbines
Utility-scale wind turbines are large and getting even larger. (Source: Ruth Baranowski, National Renewable Energy Laboratory.)

water on your grandfather's farm. Each requires 15–20 acres of land. A typical wind turbine has blades over 100 feet long and a total height of over 300 feet—and the next generation could be even bigger. Each is rated to produce 1.5–2.0 megawatts (MW) of peak power.[6]

Wind is also variable, but in a different way from solar. The sun does not heat our planet evenly because of the Earth's rotation and shape. This results in different atmospheric conditions. When there is a difference in air pressure between one area and the next, this causes the air to move from the high pressure area to the low pressure area. We call this moving air the wind. While it is driven by the sun, wind does not start at dawn and stop at dusk. In coastal areas, the wind blows from sea to land throughout the day, especially in the afternoons. At night, the direction often reverses, but wind turbines work no matter the direction of the wind. There are many other complexities as well that affect the speed and direction of the wind.

Solar Photovoltaic (PV) Technology

When certain materials are illuminated, they cause electrons to become free and move from atom to atom, creating an electric current from one side of the material to the other. This photovoltaic (PV) effect was discovered in the early 1800s,[7] and Albert Einstein provided a theoretical explanation in 1904, which led to a Nobel Prize in Physics. The first practical photovoltaic devices were developed for the United States space program in the late 1950s, when reliability rather than cost was the guiding principle. By the 1980s, PVs were beginning to be used for highway signs, emergency equipment, and other devices located in remote areas where running power lines from the electric grid was prohibitively expensive. By the late twentieth century, costs had declined enough that PV systems were being installed on rooftops to supplement the electric demand of the building.

In the United States, over 8,000 MW of PV systems were installed in 2015. The Solar Energy Industries Association estimates that in 2016 and 2017 more than 20,000 MW will be installed.[8] Much of the growth is in California, where the state has aggressive programs to promote the use of solar both at the building level and at the utility level. Solar accounted for 40 percent of all new electricity generation capacity added in 2013.[9] Solar is the second-largest source of new electricity generating capacity behind natural gas.

There are many types of photovoltaic panels, but the most common consist of polycrystalline or monocrystalline cells. These are made of silicon. When sunlight strikes a thin wafer of silicon, an electric current is generated from one side to the other. A delicate grid of electric conductors on the front and a more continuous conductor on the back of the cells collect the electricity that is generated. Solar cells are tricky to make, and there are lot of factors that affect performance, but once they are made they are extremely reliable, work for decades, and require little maintenance.

The silicon used for photovoltaic cells is a little different from the silicon used for other electronics. It is "doped" or "contaminated" with other elements to improve its ability to produce electricity. This just means that a tiny amount of another material is added to each side of the silicon wafer. It is common for phosphorus to be added to one side of the solar cell (about one atom of phosphorus for each 1,000 atoms of silicon). This side of the cell will have a negative charge. A material like boron is added to the other side at a much lower concentration (about one atom of boron for each 10 million atoms of silicon). This side of the cell will have a positive charge. The surface facing the sun typically has a non-reflective coating so that more of the sun's energy is absorbed.

Each solar cell is quite small, typically only about five to six inches square, and creates a charge of only about a half of a volt. For comparison, a common flashlight battery has a charge of 1.5 volts. For this reason, solar cells are commonly grouped in a panel, and the cells in the panel are wired in series so that the voltage of the whole array of cells is the sum of the individual cell voltages. A typical panel is 1 meter wide by 1.64 meters long and has sixty solar cells wired together (six in one direction and ten in the other), but many other sizes are common. The voltage produced by the whole panel is typically in the range of 30 volts, which is roughly the same as about twenty common batteries placed end to end (in series). The individual cells are bonded to a plate of glass and enclosed in an aluminum frame.

Polycrystalline solar panels represent about 60 percent of the products on the market, and monocrystalline panels represent about 30 percent, but there are other promising developments: thin-film technologies and multi-junction technologies (which make up the other 10 percent).

Thin-film materials include amorphous silicon (a-Si), cadmium telluride (CdTe), and copper-indium-gallium-selenium (CIGS). Amorphous silicon can be produced at a much lower cost, but is less reliable and has a lower efficiency. CdTe and CIGS are more expensive and are limited by the availability of the rare-earth metals used in their production. Multi-junction solar cells consist of different layers, each tuned to different wavelengths of radiation from the sun. These have the capability of

Figure 3-3: Typical Solar Panels

These monocrystalline PV panels are being installed at the RMI Innovation Center. Note that this system uses micro-inverters (one for each panel) that you can see attached to the mounting rails. (Source: Craig Schiller, Rocky Mountain Institute.)

Table 3-1 — Comparison of Photovoltaic (PV) Technologies

Solar Cell Technology	Market Share	Advantages	Drawbacks
Polycrystalline silicon	60%	Cost, Reliability	Efficiency
Monocrystalline silicon	30%	Efficiency, Reliability	Cost
Amorphous silicon		Cost	Reliability, Efficiency
Cadmium telluride		Cost	Durability, Toxicity, Cadmium Availability
Copper-indium-gallium-selenium (CIGS)	10%	Efficiency, Cost	Process, Durability, Indium Availability
Multi-junction		Efficiency	Cost, Complexity

being very efficient (having a theoretical efficiency limit of about 66 percent, which is about double the limit for silicon), but they are expensive and complex.

Modern monocrystalline solar cells have efficiency between 15 and 22 percent. Polycrystalline solar cells have a lower efficiency, typically between 11 and 15 percent. A solar cell that is 15 percent efficient means that it is capable of converting 15 percent of the total energy from the sun into electricity. The theoretical maximum possible efficiency for monocrystalline solar cells is around 33 percent.[10]

POLYCRYSTALLINE AND MONOCRYSTALLINE SILICON

Silicon (Si) is one of the most plentiful materials on Earth, but it is very rarely found in nature in a pure form. The most common source of silicon is quartz, which is silicon dioxide (SiO_2). A SiO_2 molecule consists of one atom of silicon bonded with two atoms of oxygen. Quartz represents something on the order of 10 percent of the Earth's crust, so there is no shortage of this base material. However, turning quartz into semiconductor-grade silicon is a pretty elaborate, energy intensive, and complex process.[11]

The result of this process is polycrystalline silicon, which is also called semicrystalline silicon, polysilicon, poly-Si, or simply "poly." (The literature on solar panels is confusing, and it helps to know that these are all the same substance.) About 60 percent of solar cells are made from polycrystalline silicon. Polycrystalline solar cells are perfectly square in shape and have a metal flake appearance. The panels used at the DPR office building in Phoenix are polycrystalline (see appendix).

To improve the performance of solar cells even further, the silicon molecules may be arranged in a very orderly crystalline structure. This requires an additional step, and the result is a material that is called monocrystalline silicon, single-crystal silicon, or just mono-Si (these are all the same thing). To make monocrystalline silicon, the polycrystalline silicon is melted by heating it to about 2,500°F. Crystals of monocrystalline are formed on a tiny wire that is rotated just above the molten polycrystalline. The process continues until an ingot with a diameter of about eight inches is formed. Each ingot is about six feet long.

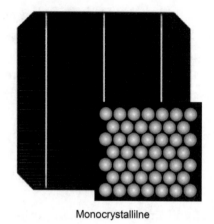 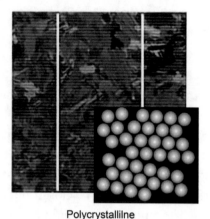

Monocrystallilne   Polycrystallilne

Figure 3-4: Polycrystalline vs. Monocrystalline Solar Cells
Monocrystalline cells are manufactured from round ingots, with the corners lopped off to save material. The inset images are conceptual diagrams of the molecular structure of the two types of crystalline.

These ingots are trimmed so they have a nearly square shape with lopped-off corners. They are then sawed into wafers that are only about 0.007 inches (7 mills) thick.[12] Monocrystalline solar cells do not have the metal flake appearance of polycrystalline silicon solar cells. These are used at the RMI Innovation Center (see fig. 3-3 and the examples in the appendix).

Monocrystalline silicon is perhaps the most important material development of the late twentieth century. Its availability at an affordable cost has been essential for the development of computers, tablets, smart phones, and other electronic gadgets that empower our modern electronic world.

RATING OF SOLAR COLLECTORS

All solar panels are tested under Standard Test Conditions (STC).[13] In a laboratory, the collectors are exposed to artificial sunlight with an intensity of 1,000 watts per square meter. (The subscript 1000 is often used to indicate this test condition—hence STC_{1000}.) The collector is also perfectly clean, the air is clean, the collector faces directly toward the source of artificial sunlight, and the temperature of the collector is maintained at 77°F (25°C). So when a collector has an STC rating of, say, 300 W, this power output would only be achieved under ideal conditions. The collector would have to be oriented to directly face the sun, the atmosphere would have to be clear, and the measurement would have to be taken at precisely solar noon. While a collector may never produce power at its STC rating, at least all panels are rated under the same conditions so they can be compared to each other. The STC rating is an input for most photovoltaic software applications. Performance is also often given as a PTC rating, which is a little closer to real-world conditions.[14]

The amount of sunlight that falls on a collector is the most important factor that affects its output. The second-most important factor is temperature. Solar panels perform best when they are cool. Performance declines when the ambient temperature is higher than the 77°F rating condition. The ideal conditions for maximum production are clear skies and cold temperatures. A clear winter day in Aspen, Colorado, would be perfect.

Besides the STC rating, the specifications for solar panels include much more information that is useful and necessary when designing the system and matching it to the inverter. Two such specifications are the open-circuit voltage (Voc) and the short circuit current (Isc). These factors help define the performance curve of the solar panel.[15] (See fig. 3-5.)

INVERTERS

Solar panels produce direct current (DC) in the same way that a charged battery does; electrons flow in just one direction. The electric grid in the United States and most of the world, however, delivers alternating current (AC): electrons move back and forth in the conductors. Early on in the history of electricity there was a "battle of the currents" between Thomas Edison (and General Electric), a proponent of DC power, and Nikola Tesla (and Westinghouse), a proponent of AC power. In spite of Edison's publicity stunts to show that AC was dangerous, which involved purposely electrocuting various large animals including Topsy, a circus elephant, AC became the standard. Most of our modern appliances run on

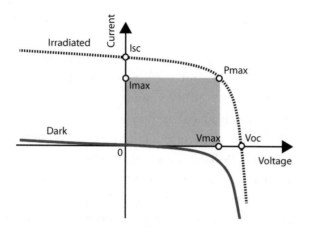

Figure 3-5: Inverter Maximum Power Point Tracker (MPPT) Function
This conceptual diagram shows how an inverter finds the maximum power point for the specific conditions represented by the dotted line. The position of the dotted line changes with sun angles and solar conditions.

AC, since that is the standard for the electric grid; therefore, solar power must be converted to AC in order to be widely useful.

An inverter is an electrical device that converts direct current (DC) from solar panels into alternating current (AC). Inverters are an essential part of all grid-connected solar systems. The inverter not only converts DC to AC, it also synchronizes AC power generated from the solar system with the voltage and alternating frequency of the grid, which is 60 cycles per second (hertz, or Hz) in the United States but 50 Hz in most other countries. The inverter performs other essential functions as well. For safety reasons, many inverters shut down the solar system if there is a power outage in the electric grid. Otherwise the grid might be powered by solar generating sources while maintenance personnel are working to correct a problem.

The inverter also performs an important optimization function. Each solar panel (or array of panels) is capable of producing various combinations of voltage (V) and current (I); power (P) is the product of voltage times current. Some combinations of V and I produce more power than others, so the inverter searches for and finds the combination that maximizes the power. The maximum power point depends on the orientation and tilt of the collectors as well as sun conditions, shading, and other factors. The adjustment is continuous, since these conditions are constantly changing.

Inverters come in different sizes and are rated according to peak power, usually in kilowatts (kW). The largest sizes are rated for 750 kW and above; these would be used for industrial-size arrays of 3,000 or more solar panels. Medium-size inverters are in the range of 85–100 kW and work with arrays of 300–400 panels. Small, multi-panel inverters for residential and small-size commercial projects are in the range of 10–30 kW and work for arrays between about 40 and 120 panels.

Larger systems tend to have a single inverter or several large inverters for the whole system. A typical arrangement is to wire the solar panels in strings (in series) such that the total voltage to the inverter is in the range of 500–1,000 V. Figure 3-6 contrasts series versus parallel wiring. Most inverters are weatherproof and can be mounted outdoors on rooftops or in other suitable locations.

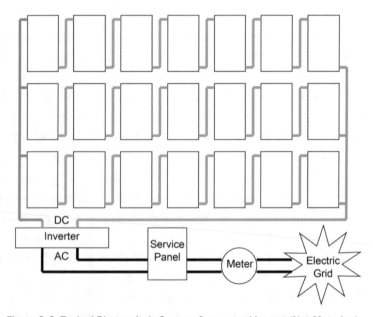

Figure 3-6: Typical Photovoltaic System Conceptual Layout (Net-Metering)
The solar panels in each row are wired in series but the separate rows are wired in parallel.

Micro-inverters are designed so that each individual solar panel has its own inverter. These are typically rated to accept up to about 270 W of DC power from the panel.[16] For smaller jobs micro-inverters are cost-competitive, since their cost scales with the number of panels. They also have a number of advantages over multi-panel inverters. They find the maximum power point separately for each solar panel, so performance is increased if the individual panels have different orientation or tilt or if one or more of the panels are shaded. Also, if there is an inverter or solar panel failure, the power from only one panel is lost, not the whole array. If you are the type of person who likes to track the performance of your system, micro-inverters offer the opportunity see how each individual panel and inverter is performing. Micro-inverters are also very easy and safe to install; whips from the collectors plug into the inverters and the inverters plug into a buss mounted beneath the solar panels.

ORIENTATION, TILT, AND TRACKING SYSTEMS

The more directly solar panels face the sun, the more energy they collect, which is why some systems have motors that rotate and/or tilt the panels so that they always face directly toward the sun as it moves through the sky. These are called tracking systems and there are two types: single axis and double axis. *Single-axis tracking systems* rotate the panel(s) in just one direction. A typical single-axis tracking system would rotate the panel on a vertical axis so that it faces east in the morning and west in the after-noon, while maintaining the same tilt. Alternatively, a single-axis tracking system could rotate the panel on a horizontal axis or even a sloped axis. (See fig. 3-7.) Single-axis tracking systems improve the orientation of the solar array, but do not achieve a constant normal incidence. A *double-axis tracking system,* by contrast, adjusts both the orientation and the tilt of the collector such that the panel faces directly toward the sun at all times.

Tracking systems can increase solar production by as much as 33 per-cent,[17] but more typical production increases are in the range of 20–25 per-cent. However, they are mechanical devices that increase costs, require maintenance, and add an element of unreliability. Typically, they make sense only if the site is constrained or if special concentrating collectors

73

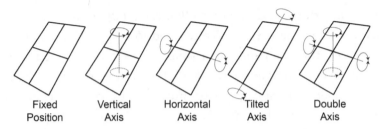

| Fixed | Vertical | Horizontal | Tilted | Double |
| Position | Axis | Axis | Axis | Axis |

Figure 3-7: Solar Panel Tracking Methods

The three options in the center are all single-axis tracking systems. A double-axis tracking system pivots on two axes, as shown on the far right.

are used. When space is not a problem, installing more panels in a fixed position is usually a more cost-effective option. The benefit of tracking systems is greatest when the sun is low in the sky, i.e., in northern locations (high latitude) and during the winter.

The traditional rule of thumb for fixed solar panels is to face them toward the south and tilt them at an angle equal to the latitude; add 15 degrees for maximum winter production and take away 15 degrees for maximum summer production. However, more detailed studies show that to achieve maximum annual production, the optimum tilt should be flatter than the angle of the latitude. This is especially true for areas with predominantly overcast conditions (for overcast conditions, the best tilt is dead flat). A better rule of thumb is to set the tilt equal to 65 percent of the latitude plus 7 degrees.

When it is not possible to face collectors due south (in the northern hemisphere), the penalty is fairly modest in lower latitudes, getting larger in northern latitudes. For most cities in the lower forty-eight states, the penalty for rotating the orientation to the southeast or the southwest is in the range of 3–7 percent. If the deviation from south is greater, i.e., facing east or west, greater production is achieved by installing the panels horizontally.

If the goal is to minimize cost through net metering, and a time-of-use utility rate applies, it may be more beneficial to face the collectors more to the west and give them a shallower tilt, since this will increase production when the utility is buying back power at a higher rate.

Table 3-2 — Performance Comparisons for Various Orientations and Tilt

These data represent estimated kWh/yr of energy production per kW of STC-installed PV capacity. These typical production values are calculated using weather data for each of the representative cities. The lighter shades indicate higher production. The boxed figures indicate the maximum production for each city. Note that for San Francisco, production is significantly greater for west-facing panels than for east-facing panels (summer mornings are often foggy in San Francisco). For Boulder, the opposite is the case, which is probably because of the Front Range of the Rocky Mountains to the west. (Source: PV-watts calculations by the author.)

Climate Region	Orientation	0° Tilt	10° Tilt	20° Tilt	30° Tilt	40° Tilt	50° Tilt	60° Tilt
Warm and Dry	East	1,414	1,385	1,336	1,269	1,191	1,105	1,013
(2b, 3b, 4b)	Southeast	1,414	1,470	1,493	1,486	1,450	1,383	1,292
City: Los Angeles	South	1,414	1,518	1,581	1,605	1,594	1,540	1,451
Latitude: 34.0	Southwest	1,414	1,498	1,545	1,560	1,537	1,483	1,399
Flat Penalty: 12%	West	1,414	1,425	1,409	1,368	1,310	1,236	1,149
Hot and Humid	East	1,359	1,361	1,336	1,290	1,231	1,157	1,070
(1a, 2a)	Southeast	1,359	1,411	1,431	1,421	1,382	1,317	1,230
City: Miami	South	1,359	1,427	1,462	1,460	1,426	1,358	1,256
Latitude: 25.8	Southwest	1,359	1,400	1,411	1,391	1,345	1,277	1,185
Flat Penalty: 7%	West	1,359	1,344	1,306	1,249	1,180	1,101	1,014
Pacific Coast	East	1,378	1,353	1,304	1,244	1,172	1,092	1,010
(3c, 4c)	Southeast	1,378	1,437	1,467	1,466	1,434	1,373	1,289
City: San Francisco	South	1,378	1,485	1,553	1,582	1,571	1,523	1,436
Latitude: 37.8	Southwest	1,378	1,464	1,518	1,534	1,518	1,466	1,389
Flat Penalty: 13%	West	1,378	1,389	1,372	1,336	1,282	1,213	1,132
Warm and Humid	East	1,316	1,312	1,286	1,244	1,187	1,119	1,039
(3a, 4a)	Southeast	1,316	1,368	1,410	1,412	1,386	1,333	1,255
City: Atlanta	South	1,316	1,404	1,457	1,475	1,458	1,408	1,324
Latitude: 33.6	Southwest	1,316	1,374	1,402	1,401	1,370	1,316	1,237
Flat Penalty: 11%	West	1,316	1,306	1,274	1,227	1,166	1,096	1,018

Table 3-2 — continued

Climate Region	Orientation	0° Tilt	10° Tilt	20° Tilt	30° Tilt	40° Tilt	50° Tilt	60° Tilt
Cold and Dry	East	1,311	1,330	1,329	1,308	1,270	1,217	1,150
(5b, 6b)	Southeast	1,311	1,417	1,489	1,527	1,531	1,501	1,441
City: Boulder	South	1,311	1,438	1,528	1,578	1,589	1,561	1,495
Latitude: 40.0	Southwest	1,311	1,385	1,429	1,443	1,429	1,386	1,318
Flat Penalty: 17%	West	1,311	1,284	1,243	1,191	1,132	1,066	994
Cold and Humid	East	1,138	1,134	1,112	1,075	1,029	975	910
(5a, 6a, 7)	Southeast	1,138	1,198	1,233	1,241	1,227	1,188	1,127
City: Chicago	South	1,138	1,223	1,279	1,304	1,299	1,265	1,201
Latitude: 41.8	Southwest	1,138	1,195	1,227	1,232	1,215	1,175	1,115
Flat Penalty: 13%	West	1,138	1,129	1,102	1,065	1,016	959	894
Arctic	East	748	751	751	749	738	723	695
(8)	Southeast	748	819	875	917	938	939	922
City: Fairbanks	South	748	845	923	978	1,012	1,022	1,007
Latitude: 64.8	Southwest	748	816	867	906	925	926	909
Flat Penalty: 27%	West	748	746	740	732	720	702	676

SHADING

Shading of photovoltaic systems is a problem that needs serious attention. The loss of power is not proportional to the area of the collector that is shaded. Seemingly minor shading can cause a 50 percent or more loss of production. Each solar cell in a panel is wired in series with the next, and when just one cell is shaded it affects the performance of the entire panel. And since solar panels also are often wired in series, when just one panel is shaded the performance of all the panels in the string is affected. The impact of shading is a little like the proverb "a chain is only as strong as its weakest link." When just a few cells in the string are shaded, the whole system is seriously degraded.

Fortunately, it is very easy to determine the position of the sun in the sky for any hour of the day and any time of the year and to locate the panels where shading is less of a problem. Figure 3-8 shows the two common ways that sun paths are diagramed. Using Cartesian coordinates (on the left), the altitude of the sun is plotted on the vertical axis and the azimuth on the horizontal axis. Solar noon is in the center of the diagram, with the east on the left and the west on the right, just as if you were looking south. The lines on the graph shaped like domes are the months of the year and the lines radiating from center-bottom are the times of day. From this graph, you can read the solar altitude and azimuth for any time of the day or month of the year. Shading from adjacent buildings or trees can be overlaid on this diagram to identify the times of day when shading is a problem.

The information can also be plotted using polar coordinates, as shown on the right of figure 3-8. The bowl-shaped lines are the months of the year and the solar altitude is read by the distance from the origin. The near-vertical lines are the times of the day. The polar coordinate plot contains the same information as the Cartesian coordinates, just in a different format. Again, the outline of buildings and trees can be plotted on this diagram to identify problem times during the day or year. These plots are for 38 degrees north latitude, but similar charts are available for any location.

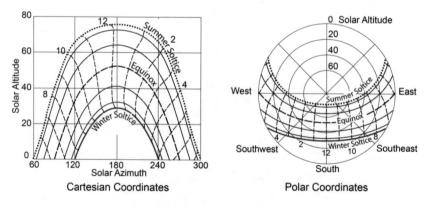

Figure 3-8: Typical Sun-Path Diagrams

Diagrams like this may be generated for any location. The University of Oregon has a very useful website where you can enter your zip code and get site-specific sun path diagrams plotted with either Cartesian or polar coordinates (see: http://solardat.uoregon.edu/).

Various instruments are available to locate buildings, trees, and other shading elements and to plot them on either the Cartesian or polar charts. Physical devices like the Solar Pathfinder have been around for decades,[18] but electronic devices and software that use a fish-eye camera lens are finding favor, too, since these are more portable, provide greater accuracy, and are easier to use.[19] Plots may also be made through manual observations, but this is a tedious and time-consuming process. Google maps has initiated Project Sunroof that will give you a quick assessment of solar potential, but this is not very detailed and should only be used for a preliminary feasibility analysis.

When solar panels are mounted on a flat surface and tilted, the rows must be spaced such that they do not shade each other. The spacing needed between the collectors is determined by the altitude of the sun at noon on the winter solstice. If the vertical height of the collectors is four feet and the solar altitude at noon on the winter solstice is 27 degrees, then collectors would need to be separated by about eight feet (that is, four feet divided by the tangent of the solar altitude). The necessary spacing to avoid self-shading can significantly reduce the collector area on a roof. Table 3-3 shows the ratio of solar collector area to roof area for different latitudes and solar collector tilts. For all locations (even in the Arctic), the loss of collector area due to spacing is much greater than the penalty for mounting the solar panels horizontally, so if the goal is

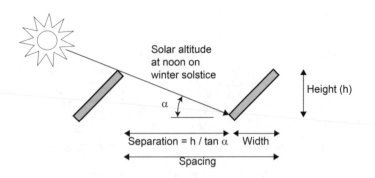

Figure 3-9: Spacing of Solar Panels to Prevent Self-Shading
When solar panels are tilted, they must be spaced in a manner that does not result in self-shading.

Table 3-3 — Ratio of Solar Collector Area to Roof Area

This table gives estimates of the ratio of the collector area to the roof area for different latitudes and collector tilts. These data may be used in combination with the data in table 3-2 to estimate the maximum solar potential for rooftop solar systems.

Latitude	Solar Altitude at Winter Solstice	Tilt of Collectors		
		20°	30°	40°
24	41.6	75%	70%	67%
28	37.7	72%	66%	63%
32	33.8	69%	62%	58%
36	29.9	65%	58%	53%
40	25.9	61%	53%	48%
44	22.0	56%	47%	42%
48	18.0	50%	42%	36%

to maximize production from the renewable-energy system, it is best to mount the collectors horizontally so they do not shade each other and more of the roof can be used for collection. Note that collectors should not be dead flat but always gently sloped so that rain will help to keep them clean. (See fig. 3-10.)

The Bullitt Center in Seattle positions the solar collectors in a near-horizontal position in order to maximize production. Since Seattle is overcast for much of the time, this works quite well. Snow accumulation on the collectors can be an issue in some climates, and this is a reason to tilt the collectors a little more steeply. The RMI Innovation Center is located in snow country. The design team investigated various methods of avoiding a loss of power due to snow coverage, including special coatings to make the glass surface more slippery and heat tape to melt the snow. Their studies showed that additional energy production would more than offset the energy used by the heat tape, but in the end they decided to just accept the loss of production from snow coverage. The options they looked at would have voided the warranty offered by the solar

Figure 3-10: Near-Flat Solar Array at the Bullitt Center
The solar collectors are located in the same plane to avoid self-shading. Under overcast conditions (typical of Seattle), a horizontal orientation is optimal. (© Brad Kahn, Flickr.)

collector manufacturer, and their attorneys cringed at the idea of workers on the roof pushing the snow away.

Cost-Effectiveness and Financing

At the turn of the millennium, solar energy was expensive and rarely installed to offset building energy use. In recent years, though, the cost of PV panels and inverters has declined and the industry has introduced a number of financial innovations that make the technology accessible to almost all of us.

DECLINING COSTS

The cost of photovoltaic solar-power systems has declined significantly since they became a practical application as part of the space program in the 1960s and 1970s. In 1977, the cost of a PV panel (without installation, mounting, the inverter, and other balance-of-system [BOS] costs) was a whopping $76/W.[20] At that price, a modern 250 W panel would cost almost $20,000. Today the cost of that panel would be around $250. The most dramatic cost declines were in late 1970s and 1980s, when costs dropped from $76/W to less than $10/W, but the steady decline has continued. Figure 3-11 shows how the global cost of silicon PV modules (the key component of the system) has declined from about $5/W in 1998 to less than $1/W today. These costs do not consider tax benefits to consumers or other incentives, but such programs have contributed to the cost decline by increasing demand and boosting production.

Of course, the total cost of a solar installation includes more than just the PV module. As mentioned earlier, an inverter is needed to convert the DC power from the panels to AC and to synchronize the power frequency with the grid; a racking system is needed to support the panels and to resist wind and other loads; and the system needs to be connected to the electrical service panel. Depending on configuration, the system may need a disconnect switch on the DC side. There is also labor to install the system and soft costs to design it, obtain the permit, etc. In the solar PV world, these additional costs are referred to as the balance-of-system (BOS) costs. The BOS costs have also declined, but not as much as the panel costs. Except for the inverter, the BOS costs more closely track general construction costs.

Figure 3-11 shows the median installed price of residential and commercial PV systems from 1998 through 2013. Data are given for three sizes: smaller than 10 kW, 10–100 kW, and larger than 100 kW. Larger systems have a lower median cost, demonstrating economy of scale. The installed price was stagnant between about 2003 and 2009, but has dropped considerably since then. Median costs for 2013 were between about $4/W and $5/W, depending on the size of the system. Since about 2010, the BOS costs have also fallen considerably as contractors, laborers, designers, and others have become more familiar with the technology and systems have become more of a commodity.

Figure 3-11 shows the decline in median installed cost, but for each period, there is considerable variation, as shown in figure 3-12. In this

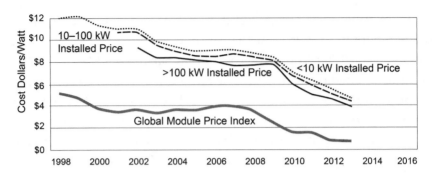

Figure 3-11: Installed Price of Residential and Commercial Photovoltaics Over Time
(Source: "Benchmarking the Declining Cost of Solar," Solar Today, January 27, 2015.)

graph, the installed price for smaller systems (less than 10 kW) is shown on the horizontal axis and the frequency distribution is shown on the vertical axis. The decline in the median cost is shown as the peak of each curve moves to the left with time. If you look at the cost curve for 2013, the median is about $4.50/W, but some prices are as low as $2/W and others are as high as $8/W. The standard deviation is roughly $2/W, which means that about two-thirds of the installed systems cost between $3/W and $7/W. Another thing to note is that over time, the standard deviation (or variance) is becoming smaller, perhaps because there is more certainty about the design and construction process for PV systems.

The cost of solar systems is becoming more competitive with traditional electricity generation sources. Levelized Cost of Energy (LCOE) is the metric most often used when comparing the cost of alternative methods of electricity generation. The LCOE is the net present value of all the costs incurred over the life of the system, including initial investment, financing, operation, maintenance, and fuel, divided by the kWh of electricity produced. The units of LCOE are dollars per kWh. A generating system that has an LCOE of, say, $0.08/kWh would need to sell electricity at an average cost of $0.08/kWh in order to break even.

Figure 3-13 shows LCOE projections from the US Energy Information Agency (EIA) for the last five years.[21] These data are EIA's best estimates for new plants to be constructed in the future. Concentrating solar plants and offshore wind have the highest LCOE at well above $0.20/kWh. Coal

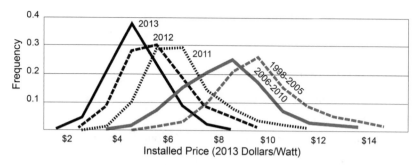

Figure 3-12: Installed Price Distribution for Residential and Commercial Photovoltaics (≤10 kW Systems)
(Source: "Benchmarking the Declining Cost of Solar," Solar Today, January 27, 2015.)

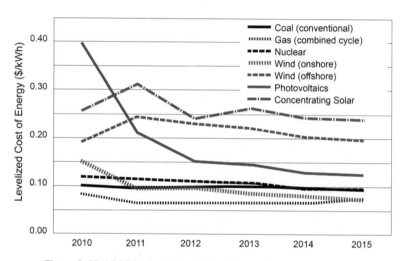

Figure 3-13: LCOE Projections for New Electricity-Generation Plants
(Source: US Energy Information Administration.)

is right around $0.10/kWh and is not declining. The generating source with the lowest LCOE is gas, which is right around $0.07/kWh. Onshore wind has dropped from about $0.15/kWh in 2010 to around $0.07/kWh in 2015, making it about equal to gas and the least expensive method of generating electricity. The most rapid cost decline belongs to solar photovoltaic, with the cost declining from about $0.40/kWh in 2010 to about

$0.12/kWh in 2015, making it only slightly more expensive than coal and gas, but with far fewer adverse environmental impacts.

FOR MORE INFORMATION

- See: http://solartoday.org/2015/01/benchmarking-the-declining-cost -of-solar/.
- See also: https://en.wikipedia.org/wiki/Cost_of_electricity_by_source.

SOLAR POWER PURCHASE AGREEMENTS AND SOLAR LEASES

Renewable-energy systems on many buildings are not owned by the same entities that own the actual buildings. For various reasons, building owners often enter into solar lease arrangements or solar-power purchase agreements (sPPA) with third parties that actually own the solar systems. There are subtle differences between sPPAs and solar leases, but they have lots of features in common.

A solar-power purchase agreement (sPPA) is a financial arrangement in which a third party owns, operates, and maintains the solar system, and the building owner agrees to provide a place for the system either on the building roof or elsewhere on the property.[22] The building owner also agrees to purchase electric power from the system at a negotiated rate and for a predetermined period. After the sPPA has expired, the owner can buy the system, renew the lease, or have the system removed.[23] During the period of the agreement, the third party maintains and operates the system. This arrangement allows the host customer to receive stable-cost and sometimes lower-cost electricity than would be available from the local utility, while the third party acquires valuable financial benefits such as tax credits, depreciation, and income generated from the sale of elec-tricity. There are generally no (or small) up-front costs for the building owner, just a commitment to buy power from the system for a specified period of time and abide by other terms of the agreement.

With this business model, the host customer buys the services produced by the PV system rather than buying the PV system itself. This framework is also referred to as the "solar services" model, and the developers who offer sPPAs are known as solar services providers. Such sPPA arrangements enable the host customer to avoid many of the traditional barriers to adoption by organizations looking to install solar systems: up-front capital costs, system performance risk, and complex design and permitting processes. In addition, sPPA arrangements can be cash-flow-positive for the host customer from the day the system is commissioned.

With an sPPA, the building owner agrees to buy the output from the solar system and only pays for the electricity that is delivered by the system. With a solar lease, by contrast, the building owner leases the system (like a car) and takes whatever power is generated; however, solar leases usually have a guarantee of some minimum level of production. The term for both sPPAs and solar leases is typically seven to fifteen years for commercial systems and typically twenty years for residential systems.[24]

Solar leases and sPPAs are especially popular for schools, institutions, and government buildings that may be short on cash and are not in a position to take advantage of tax credits and/or other financial benefits like depreciation that are available to for-profit companies. For them, sPPAs and solar leases provide the benefits of the solar system with little or no capital outlay. Scott Shell, a San Francisco architect with the firm of EHDD, reports that many of his clients install solar systems through power-purchase agreements at no up-front cost, and they pay less for electricity than they would through the local utility. He characterizes this as a "no-brainer."

A variety of financial tools are used for all aspects of commercial buildings. While sPPAs and solar leases are getting a lot of press, similar financial arrangements have been used for other building systems for decades. Energy service companies (ESCOs) often own the chillers and boilers in buildings and sell chilled water and/or hot water (services) to the building owner. An old financial tool is simply being reestablished for a new product, solar systems, which at present are less common than some of the other systems that have been previously financed in this manner.

In evaluating whole-building performance and zero net-energy, the ownership of the renewable-energy systems and the way they are financed should have no bearing. In the case of a lease, the owner uses the power from the leased system. In the case of a sPPA, the owner agrees to also buy the power, but with different terms. It is possible that the solar panels will be removed after the term of the lease, but even if the building owner also owns the PV system, there is no guarantee regarding how long they will maintain and operate the system. The benefits of solar will increase over time, so permanency is a small concern. The important factor is that additional capacity be added to the existing renewable-energy infrastructure when the ZNE building is constructed. Whether this is achieved through a power-purchase agreement, a solar lease, or other financial mechanism is unimportant.

ZNE Feasibility

From the EUI information in the previous chapter and the solar production data in this chapter, it is possible to make a first-order assessment of ZNE feasibility for typical building types and climate regions. Table 3-4 calculates the renewable-energy production that is possible for horizontally oriented solar collectors in each of the climate regions. Production in kWh is converted to kBtu/ft²·yr (of collector area) to be consistent with the EUI data in tables 2-6 and 2-7. This is based on a kW of rated PV power requiring 65 square feet of surface area, which is typical of modern monocrystalline collectors.[25] Solar production is in the range of 60–74 kBtu/ft²·yr of horizontal collector area except for the Arctic, which is 39 kBtu/ft²·yr.

If you multiply the solar production values from table 3-4 times the area of the site, this approximates the maximum renewable-energy potential for the site, but this would be an extreme situation equivalent to covering the entire site with an array of solar collectors, i.e., the theoretical maximum solar-energy production for the site. A better way of looking at the data, though, is in terms of the collector area needed per square foot of floor area, which is the information presented in table 3-5. This ratio is presented both for buildings that are in minimum compliance with ASHRAE Standard 90.1-2013 and also for the lowest maximum technical potential EUI.

Table 3-5 is shaded to indicate the difficulty in achieving ZNE. The darkest shade marks buildings that require a collector area larger than the

Table 3-4 — Annual Solar Production per Square Foot of Roof/Site Area (kBtu/ft²·yr)

The following data are based on 65 square feet of collector area per kW (STC). The annual production is taken from table 3-2 for a horizontally mounted solar panel.

	Climate Regions (see figure 2-3)						
	Pacific Coast	Warm and Dry	Hot and Humid	Warm and Humid	Cold and Dry	Cold and Humid	Arctic
Horizontal Production (kWh/yr)/kW (stc)	1,378	1,414	1,359	1,316	1,311	1,138	748
Horizontal Production (kBtu/yr)/kW (stc)	4,702	4,825	4,637	4,490	4,473	3,883	2,552
kBtu/ft²·yr of Collector Area	72	74	71	69	69	60	39

floor area. If these buildings were one story in height, covering the roof with collectors would not be enough. The next lighter shade marks buildings and climates with a collector-area to floor-area ratio between 0.5 and 1.0. If such a building were one story, the roof would provide space for enough solar panels to achieve on-site ZNE. The next lighter shade shows building types and climates that could achieve ZNE with a two-story configuration; the next for three stories, etc.

A quick review of the data shows that ZNE will be very difficult to achieve in some climates and for some building types. Restaurants, for instance, would need a solar collector area that is four to six times the floor area, except in the Arctic, where the ratio is almost 10:1. The good news is that restaurants represent only about 1 percent of expected building construction. Furthermore, this building type has many opportunities for savings that were not investigated in calculating the maximum technical potential EUIs presented in chapter 2.

Offices with a data center, as well as hotels and health care facilities, all have trouble in the Arctic climate region, but this region only represents less than one-tenth of 1 percent of expected building construction. While not represented in the PNNL models, supermarkets are another building type that will have difficulty reaching on-site ZNE, because of refrigerated casework and food preparation. Many supermarkets these days are a lot like take-out restaurants.

Table 3-5 — Collector Area to Floor Area Ratio Needed to Achieve ZNE

	Climate Regions (see figure 2-3)						
	Pacific Coast	Warm and Dry	Hot and Humid	Warm and Humid	Cold and Dry	Cold and Humid	Arctic
Buildings in Compliance with Standard 90.1-2013							
Warehouses	0.22	0.21	0.17	0.24	0.28	0.44	0.84
Offices	0.30	0.42	0.46	0.46	0.45	0.56	1.04
Retail	0.49	0.66	0.67	0.72	0.77	0.98	2.07
Schools	0.48	0.62	0.68	0.69	0.69	0.84	1.72
Apartments	0.49	0.64	0.67	0.74	0.76	1.02	1.93
Offices/Data Centers	0.85	0.94	0.99	1.02	1.05	1.29	2.25
Hotels	0.78	1.01	1.12	1.13	1.12	1.38	2.55
Health Care	1.40	1.45	1.64	1.68	1.61	2.01	3.57
Restaurants	4.97	5.80	5.81	6.82	7.46	9.60	19.34
Maximum Technical Potential							
Warehouses	0.08	0.08	0.07	0.09	0.10	0.13	0.19
Offices	0.11	0.14	0.15	0.15	0.15	0.18	0.30
Retail	0.18	0.24	0.25	0.25	0.26	0.32	0.67
Schools	0.22	0.28	0.32	0.32	0.31	0.38	0.66
Apartments	0.33	0.40	0.41	0.44	0.47	0.57	0.90
Offices/Data Centers	0.59	0.63	0.66	0.64	0.68	0.77	1.19
Hotels	0.55	0.66	0.69	0.74	0.75	0.90	1.48
Health Care	0.87	0.86	0.96	0.96	0.95	1.15	1.83
Restaurants	3.66	4.35	4.53	4.87	4.99	5.91	9.61

Shading Legend for Table 3-5

≥ 1.00	Most difficult. For one-story buildings, the collector area would need to exceed the roof area.
0.50 – 1.00	Rooftop PV will achieve ZNE for one-story buildings.
0.33 – 0.50	Rooftop PV will achieve ZNE for two-story buildings.
0.25 – 0.33	Rooftop PV will achieve ZNE for three-story buildings.
≤ 0.25	Rooftop PV will achieve ZNE for four-story buildings.

To achieve ZNE for these challenging building types and climates, one of two things must occur. First, some sort of radical action would be needed to reduce the EUI, such as eliminating walk-in freezers and bringing fresh supplies to the restaurant each day. Such steps would drastically change the nature of the activities going on in the building, and thus they are unlikely to occur. The other option, which is more reasonable, is to expand the boundary for PV production beyond the roof. PV panels can be installed over parking areas, for instance, and when this is not possible, there are opportunities to install renewable-energy systems on remote sites, to buy shares in community solar systems, or to purchase renewable-energy certificates. These and other options are discussed in chapter 6.

CHAPTER 4

Energy Modeling: Evaluating ZNE before the Utility Bills Arrive

Lighting, heating, cooling, and other building systems don't operate independently of each other; they interact in complex ways. Consider the following examples:

- Electric lighting provides illumination, but also adds heat to the space that must be removed by air conditioners. Heat is also added by computers and office equipment. Internal heat gain lowers the balance-point temperature, the outdoor temperature above which a building needs to be cooled. Internal-load-dominated buildings may require cooling even when it is cool or even cold outside.

- Making windows larger brings in more daylight, which can reduce the energy for electric lighting, but larger windows also add heat to the space, which will increase the energy to be used by cooling and ventilation systems.

- Letting the space temperature drift at night and on weekends will save energy during those periods, but can cause more energy to be used on Monday morning when the building needs to be warmed up or cooled down prior to occupancy.

With products like cars, smart phones, and computers, designers can build full-scale prototypes and try things out until they get the product to perform the way they want. This approach can be used with some building components, like lighting fixtures and mechanical equipment, but it is not feasible for the whole building. Instead we use models. Energy modeling is a procedure for looking at the interactions between building systems and understanding how a building functions as a whole. Models can be used throughout the design process from schematic design through construction, but the models become more detailed in later phases.

Models may be used to study design options, to find cost-effective insulation levels, and to assist the building design process in many other ways. Models help us understand the interactions between building systems and find a balance that achieves optimal and cost-effective performance. Sometimes the right balance is non-intuitive. Rules of thumb and prescriptive standards can take us only so far. To achieve deep energy savings, it is necessary to look at the whole building and understand the interactions between building systems. Energy models are an essential tool in this process. Through modeling, cost savings can sometimes be achieved by downsizing heating, ventilation, air-conditioning (HVAC), and other equipment, and these savings can more than offset the additional cost of better windows and lighting systems.

Models are a simplified representation of reality. For new buildings, the reality does not yet exist and models can anticipate what that reality will become. Models can be mental, verbal, graphical, physical, or mathematical. Mental models are abstractions that exist in our heads. They can't be shared easily with others, except through extended conversation. Yet mental models are very powerful and they affect every decision we make. When we share a mental model with others through writing or speech, it becomes a verbal model. When a mental model is drawn up, it becomes a graphic model. When the drawings are translated to cardboard or foam board, they become physical models. Precision is added at each step of the process. Mental and verbal models are vague and undefined; graphic and physical models are explicit and detailed.

With modern software applications, the distinctions among graphic, physical, and mathematical models is blurred. When we develop a representation of a building in computer-aided design and drafting (CADD) software like SketchUp or Revit®, it exists fundamentally as a mathematical model, but the software allows us to view floor plans, sections, elevations, perspectives, and other graphic representations. With a 3-D printer, we can even generate a physical model.

Energy models, by their very nature, are formal mathematical models that are replicable and can be directly viewed and manipulated by others. However, many software applications have sophisticated graphic capabilities to display not only the building form and configuration but also patterns of expected energy use. In an energy model, each surface (wall, roof, or floor) is represented by coordinates and numbers that describe its position in space, its height, width, tilt, and orientation. Each surface references a construction assembly that describes the amount of insulation, its ability to store heat (thermal mass), and surface properties (rough or smooth, light or dark). Surfaces enclose zones, which are separate areas within buildings that each have their own thermostat. Zones have lighting systems and equipment that directly use energy and produce heat. Assumptions are made about when lights are turned on or off, when people enter and leave the building, and when equipment is used. HVAC systems and their performance are also specified, including the maximum rate that heat can be added or removed, how the equipment responds to changing outdoor temperature, and how the systems can modulate between peak operation and partial operation.

Energy models can become quite complex, and a big challenge is finding the right balance between simplification and detail. A model that is too simple overlooks important interactions, but a model that is too complex is expensive to develop, slow to run, and burdened with extraneous information; further, the results can be difficult to interpret. There are many techniques, gained through experience, for simplifying models. For instance, typical spaces can be modeled once and the results then scaled for all similar spaces. Thermal zones can be grouped together if they have a similar solar exposure and provide the same level of energy services to the occupants. Modelers can find thermodynamic approximations for more-complex heat transfer. All of these simplifications require the kind of reasoned judgment that comes with experience.[1]

As will be described later in this chapter, there are many advantages to using energy models, but a big plus is that our mental models are improved as we develop, study, and understand formal mathematical energy models. Models help us become better designers and they enable us to better understand the factors of building design that are important for energy efficiency as well as those that are not.

Table 4-1 — Energy Model Taxonomy

See also: http://www.buildingenergysoftwaretools.com/. For a good history of energy models, see: http://www.bembook.ibpsa.us/index.php?title=History_of_Building_Energy_Modeling. This has a good graphic showing activities chronologically.

	Examples	Description
Calculation Engines Calculation engines commonly accept input as a text file and produce results as a text file. The basic calculation engines have no graphic user interface. They simulate how a building will use energy for a whole year. They can operate at hourly or sub-hourly increments of time.	DOE-2.1E	DOE-2.1E was the workhorse in the computer modeling world for decades. It was developed primarily by the national laboratories with funding from the US Department of Energy. An input text file is created using a language called BDL (Building Design Language) that describes the building to be modeled in great detail. This input file is then processed by the calculation engine and the results of the simulation are written to a results file, which is also in a text format. The beginnings of DOE-2 pre-date modern personal computers so there is no user interface, although several third-party interfaces were developed over the years.
	EnergyPlus	EnergyPlus is the successor to DOE-2.1E and receives the DOE support that had gone to DOE-2.1E. EnergyPlus also works from text files, but the format is different. It uses IDF (Input Data Format), which is even terser than the BDL used by DOE-2.1E. However, EnergyPlus was never meant to be a stand-alone application, but rather to serve as the engine under the hood of more-robust user interfaces.
	DOE-2.2	DOE-2.2 is a private-sector spin-off of DOE-2.1E and serves as the calculation engine for the EQuest user interface.
	Others	Many software applications have proprietary simulation engines: IES's Apache, TAS, Trnsys, HAP, and TRACE are the most prevalent.

Table 4-1 — continued

	Examples	Description
Middleware Middleware is a software layer between the calculation engine and the user interface.	OpenStudio®	OpenStudio® is a collection of software tools developed by the National Renewable Energy Laboratory to support whole-building energy modeling using EnergyPlus and advanced daylight analysis using Radiance. The tools include a plug-in to SketchUp for creating geometry; an application for reviewing EnergyPlus results files, and a parametric analysis tool. OpenStudio is also used as a software development kit (SDK) with a robust set of developer-focused tools designed to make it easier for third parties to integrate with EnergyPlus.
	CBECC-Com	CBECC-Com is a software application developed by the California Energy Commission for use with the state's energy performance standards. It uses its own text data format, based on gbXML, for both input and results. The primary function of the software application is to automatically generate the baseline building and to perform simulations in EnergyPlus. The application has only a rudimentary user interface, but it is intended to be used as part of a more robust graphic interface developed by the private sector.
Select User Interfaces User interfaces are fully functioning software applications that reside either on the Web or as stand-alone applications. Many incorporate one of the calculation engines described above and some use the middleware.	Trane/TRACE	Trane TRACE is a software application offered by the Trane company, a major manufacturer of HVAC equipment. The application is popular because it may be used both to size equipment and to perform annual energy simulations.
	EQuest	EQuest is a stand-alone user interface developed with significant funding from Southern California Edison. It is widely used, partly because it is offered for free.
	EnergyPro	EnergyPro has been used in California for decades to perform calculations needed for the state's energy-performance standards. The most recent versions build on top of CBECC-Com.
	Carrier/HAP	Carrier HAP is a software application offered by Carrier Air-Conditioning that has its own proprietary calculation engine and user interface.

Table 4-1 — continued

	Examples	Description
Select User Interfaces continued	IES Virtual Environment	IES-VE is a comprehensive package of software applications with a robust graphic interface. Separate versions are offered to meet the specific needs of architects vs. those of engineers. The most recent version incorporates CBECC-Com and has been approved for use with the California energy-performance standards.
	Design Builder	Design Builder is a comprehensive package of software applications that uses EnergyPlus and includes a robust graphic interface.
	Safaira	This software application focuses on the needs of architects during the early design phase.
	Green Building Studio	This Web-based software application is offered by Auto desk and integrates with their CADD programs, in particular Revit®. It uses DOE-2.2 as the calculation engine.
Special Purpose Software	Radiance	Radiance is a suite of tools for performing lighting and daylight simulation. It includes a graphic renderer as well as many other tools for simulating light levels.
	CFD Engines	CFD, or computational fluid dynamics, is a procedure for evaluating airflow in buildings, taking into account the velocity of air leaving the diffuser, its temperature, and other factors. CFD is also useful for evaluation of natural ventilation strategies and air quality analysis, e.g., CO_2 levels in a space.

Comparing Options

Energy models are very precise, but not always accurate. *Precision* refers to the ability of models to produce the same results over and over again with little variation, while *accuracy* refers to the ability of a model to match a reference value, e.g., the actual utility bills after the building is constructed, commissioned, and operated (see fig. 4-1). To use models effectively, modelers need to learn how to take advantage of the precision and to understand and manage the accuracy—and inaccuracy.

Three factors affect the accuracy of models or their ability to predict

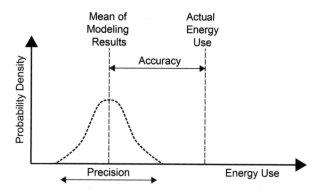

Figure 4-1: Precision vs. Accuracy

In the context of energy modeling, accuracy refers to how well the model predicts actual energy use, while precision is a measure of reliability or consistency.

actual energy use (see fig. 4-2). They are listed below in descending order of importance:

Predictions of Weather and Building Operation. How well is the modeler able to estimate the conditions that the building will experience after it is built? What will the weather be? How many hours a day, week, or year will the building be operated? How many people will use the building? How many computers, monitors, copiers, and other pieces of equipment will be located in the building? At what temperature will the building interior be maintained, and how much outside air will be brought in for ventilation? Will the managers maintain the building so that fans, chillers, boilers, and other equipment operate efficiently? These factors are what we refer to as operating conditions, and they are generally the most significant sources of inaccuracy in modeling.

Physical Description of the Building. How well do the building characteristics specified in the model agree with the actual building as constructed? Were energy-efficiency features eliminated during the construction phase through "value engineering" or other cost cutting? Did the modeler take shortcuts or make unreasonable simplifications? Are the thermal, solar optic, and geometric properties of windows specified accurately? Did the model include everything in the building that uses energy, e.g., elevators,

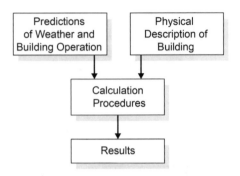

Figure 4-2: Factors Affecting Model Accuracy

Of the three factors affecting model accuracy, the most significant is our ability to predict how the building will be used and what weather conditions it will be subjected to.

outdoor lighting, garage ventilation, etc.? Creating a physical description of the building takes the majority of the modeler's time and can also be a significant factor in inaccurate models, especially when the modeler takes shortcuts or makes unreasonable simplifications.

Calculation Procedures. Do the calculation algorithms used in the model mirror the patterns of heat transfer and equipment operation in the real world?

Software developers and researchers give a great deal of attention to the calculation procedures, as they should, because this is the only part of the process that they can control. As a result, our energy calculation procedures are getting better and better. The interesting part, however, is that of the three factors described above, the correctness of the calculation procedures is the least significant. If our goal is to match the actual energy use of the building, by far the most important and difficult factor is predicting the weather and how the building will be operated.

When good energy modelers have the opportunity to go back and adjust their assumptions on building operation to match what actually took place and to use the weather history for the same year as the utility bills, much of the inaccuracy is eliminated.[2] Even more accuracy can be achieved when they are able to audit the constructed building and make adjustments to the physical description in the model to account for changes made during construction. The result of these adjustments is what we call a calibrated model.

Calibrated models are rare, as they are expensive to develop and the energy modeler is rarely retained after the design and construction phase. A good calibrated model requires careful measurement of plug loads, occupancy patterns, lighting operation, temperature control, HVAC operation, and many other factors. Sometimes modern energy-management systems can provide some of the data needed for model calibration if they are set up to do so, but often the energy modeler must install short-term monitoring equipment to record the on/off status of fans and other equipment and take spot measurements of temperature, air and/or water flow, power usage, and many other conditions needed for calibration.

Attempting to calibrate models against utility bills when little or no information is known about actual building operation is a non-deterministic challenge. Think of a soundboard at a rock concert, where each lever represents a model input. The sound engineer can find multiple combinations that will achieve the overall decibel level (analogous to the utility bill), but it is a much greater challenge to find the perfect combination where every instrument and voice is in clear balance. In exactly the same way, the only way to find the right balance of model inputs for building design is to monitor plug loads, schedules, occupants, and dozens of other details, and use this data for model calibration.

During the design and construction process, models are most useful in evaluating design alternatives and in comparing these alternatives to a baseline building. In these cases, the only thing that varies is the physical description of the building. The predictions on weather and building operation are held constant, and the same calculation procedures are used for the baseline and all the design alternatives. If the prediction on hours of operation is high, it is high for all the design alternatives as well as the baseline. If a design alternative is 25 percent better than the baseline condition for one set of operating assumptions, this ratio will change very little for a different set of operating conditions, since variations will push both the baseline and the proposed design in the same direction. Constraining the model in this way takes advantage of the precision of energy models and manages the inaccuracy. While the absolute predictions of energy use may be off, the comparisons are very precise. This process has many advantages, which are discussed below.

All of the zero net energy (ZNE) buildings described in this book, as well as practically all others, use modeling to estimate the energy use and to size the renewable-energy system to offset this demand. Ed Dean has developed case studies for Pacific Gas and Electric on ZNE buildings in the service territory and compares the modeled energy utilization index (EUI) with the actual EUI. In most cases there is excellent agreement.[3]

Energy-Performance Standards and Building Ratings

Virtually all mandatory energy standards have a performance option that provides more flexibility to designers to meet the varying needs of their clients and the special circumstances of their building sites and microclimates. Early performance standards were based on fixed energy targets expressed in terms of $Btu/ft^2 \cdot yr$ or $kWh/ft^2 \cdot yr$.[4] The format of these targets took account of both building type and climate and was similar to the EUI tables presented in chapter 2. Building designers who used the performance approach developed energy models to demonstrate that the predicted energy use of their buildings would be less than the target. While the concept was simple, it had many loopholes and simply did not work. The fundamental flaw was that it depended on model accuracy, not precision.

Different calculation procedures produce different results, so engineers would sometimes achieve compliance by picking a different computer program. The California Energy Commission (CEC) attempted to address this by giving each approved computer program a multiplier or adjustment factor, i.e., you took the results from your model and scaled them up or down depending on whether the adjustment factor for a particular software application was greater than or less than one. Energy use could also be reduced by raising the cooling setpoint temperature, reducing the hours of operation, lowering ventilation rates, or assuming less office equipment. To address this problem, the CEC specified "fixed and restricted" for energy performance calculations used for code compliance. These actions by the CEC improved the process, but the inner circle still had little confidence that energy efficiency was being achieved or that the loopholes had been closed.

Due to these and other problems, modern energy-performance standards have abandoned the fixed energy budget approach in favor of a two-model approach that capitalizes on the precision of energy models. The goal is to achieve code compliance, not to accurately predict future energy use. This approach was first adopted by the CEC in the mid-1980s and was called the "custom budget approach." A similar approach was subsequently adopted by ASHRAE Standard 90.1 in 1989.

With the two-model approach, one model is developed to represent the proposed design, which is a candidate for compliance using the performance approach, and a second model is developed for the baseline building. Results are computed using the same calculation procedures, weather,

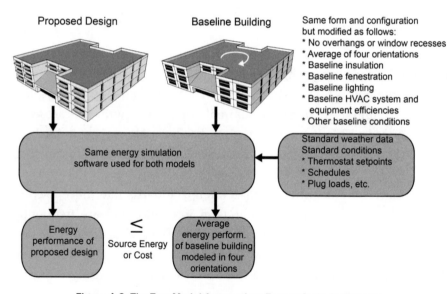

Figure 4-3: The Two-Model Approach to Energy Code Compliance
The same energy-simulation tool, weather data, and operation assumptions are used for both the baseline building and the proposed design. The only thing that changes are the building features. The baseline building is modeled once in each cardinal orientation and the results averaged, in order to credit the proposed design for good orientation and penalize it for poor orientation.

and operating conditions. Many of the physical characteristics of the building are also neutral, such as the size and shape of the building. Only energy-efficiency features regulated by the standard are allowed to change. This approach does not attempt to predict actual energy use (it acknowledges the inaccuracy), but rather it provides a consistent and reliable procedure for evaluating comparative whole-building energy performance.

Reliability and replicability can be improved if the baseline building is automatically generated by the software. Automatic generation of the baseline building has for decades been a requirement for software used for performance calculations in California and is an important factor for confidence in the procedure. The two-model approach has become the standard for energy-performance standards since it solves so many problems. The problem is that modelers must create two models, but this inconvenience and extra work can be avoided when this job is performed automatically by the software.

Fixing the Baseline

The two-model approach to code compliance works much better than the fixed-budget approach, but it is not without its problems. One of the largest problems is that the baseline is constantly changing. The baseline is most commonly defined as minimal compliance with the prescriptive standards. This is the case with either the California standards or ASHRAE 90.1. A new version of ASHRAE Standard 90.1 is published every three years, and the development committee makes changes to the standard on a continuous basis. State standards like those used in California are also under continuous maintenance and are frequently updated, usually on a three-year cycle. This places a burden on the software developer and energy modeler to know which version of the standard must be used for defining the baseline and to correctly interpret these requirements.

A related problem is that as energy standards become more stringent, the prescriptive requirements become more complex. To provide flexibility, there are multiple ways to legally comply with the thorny prescriptive requirements, and each method of compliance does not achieve the same energy performance. This presents opportunities for "gaming the system"; i.e., an astute modeler would choose the method of compliance that causes the energy performance of the baseline building to be the greatest. Keep in mind that compliance can be achieved by reducing energy use in the proposed design or by increasing energy use in the baseline building.

For example, both the California and ASHRAE standards require that large, high-ceiling spaces have skylights that cause at least half the space to be daylighted. There are many ways to meet these criteria, each providing potentially different levels of savings. Should the baseline building have one big skylight or many small ones? What about skylight spacing? Should the baseline building optimize skylight area and layout to achieve maximize lighting savings while minimizing heat gain and loss? What is the target illumination level in the space? Where are daylight sensors located and how are the controls configured and operated? None of these details is addressed by the standard. As this example shows, defining the baseline building becomes a design problem, with many acceptable solutions. But this is not the only complex prescriptive requirement. There are many others, such as building orientation, perimeter daylighting, and exterior shading.

Recognition programs such as LEED and Green Globes offer credits for achieving energy savings that exceed code minimum. Energy-efficiency incentive programs operated by enlightened utility companies like Pacific Gas and Electric offer cash to building designers and owners who produce buildings that use less energy than code minimum. For utilities, it is almost always cheaper to save energy through incentive programs than it is to build new power plants and/or upgrade the grid. The credits offered by recognition programs and cash offered by incentive programs are generally based on energy savings beyond code minimum. While this seems like a simple concept, the moving baseline that results in the near continuous update of energy codes creates considerable confusion and uncertainty.

A few years back, I wrote a paper called "Rethinking Percent Savings" in which I laid out the problems described above in greater detail and proposed a new metric for consistently measuring energy performance, the Zero-Energy Performance Index (zEPI).[5] This is a scale that is stable over time and is not dependent on the latest changes to either ASHRAE Standard 90.1 or California Title 24. The zEPI scale can be used as the basis for incentive programs, green building rating systems, and energy labels. Updates to energy codes can be evaluated on the scale, as opposed to having code updates redefine the endpoints of the scale. The zEPI scale works for all building types, from offices and schools to energy-intensive building types such as supermarkets and laboratories.

The zEPI concept is simple. It is the ratio of the energy performance (EUI) of a candidate building to the energy performance of a baseline building. The baseline building is a typical building at the turn-of-the-millennium as defined by CBECS 2003, a nationwide survey of building energy use.[6] The energy performance of both the candidate building and

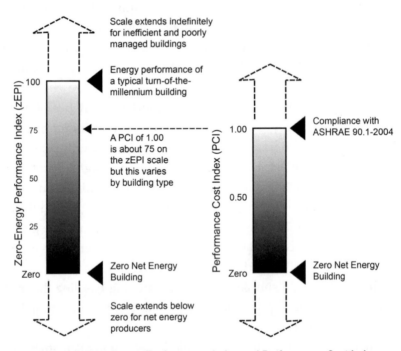

Figure 4-4: Zero-Energy Performance Index and Performance Cost Index

Both zEPI and PCI establish a stable baseline building. The baseline building for zEPI is CBECS 2003, while the baseline building for PCI is ASHRAE Standard 90.1-2004.

the baseline building is determined using the same procedures, weather, and operating conditions, in order to take advantage of the precision of energy modeling and to manage the inaccuracy.

One hundred on the zEPI scale represents average energy consumption at the turn-of-the-millennium and zero on the scale is a zero net energy building. New buildings that comply with the latest energy-efficiency standards would get a zEPI score less than 100. All energy use is included in the zEPI calculation, not just that which is addressed by energy standards.[7] Buildings that use half as much as the average get a 50 on the scale. Buildings that use twice as much as the average get 200 on the scale. A zero net energy building gets zero on the scale. A building that is a net energy producer (like the RMI Innovation Center and many of the other examples) gets a negative score. The scale is stable over time because the zero-marker and the 100 marker do not change.

The recommended zEPI scale enables the energy standards development process to become more of a top-down, goal-oriented process to replace the current bottom-up process. The latter is characterized by adding or modifying prescriptive requirements one by one, which continually redefines the baseline for performance calculations. The top-down process sets a goal on the zEPI scale, and then prescriptive packages are developed to achieve the goal.

Since zEPI was introduced, a similar scale has been adopted in the latest version of ASHRAE Standard 90.1.[8] This scale is called the Performance Cost Index (PCI) and has most of the benefits of zEPI, but works a little better in the energy-modeling world. PCI is included in appendix G of Standard 90.1, which is called the Performance Rating Method. The most significant difference with PCI is that the 1.00 marker on the scale is defined to be roughly equal to minimum compliance with the 2004 version of Standard 90.1, instead of CBECS 2003. The second difference is that energy performance is defined in terms of cost, where zEPI commonly uses source energy (these metrics are discussed in greater detail in chapter 6). Standard 90.1 has PCI targets for compliance with the code. Recognition and incentive programs can set their own PCI targets and associate credits with different targets. For programs like Architecture

Table 4-2 — Converting PCI to zEPI

These values represent the zEPI score for the PCI baseline building. Multiply the calculated PCI by these values to obtain a zEPI score. These conversions are valid when the relative cost of electricity on a per-Btu basis is roughly three times the cost of gas on a per-Btu basis. These values are calculated by the author and are based on the PNNL progress indicator work and simulations of pre-1980 and post-1980 buildings by the NREL.

Climate Regions (see figure 2-3)

	Warm and Dry	Hot and Humid	Pacific Coast	Warm and Humid	Cold and Dry	Cold and Humid	Arctic	Average
Warehouses	n. a.	n. a.	81	77	69	64	52	68
Apartments	76	75	60	62	61	60	56	64
Offices	76	79	80	78	77	78	76	78
Schools	84	87	87	87	88	87	81	86
Retail	62	65	65	63	63	64	64	64
Hotels	84	80	87	84	87	85	85	85
Health Care	83	84	86	85	86	86	83	85
Restaurants	97	97	97	97	97	97	94	96
Average	87	87	88	87	87	86	81	86

2030 and ENERGY STAR that are based on a CBECS baseline, there is an easy conversion. (See table 4-2.)

Scenario Analysis

The two-model approach solves many problems with regard to current energy performance standards and recognition programs. The process focuses on the difference between the rated building and the baseline building, not an absolute prediction of energy use. When we set our goal to be zero net energy and when the assessment is made at the meter after the building is in operation, this represents a return to the fixed-budget approach. We don't need tables to specify a different target for different building types and climates; they all have the same target—zero. With a return to the fixed-budget approach, the assumptions we make about building operation are no longer neutral, they are critical. The choices of energy-modeling tool and of weather data are also critical.

An energy services index (ESI) is a metric that may be used to characterize various sets of operating assumptions by a single number.[9] The ESI is the ratio of energy performance for an alternative set of modeling assumptions to the energy performance with a reference set of modeling assumptions, keeping everything else equal. An ESI of 1.0 means that modeling assumptions are delivering the same level of energy services as the reference case, even though many of the assumptions may be different, some predicting greater energy use and some predicting less. For instance, if the hours of operation are lower, but the heating setpoint is higher, this may result in the same ESI as the reference case.

An ESI of less than 1.0 means that the rated building is providing fewer energy services than the reference case. This could be because of fewer hours of operation, less or more efficient office equipment, fewer occupants, or some combination of these and other operating assumptions. An ESI greater than 1.0 means that the building is providing a higher level of energy services because of longer hours of operation, more equipment, more people, or more of some other service.

The greatest uncertainty in energy modeling is our prediction of how the building will be used in the future: will the energy services index be larger than 1.0, less than 1.0, or equal to 1.0? Typical energy models are run with just one set of building operation assumptions, which usually represent the energy modeler's best guess about how the building will be operated in the future. But, since this is the greatest uncertainty in the modeling process, another approach should be considered. Designers and owners should try to design their buildings to achieve ZNE for a range of plausible operating conditions or at least try to understand the extreme operating conditions for which achieving ZNE will be difficult. At the RMI Innovation Center, the designers oversized the renewable-energy system by about 20 percent in order to accommodate a possible energy-services level greater than what they now anticipate.

What I am recommending is a scenario analysis that asks questions such as: What if half of the building occupants worked late every night?

What if the building were used for fewer hours? What if half the occupants switched from desktop or notebook computers to tablets? What if the office became completely paperless and all printers were eliminated? What if half the occupants telecommuted? What if the organization expanded and took on a software development division and the coders stayed up all night, worked weird hours on the weekend, and all had powerful workstations with three large monitors? With the two-model approach, each of these changes of assumptions would be implemented in both the rated building and the baseline building, and they would tend to cancel each other out. The EUI of both the rated building and the baseline building would together trend up or trend down and the difference would be relatively unchanged. But, when our goal is ZNE, these varying assumptions make a world of difference. With a higher energy service index, the renewable-energy system will need to be larger in order to achieve ZNE; with a lower energy service index, the renewable-energy system can be smaller.

This type of scenario analysis is recommended in a broader context by Stewart Brand in his terrific book *How Buildings Learn*, and is related to "long life, loose fit" (see chapter 2). Through examples like Building 20 on the MIT campus (see fig. 2-1) and many other cases, Brand shows that buildings last through major paradigm shifts like personal computers and tablets, the transition to a service economy, and the Internet. Future owners modify buildings to accommodate these changes in ways that the original designers could not possibly have anticipated. The message is that we can't foresee how our buildings will be used in ten or twenty years, so we should make them as flexible as possible so they can respond to future pressures, whatever they are.

The scenario analysis I am recommending for energy modeling is far simpler than the broader scenario analysis recommended by Brand. With energy modeling, the basic model is typically unchanged; it is not necessary to modify the physical structure, the zoning, the basic lighting, or HVAC equipment. It is only necessary to substitute different assumptions regarding how many hours a week the building will be operated, the number of workers or employees that occupy the building, the power requirements of the equipment they use, how intensively they use the equipment, and other similar assumptions. With scenario analysis, energy models should be run with at least four sets of operating assumptions, described below:

- *Standard Reference.* This is a standard set of operating conditions for the basic building type. It provides a common "test track" that enables us to compare one building to another. However, the results should carry the caveat "Your mileage may vary." At present, the closest thing we have to a set of standard operating conditions that are universally recognized for offices, retail stores, or other building types are the default schedules and conditions recommended for Standard 90.1. These are published in great detail by COMNET (see www.com net.org). They are consistent with national surveys of building occupancy,[10] as well as the recommendations in the ASHRAE Standard 90.1 User's Manual.[11] This is the set of conditions used as the basis for calculating the energy service index.

- *Best Guess.* If the initial tenants are known, the energy modeler and designer should interview or survey this group to estimate the typical hours of operation, plug loads, and other operational factors. These assumptions should define the initial best guess.

- *Minimum ESI.* Imagine a tenant for the building that would use the building the least and require the fewest energy services. Such a tenant would have lower plug loads (fewer computers) and fewer hours of operation, and perhaps they would raise the cooling thermostat for some areas of the building. Examples include a company that encourages telecommuting, an optometrist's office that is open from, say 10:00 a.m. to 5:00 p.m., or a specialized showroom that is open by appointment only.

- *Maximum ESI.* Now imagine a tenant for the building that would use the building the most and require the greatest level of energy services. Think of a high-tech company with energetic employees who stay late, work weekends, and take their meals at the office. Each employee might have multiple monitors and powerful computers at their desks.

An EUI (without consideration of on-site renewable energy) will be calculated for each of the recommended scenarios. This can be plotted on the vertical axis against the energy service index on the horizontal axis, as shown in figure 4-5. The points will, by definition, form a straight line, since the ESI is the EUI of the scenario divided by the EUI of the reference scenario. Alternative scenarios can also be developed for on-site renewable-energy production. These will be horizontal lines, since the production is constant for each of the operational scenarios. In the hypothetical example shown in figure 4-5, PV on the roof would achieve ZNE if the building is used the way we anticipate, but if the ESI is near the maximum scenario, PV would have to be added over the parking area as well.

Our buildings last for a long time and we should understand the conditions within which we will be able to achieve ZNE as well as the conditions that would require acquiring additional renewable-energy capacity.

FOR MORE INFORMATION

- www.COMNET.org
- www.bembook.ibpsa.us

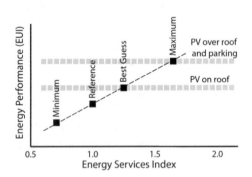

Figure 4-5: Scenario Analysis

Energy models should be run with a range of operating conditions representing possible building-use patterns, and these should be compared with renewable-energy production to evaluate ZNE feasibility for these conditions.

Making It All Work: Integrated Project Delivery, Commissioning, Intelligent Controls, and Mobile Devices

Zero net energy (ZNE) requires that the owner, design team, and builder all work together in a highly collaborative way; that critical building systems be systematically tested prior to occupancy; that controls and monitoring equipment be installed to verify that ZNE is being achieved after occupancy; and that procedures exist to manage and control the amount and type of equipment used by the occupants. In this chapter, methods and procedures are recommended to help achieve these goals.

Project Delivery Methods

Designing and constructing buildings is a complex process that involves dozens of specialties and skills. Communication and teamwork are essential for success, and the contractual relationships among the owner, the designers, and the builders are critical. Each of the common project delivery methods has advantages and disadvantages and can be a vital factor in successfully achieving ZNE.

DESIGN-BID-BUILD

Every architect and engineer can share horror stories about how their designs get messed up during the construction phase through design changes, value engineering, or other cost-cutting techniques. Likewise, general contractors and construction managers can share stories of their own about how the construction drawings from the design team are not specific enough and create problems of constructability. The fee for heating, ventilation, and air-conditioning (HVAC), as well as lighting and other design specialties, is traditionally a multiplier on the value of construction they are responsible for, so their fee is larger for more complex and costly systems that may not be in the best interest of the project. Too frequently, the various design and construction specialties each work in their own little worlds, with little communication with the rest of the team. The project is passed from silo to silo with a minimum of cross-disciplinary interaction. The result is often a project that is over budget and over schedule, and fails to meet the most basic project goals, including energy efficiency.

To meet the goal of ZNE, the owner, design team, and construction team need to look for ways to more effectively work together. Designers and constructors typically have an adversarial relationship that is fostered in large part by the way we commonly organize to build a building. With the traditional process, known as *design-bid-build* (see fig. 5-1), the owner has separate contracts with the design team and the construction team. There is no contractual relationship between the design team and the construction team. To make things worse, the construction team is often not selected until the building is completely designed and "put out for bid." This traditional project-delivery method offers few opportuni-

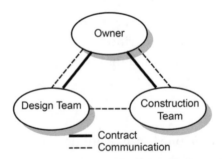

Figure 5-1: Traditional Design-Bid-Build Project Delivery Method
(Source: Integrated Project Delivery: A Guide, AIA National and AIA California Council, 2007 http://www.aia.org/groups/aia/documents/pdf/aiab083423.pdf.)

ties for communication and collaboration. It is difficult or impossible to obtain early involvement of the construction team, which is an essential channel of communication. Yet, for many public projects, this method of project delivery is required by law on the grounds that competitive bidding will yield a lower price.

In spite of the inherent difficulties of the design-bid-build process, a good architect—coupled with the right client—is able to produce excellent ZNE work with this project-delivery method. The Packard Foundation by EHDD and the Iowa Utilities Board by BNIM (see appendix) are examples of integrative design and collaboration, albeit without the participation of the builder during the design phase.

DESIGN-BUILD

Design-build is an alternative project-delivery method and one that was used successfully for the zero net energy NREL RSF (see appendix). With design-build, there is a single contract between the owner and a design-build firm (see fig. 5-2). The design-build firm is often a single-purpose joint venture with the general contractor as the lead. The architect and the rest of the design team are subcontractors to the general contractor. An advantage of design-build is that the design team and construction team are "in the same room." When done right, design-build can encourage collaboration and produce successful results, as demonstrated by NREL.

Lisa Dal Gallo, an attorney who works on structure construction contracts for owners, designers, and constructors, conveys that the design-build process can be structured in many ways and lead to different results depending on how it is set up. In putting together the request for proposals to select a design-build firm, the owner or his representative sometimes develops a set of bridging documents or a preliminary design that all competitors in the design-build process use to base their bids. The design team that develops the bridging documents is typically excluded from competing for the main construction contract.

Lisa argues against the use of bridging documents, however, because the procurement method often provides even less collaboration and design integration than the traditional design-bid-build process.[1] Most

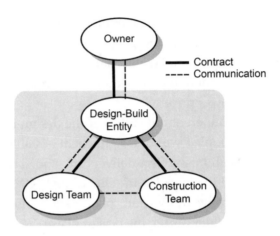

Figure 5-2: Design-Build Project Delivery Method
*(Source: Integrated Project Delivery: A Guide, AIA National and AIA California Council, 2007,
http://www.aia.org/groups/aia/documents/pdf/aiab083423.pdf.)*

of the critical decisions are made when the bridging documents are prepared, leaving little opportunity for optimization and innovation by the
design-build team. There is little communication or knowledge transfer between the architect who prepared the bridging document and the
design-build team; there is often repetition of work; and the second architect has no sense of "ownership." Furthermore, when the design-build
team is selected solely based on a guaranteed maximum price (GMP), the
design-build team will price exactly what is represented on the bridging
documents, and cost savings are often achieved at the expense of quality.
As the general contractor is under great pressure to achieve aggressive
cost savings, the architects and engineers are often treated as vendors
instead of partners.[2]

At the other end of the spectrum is what Lisa calls "integrated design-
build," which is much closer to the variety of design-build used for the
NREL RSF. First, the owner chooses an experienced design-build team
that is proven and committed to collaboration and integrated design.
Instead of developing bridging documents, the owner creates scoping
criteria that provide detailed performance and owner requirements, but
allow the design-build teams to collaborate on the design and present

their own concepts to achieve the owner's goals. Three or so design-build teams are selected based on their qualifications and are invited (with compensation) to participate in a mini–design competition. A design-build team is then selected based on best value, not lowest cost. After selection, the owner works with the design-build team to set the price. This form of design-build has many advantages to the owner, but the process is risky for design teams since the conceptual designs they generate for the design competition usually cost much more to develop than the fixed compensation they are offered.

With the design-build project-delivery method, there is one entity that can be held accountable for building performance. I was an advisor to the City of Oakland when they were constructing a new administrative building more than two decades ago. The project was procured through a design-build contract, and we added a clause to the contract that rewarded the design-build team with additional money if the building had an energy use less than a predetermined target. If it exceeded the target, there would be a penalty. Of course, there was a "deadband" around the energy-performance target where no compensation was granted either to the city or the design-build team. This was probably the first such contract and was possible because of the design-build project delivery method.[3] The idea has not taken off, but it is still being used in a few instances, like the NREL RSF and the RMI Innovation Center.

INTEGRATED PROJECT DELIVERY

Both the design-bid-build and design-build project-delivery methods can be used to achieve ZNE, but they work because of the integrity and commitment of the architects, engineers, and builders who participate on the teams, not because the project-delivery methods encourage integrated design and collaboration. In order to achieve our goals of outcome-based sustainability and ZNE, we need to find a way to address the challenges inherent in the traditional design-bid-build and design-build methods of project delivery. We need a method that fosters better collaboration, communication, and trust among the owner, the design team, and the construction team. The organizational struc-

---

Integrated Project Delivery (IPD)

Recommended by the American Institute of Architects, Integrated Project Delivery (IPD) is a project-delivery approach that "integrates people, systems, business structures, and practices into a process that collaboratively harnesses the talents and insights of all participants to optimize project results, increase value to the owner, reduce waste, and maximize efficiency through all phases of design, fabrication, and construction." IPD projects are distinguished by effective collaboration among the design team, the construction team, and the owner, beginning at early design and continuing through to project handover.

---

ture should encourage a collaborative process whereby information is openly shared with other team members and risk is managed collectively. Compensation and reward should be value-based and keyed to the overall success of the project. Teams should also take advantage of modern digital tools and building information modeling (BIM) to facilitate communications.

This alternative project-delivery method already exists: it is called Integrated Project Delivery (IPD). The concept was first advocated by the American Institute of Architects (AIA), California Council, but is now recommended by AIA for all projects. This project-delivery method was used for the RMI Innovation Center (see appendix) and in many other projects. It has special appeal for complex projects, like hospitals, that involve a lot of expert disciplines.[4] It is particularly appropriate for projects that want to achieve ZNE because of the high need for collaboration among the design and construction disciplines.

With IPD, the key participants (owner, architect, and contractor, along with their major subcontractors):

- are bound together as equals,
- share financial risk and reward based on how well the project meets its goals,
- agree not to sue each other (i.e., they sign liability waivers),
- open their books to each other and provide fiscal transparency,
- participate with each other early in the design process,

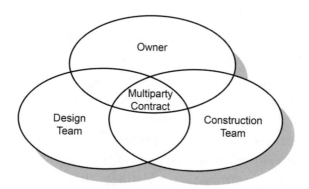

Figure 5-3: Integrated Project-Delivery Method
(Source: Integrated Project Delivery: A Guide, AIA National and AIA California Council, 2007,
http://www.aia.org/groups/aia/documents/pdf/aiab083423.pdf.)

- jointly develop project goals, criteria, and measures of success, and
- engage in collaborative decision making.

In order for the IPD process to work, the participants must have mutual respect and trust, be willing to openly share information, and collaborate in decision making. IPD is fairly new, and most design professionals, contractors, and owners are still getting used to it. As a result, some owners and architects are easing into the process. Clay Goser, who served as the "owner" for BJC Healthcare, makes reference to the Gartner Hype Cycle and notes that IPD may now be at the "peak of inflated expectations" and headed toward the "trough of disillusionment" before it climbs the "slope of enlightenment" and settles on the "plateau of productivity." All new technologies and ideas go through these cycles before they become mature.[5]

There are different flavors of IPD, but most have some sort of multi-party contract that is distinct from traditional design-bid-build or design-build contracts; most have some means of sharing risks and rewards based on overall project outcome, and most provide for fiscal transparency. Liability wavers and integrated project insurance are often omitted. Some but not all IPD projects tie financial incentives to the project goals.[6]

Some IPD projects have an incentive compensation layer (ICL) in which the profits of the key participants (architect, major consultants, contractor, and major subcontractors) are put at risk. Some of the profits are held back and then paid contingent on the project achieving its goals. If specific goals are met, designers and builders receive their normal profit, but jointly, not separately. If the goals are exceeded in measurable ways, the firms are eligible for additional compensation (or profit). The ICL can adjust the profits from minus-20 percent to plus-20 percent, depending on whether project goals are met or exceeded.[7] The RMI Innovation Center used an ICL but also added an energy performance pool of $50,000, which is paid to the key participants on a sliding scale based on the measured energy utilization index (EUI) of the building after it is operational. The target EUI was 19 kBtu/ft$^2\cdot$yr, and if the EUI is as low as 11 kBtu/ft$^2\cdot$yr the team receives the entire pool. If the EUI is 15 kBtu/ft$^2\cdot$yr, they get half. There is no penalty in the RMI contract if the building exceeds the target.[8]

Commissioning

Commissioning is a formal and rigorous quality-assurance process that has been applied to buildings since the early 1990s.[9] The term *commissioning* originates from the navy and shipbuilding; a commissioned ship is one that has been thoroughly and methodically tested and is deemed to be seaworthy. Commissioning works with any of the project-delivery methods described above, but is it especially beneficial with the design-bid-build model. As building controls and other systems have become more sophisticated and complex, the need for commissioning has increased. While commissioning has been around for two or more decades, it is still not part of the mainstream of design and construction practice.

THE COMMISSIONING LEAD

The key to successful building commissioning is the commissioning lead. Other titles for this individual are "commissioning coordinator," "commissioning authority," and "commissioning agent." The commissioning lead should be independent of both the design team and the construction team. The ideal arrangement is for the lead to be hired directly by the owner or to be a member of the owner's staff. The latter is common for organizations that construct and manage multiple buildings such as colleges, school districts, corporate campuses, etc. Sometimes a third-party commissioning lead is hired by the owner through the architect's general services contract, but this arrangement should be structured to enable the lead to play an objective role. The commissioning lead can also be an employee of one of the firms that are part of the design team or the construction team, but this is less than ideal since it is more difficult to maintain objectivity. When the commissioning lead works for a member of the design team or the construction team, at a minimum the person should not be directly involved in project delivery.

The commissioning lead should have direct experience with the type of building that is being designed and constructed. The lead does not need to be an expert in all the building systems, but should understand the building systems well enough to coordinate and manage specialists who work for the design team or the construction team. At a minimum, the commissioning lead should have a good technical knowledge of the fundamentals, design, and operation of the HVAC system and the implementation of control systems, since these are areas where many of the problems occur. A good commissioning lead is the type of person who is comfortable on a construction job site and familiar with construction processes, and who has a sound grasp of engineering and control principles.

THE COMMISSIONING PROCESS

An effective commissioning process begins in the pre-design phase and continues through the first year or so of building occupancy and operations. Table 5-1 lists the principal activities in each phase of project delivery. The process is built around several documents or deliverables, which are updated and maintained as the building is designed and constructed. The commissioning lead is responsible for writing and maintaining these documents and for conducting or observing the functional tests.

Owner's Project Requirements (also called Project Intent). A document that details the functional requirements of the building and the expectations of how it will be used and operated. This is similar to the architectural program but is more quantitative with project goals, measureable performance criteria such as EUI or zEPI targets, cost considerations, etc.

Basis of Design. A document that records the concepts, calculations, decisions, and product selections used to meet the Owner's Project Requirements. The document includes a narrative description as well as individual items that support the design process.

Commissioning Plan. A document that outlines the organization,

Table 5-1 — Overview of Commissioning Process

Source: California Commissioning Guide, California Commissioning Collaborative, 2006.

Phase of Project Delivery	Activity
Pre-Design and Planning	Select a commissioning lead.
	Pre-design phase commissioning meeting.
	Begin developing owner's project requirements.
	Develop initial commissioning plan outline.
Design	Design phase commissioning meeting (if pre-design meeting didn't occur).
	Perform commissioning-focused design review.
	Update commissioning plan.
	Develop commissioning requirements for the specification.
	Begin planning for verification checklists, functional tests, systems manual, and training requirements.
Construction	Construction-phase kick-off meeting.
	Review submittals, monitor development of shop and coordination drawings.
	Review O&M manuals.
	Perform ongoing construction observation.
	Perform verification checks.
	Perform diagnostic monitoring.
	Perform functional testing.
	Develop commissioning report and systems manual.
	Develop recommissioning plan.
	Verify and review training of owner's staff.
Occupancy and Operation	Resolve outstanding commissioning issues.
	Perform seasonal/deferred testing.
	Perform near-warranty-end review.

schedule, allocation of resources, and documentation requirements of the commissioning project. The commissioning plan identifies the functional tests that are to be performed, who is responsible for performing the tests, and when they will be performed during the construction process.

Issues Log. A formal and ongoing record of problems or concerns, and their resolution, that have been raised by members of the commissioning team during the course of the commissioning process. A separate log is typically maintained for design review, construction observation, and functional testing.

BENEFITS AND COSTS

Everyone involved in the delivery of the project benefits from an effective commissioning process. When commissioning begins during the design phase, commissioning can result in significant construction cost savings. Independent plan review will often find errors or potential problems that are relatively easy to correct on paper, but could be very costly if they are not discovered until the construction phase, when they might result in costly change orders or contractor call-backs. These reviews help keep the project on schedule and on budget.

Commissioning improves communication and coordination among design team members and the construction team. This is especially important with the traditional design-bid-build delivery model. The commissioning process tracks, prioritizes, and resolves issues. Better communication results in fewer system deficiencies at the completion of construction. Undiscovered deficiencies can negatively affect building control, energy use, equipment reliability, and occupant comfort for years to come.

In design review, issues that might lead to inefficient system operation and wasted energy can be identified and resolved. The commissioning process also identifies equipment or systems that will be prone to failure once they are integrated with the rest of the system. During construction, the commissioning lead makes sure that the right equipment is installed, that it is maintainable, and that it is working correctly. Functional testing extends this quality assurance to establish that building systems work together and perform effectively.

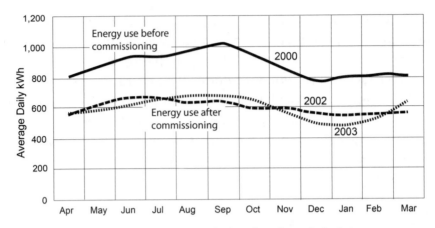

Figure 5-4: Typical Energy Savings from Commissioning

These are actual energy savings that followed commissioning of the Pacific Energy Center in San Francisco. (Source: Ryan Stroupe, Pacific Energy Center, Pacific Gas and Electric Commissioning Savings.)

Commissioning is essential in order to assure that the building is energy-efficient and that the renewable-energy system can produce enough to offset use. But commissioning is cost-effective on its own. Studies by Lawrence Berkeley National Laboratory estimate that the annual monetary benefits of commissioning can range between $0.25/ft² to more than $7.00/ft².[10] Commissioning costs are affected by many factors, including the complexity of the building (hospitals and laboratories cost more than schools and offices) and the size of the building (there are economies of scale). Based on a review of sixty-nine commissioning projects, commissioning costs ranged between $0.49/ft² and $1.66/ft².[11] Using these data, commissioning has a simple payback between three months and two years. Much of the additional cost is related to the services provided by the commissioning lead. The LBNL study estimates that almost 75 percent of these costs are related to construction observation and functional testing.[12]

FOR MORE INFORMATION

- California Commissioning Guide, California Commissioning Collaborative, 2006
- https://www.wbdg.org/project/buildingcomm.php

- ASHRAE Guideline 0-2013: The Commissioning Process and/or ASHRAE Guidelines 1.1-2007 and 1.5-2012
- General Services Administration Commissioning Guide, http://www .gsa.gov/portal/category/21595
- California Commissioning Collaborative, California Commissioning Guide: New Buildings, http://cacx.org/resources/documents/CA _Commissioning_Guide_New.pdf and California
- Commissioning Guide: Existing Buildings, http://cacx.org/resources /documents/CA_Commissioning_Guide_Existing.pdf

Building-Management Systems

Traditionally, each building system or piece of equipment had its own control. Each lighting system had a switch. Each heating system had a thermostat. Things were simple. Traditional buildings had very little automation, apart from an occasional time clock. These local controls still exist in modern buildings, but they are now supplemented and sometimes replaced by sophisticated building-management systems (BMS). A reason for this is that equipment and systems in a modern building must work in harmony with each other in order to achieve energy-efficiency, thermal comfort, and a healthy indoor environment. When a fan is on, a separate pump needs to push water through a heating or cooling coil; a boiler or chiller needs to be operating to maintain water temperature; and a cooling tower needs to reject heat. All of these separate pieces of equipment need to be controlled to work together effectively and efficiently.

CONTROL FUNDAMENTALS

Building-management systems can be complicated, but the fundamentals of controls are simple. A *control variable* is the thing that is being controlled, e.g., temperature, lighting level, airflow, pressure, or humidity. The *setpoint* is the desired state of the controlled variable. A *sensor* measures the current state of the control variable and passes this information to a *controller*, which compares the input from the sensor to the desired setpoint. The controller sends a signal to the *controlled device* (a valve, dimmer, fan, etc.) which initiates a process to reduce the difference between the controlled variable and the setpoint. This sequence is known as a *closed control loop* and is illustrated in figure 5-5. Modern buildings will have thousands of these control loops.

To put the abstract representations from figure 5-5 in context, consider a daylighting system. The setpoint for a room is a lighting level of 40 footcandles. A light meter (the sensor) measures 30 footcandles in the space. The controller compares 30 to 40 and determines that more light is needed, and it then gives this information to the dimmer (the controlled device). The dimmer then initiates a process, i.e., it tells the lamps and ballasts to increase output. The added light modifies the control variable (the lighting level) and the control loop repeats itself.

Another example of a control loop is a constant-volume, variable-temperature fan coil. A temperature sensor measures the temperature in a room to be 65°F, but the setpoint is 70°F. The controller compares the state of the control variable (room temperature) to the setpoint and determines that more heat is needed. A valve (the controlled device) is signaled by the controller to open up and increase water flow from the boiler and pumping system (the process). The result is that the temperature leaving the heating coil is increased, which raises the room temperature to be closer to the setpoint. And the loop continues as long as the heating system is on.

Most control loops are based on proportional control. This just means

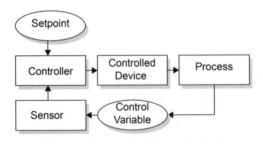

Figure 5-5: Typical Closed-Loop Control Sequence
The basic closed-loop control sequence adjusts output from a process like a heating coil to reduce the difference between the control variable and the setpoint.

that the magnitude of the response is proportional to the difference between the controlled variable and the setpoint. For instance, if the temperature setpoint for a space is 70°F and the sensor measures 50°F, then the control device (valve) would open all the way to put as much heat in the space as quickly as possible. However, if the sensor measured 67°F, the difference between the setpoint and the control variable would be only 3°F and the valve would open up just a little more.

MODERN DDC SYSTEMS

Another term used in the controls world, which can be confusing, is direct digital control (DDC). This just means that information from the sensors (which is often analog) is converted to digital information before it is passed on to the controller. Also, the controller sends out a digital signal to the controlled device, which then converts it to analog. The device that converts an analog signal to digital or a digital signal to analog can be located at the controller, the sensor, or the actuator.

Many older buildings still have pneumatic or electromechanical control systems that are analog, but these are rare in new buildings as DDC has many advantages and is becoming less expensive. DDC systems not only control equipment but also perform many building-management and system-diagnostic functions as well. A DDC system requires less maintenance and recalibration, unlike pneumatic systems. Setpoints can be controlled from a central location (with local override if desirable). Changes to control sequences can be easily modified. Building-management systems can also incorporate security, fire, and safety functions.

The way that a BMS is physically configured can get complicated, but an easy way to visualize it is as a black box that takes input from all sorts of sensors scattered around the building (see fig. 5-6). It knows the temperature of each zone, the temperature of water that is leaving or returning to the chiller, the lighting level in each space, and many other factors, limited primarily by cost. It also has the ability to control things through actuators (switches and motorized devices). It can turn equipment on or off, speed up or slow down a fan, open or close a valve or dim a lighting system. Each sensor and actuator is considered a control point, and the

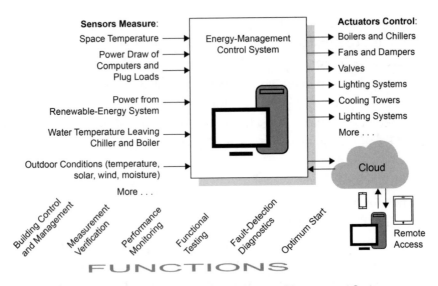

Figure 5-6: Conceptual Diagram of DDC Building-Management System

A modern building-management system performs many functions critical to achieving ZNE.

cost of a BMS is directly related to the number of control points. Costs range between $50 and $300 per point.[13]

At the core of the black box is one or more computers that process all the information provided from the sensors and make decisions on how to control various pieces of equipment in the building. In contrast to analog controls, the control algorithms in a digital system can factor in input from multiple sensors. This enables more-advanced and sophisticated control. An example of an advanced feature is the ability to determine the optimum time to start the HVAC system in order to reach comfort conditions at a particular time. With conventional systems, a time clock simply turns the system on a couple of hours before occupants are expected to arrive. But a BMS can factor in the outside air temperature, the temperature of the space, and other conditions, and it can turn on the system at the latest possible time in order to have the building comfortable when business opens.

Another feature that is beginning to emerge is fault detection and diagnostics. A BMS collects a great deal of data, and from this data, machine-learning algorithms can anticipate system failures and recommend mitigating maintenance procedures. Systems can even repeat some of the functional testing that takes place during the commissioning process.

With the proper sensors, a BMS can measure how each component of the building is using energy, including the lighting system, plug loads, various HVAC components, water heating, and more. This kind of information is critically important in order to achieve zero net energy and to understand what is wrong when ZNE is not achieved. Measured energy use from the BMS can be compared with predictions from the model to identify components that are not performing as expected. Some advanced BMS systems actually incorporate an energy model into the decision making.

MOBILE DEVICES AND OCCUPANT INTERACTION

Energy-management systems have been around for a while and several large companies dominate the market, but with pressure from building owners and managers, cross-platform standards have developed so that a building owner is not "committed for life" to a particular manufacturer and their proprietary technology, as was the case a decade to two ago. The most important of these standards is BACnet, which is a data-communication protocol for building automation and control networks.[14] BACnet has helped make it possible for smaller companies to offer innovations. One of the more exciting directions is the use of mobile devices to engage the building occupants in the management of the building.

Building Robotics is a start-up company in Oakland that provides office workers with the capability of controlling the temperature of their workspace through their smart phones or other mobile devices.[15] A Web app is also available for those who don't have a smart phone or tablet. The system, which they call Comfy, hooks up to the BMS through the BACnet protocol. Once it is set up, workers can use their mobile devices to let the system know which room they are in and to indicate whether they are hot, cold, or okay.

Lindsay Baker, president of Building Robotics and an expert on thermal comfort, notes that people are far better at judging comfort than a thermostat mounted on the wall. The thermostat may be out of calibration, located where sun is striking it, or located directly under an air diffuser, all of which can result in bad information being passed to the control system. But even if such problems don't exist, comfort depends on more than just temperature. If a person or multiple persons "vote" through their mobile devices that they are cold, this is a far better indicator than a thermostat reading that heat needs to be added to the space. The human body has a sophisticated set of sensors that can factor in temperature, humidity, mean radiant temperature, and air velocity and make a quick, accurate assessment of comfort, something that is not possible with even the best of thermostats.

The GPS in mobile devices is not sensitive enough to be able to detect a specific location (or room) within the building, but this may be possible in the future with beacon technology or WiFi. With the capability to pinpoint the room or thermal zone where the hot/cold "vote" is coming from, it would no longer be necessary for the user to pick a room when they cast their vote. Comfy would know where they are. It might also be possible to determine whether a workspace is occupied and by whom, and then deliver heat, air, and light to meet their personal preferences. An advanced control system like this would be able to identify conference rooms that are occupied and those that are not, and deliver services appropriate for the level of occupancy. Systems could be shut down for areas of the building that are unoccupied. There are privacy issues around tracking individuals (or at least their phones); Lindsay believes tracking would be something that each individual would opt into if the benefits of the system outweighed their privacy concerns. At any rate, occupancy (or vacancy) would be supplemented and verified by other sensors scattered through the building.

All of the votes submitted to Comfy are stored in memory, and machine-learning algorithms are able to figure out the best and most energy-efficient way to heat and cool the building. Lindsay reports that more "cold" votes are cast in the morning and more "hot" votes in the afternoon. As a result, the temperature of most spaces is controlled dynamically throughout the day (warmer in the morning and cooler in the afternoon). From all the votes, Comfy can infer when people arrive and when they leave and adjust the operation schedules accordingly.

The system now works just for thermal comfort, but Building Robotics is working to extend their technology to work with lighting and perhaps other building systems. LED and other modern luminaires have the capability of being individually addressable. With this technology, the BMS has the capability of separately controlling the thousands of individual lighting fixtures in each building. Software developers like a dark room; others (my wife, for instance) like to be flooded with light. The building can know who is occupying each space and adjust heat, air, and light to meet their needs.

Buildings like the Edge in Amsterdam have workspaces that are not assigned to individuals. They offer a variety of spaces with a sitting desk, standing desk, work booth, meeting room, balcony seat, or "concentration room." Each Deloitte employee (the primary building tenant) can choose a workspace each day, and their mobile app will help them find one that is suitable based on their preferences for light and temperature.

These kinds of smart systems not only improve comfort, they also save energy. With mobile devices and occupant interaction, the building-control system learns how to provide individualized comfort (light, air, and temperature) for each occupant. It does not require that a building manager diligently and constantly make adjustments to the BMS. The building learns on its own to meet the needs of the individuals who work there and to do it in the most energy-efficient manner.

DEMAND RESPONSE AND COMMUNICATION WITH THE POWER GRID

Demand response is an emerging technology that will become more important as more buildings are designed and constructed to achieve ZNE. Here is how it works. The local utility predicts that its transmission and/or distribution networks will be near capacity or that available generation will be limited for a specified time in the near future, say, this afternoon between 4:00 p.m. and 6:00 p.m., when all the commercial buildings are still being operated and people are beginning to arrive home and turning on their air conditioners. The utility notifies building operators of the expected problem and requests that they do what they can to reduce their demand for electric power during this period. Building operators can manually respond to the request by dimming non-critical lighting, slowing fan motors, temporarily raising cooling setpoints, drawing from thermal storage, drawing from battery packs, or taking other appropriate action that enables the building to keep functioning but with less power during the critical period. In exchange for a commitment to help out the grid, the building can qualify for a more favorable energy tariff (i.e., a lower price for electricity) or receive other compensation.

As we move to a smart grid (more about this in chapter 7), the signal from the utility will be in some sort of electronic form that the building-management system can detect and respond to automatically, without the need for participation by the building operator. The BMS will automatically initiate a sequence of preprogrammed steps to achieve a given amount of demand reduction. Perhaps the first step is to dim non-critical lighting and to raise the cooling setpoints by 2°F. If this does not achieve the necessary reduction, additional steps are taken until the demand-reduction goal is achieved. The BMS can also advise occupants of the situation so that they are aware of a possible temporary inconvenience.

Another way to implement demand response is through dynamic pricing of electricity. Instead of customers paying a fixed price per kilowatt, the price would change throughout the day based on demand, stress on the transmission and distribution networks, and available generation capacity. Many utilities already have time-of-use tariffs whereby the price changes for predefined peak, shoulder, and off-peak periods, but with dynamic pricing, the predefined periods would go away and the market would set the price for each hour (or sub-hour) based on supply and demand for that hour.

Most utilities experience their peak on hot weekday afternoons when air-conditioning for commercial buildings is at its maximum. As we construct and operate more ZNE buildings and bring more solar energy into the grid, the peak will shift a couple of hours into the early evening when the sun is down, commercial buildings are still being operated and people are arriving home and starting to turn things on (TV, air-conditioning, etc.). This has already happened in Hawaii, where more and more electric customers have turned to solar because of the high cost of grid-provided electricity on the islands. In response, Hawaii is reevaluating its policies on net metering and looking at other ways to integrate distributed PV systems into the grid.[16]

Dynamic pricing will create new opportunities for BMSs to respond to the price signals. Dynamic pricing will also encourage building design-ers to incorporate energy storage in the building in order to shift demand from periods when electricity prices are high to periods when they are low. Thermal storage has been used for some time. With this strategy, chillers produce chilled water at night when prices are low and tempera-ture conditions are more favorable; this chilled water is used the next day to meet the air-conditioning load. With greater use of solar panels in ZNE buildings, battery storage will also become common. A building with battery storage would still be connected to the grid, but some of the power generated by the photovoltaic panels during the day would be used to charge the batteries, and power from these batteries would be used to carry the building through the early-evening peak period, when electricity prices are high. The batteries used for storage and those used for emergency backup will likely be different. The latter would remain fully charged until they are needed, while the former may cycle each day.

MEASUREMENT AND VERIFICATION OF ZNE

The test for a ZNE building is at the utility meter, but the meter is a fairly crude measuring device. It does not break down electricity use by lighting, fans, heating, cooling, plug loads, etc., and this kind of detail is needed in order to properly manage a ZNE building. Collecting and evaluating this detailed data is a critical measurement and verification (M&V) function that can be performed by the BMS. When electricity use is higher than expected, looking at the end-uses will often identify the culprit. Perhaps a fan's energy use is high because a filter needs changing and the fan is operating against greater pressure. Maybe time clocks for outdoor light-ing are out of calibration. Many things could contribute to the problem, but without detailed information, figuring it out is mostly guesswork.

Managing the Stuff Inside

As standards and technology reduce lighting and HVAC energy, plug loads are becoming a larger percentage of energy use in buildings and finding a way to manage these loads is critical in meeting the goal of zero net energy. Plug loads include desktop computers, notebooks, monitors, copy machines, printers, smart phone and tablet chargers, break room refrigerators, vending machines, and all sorts of other devices and equipment that are scattered through our buildings and plugged into the outlets. Plug and miscellaneous loads represent almost half of the electricity use at the Bullitt Center in Seattle. The US Energy Information Agency predicts that the growth of plug loads will increase more than 90 percent by 2030, while growth of lighting, HVAC, and large appliances will be relatively flat.[17]

For typical offices, COMNET estimates that plug loads amount to about 1.7 W/ft^2, significantly higher than the power used for modern lighting systems.[18] If this equipment is operated for 3,000 full-time-equivalent hours per year, this represents 5.1 kWh/ft$^2\cdot$yr of energy use, or more than 17 kBtu/ft$^2\cdot$yr. This much energy would wreck our attempts to achieve the maximum potential EUIs identified in chapter 2.

A lot of equipment uses energy even when it is turned off. The parasitic load of chargers for notebook computers and small devices is notorious, but larger appliances like TVs, printers, and copiers can also have considerable parasitic loads. Cable boxes are perhaps the worst. I have measured the power draw of the one we have in our home, and I find that it constantly uses about 35 W whether the device is turned on or off; the only way to reduce its power use is to unplug it.

Design and construction teams have limited ability to manage plug loads. They are primarily the responsibility of the tenants and occupants who use the building after it is constructed. The trigger point for new construction projects is the building permit (when the plans are approved) and later the certificate of occupancy (when everything checks out). Opportunities to address plug loads come later in the life cycle of the building, making it a difficult issue for the design and construction teams.

While they are difficult to manage, there are many opportunities to

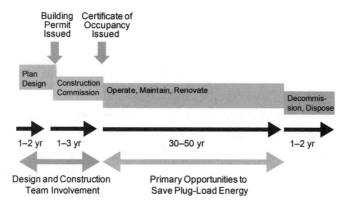

Figure 5-7: Plug Loads Related the Building Life-Cycle Phases

Opportunities for managing plug loads occur after the design and construction services have been provided.

reduce plug loads. Some studies have shown that savings of more than 40 percent are achievable without compromising utility or function.[19] The biggest opportunity doesn't cost anything at all. It simply involves using the advanced power settings available on most of our office equipment, including computers monitors, copiers, and printers. The IT systems in our buildings can be configured to maintain the power-management settings to put the machines in a "sleep mode" when they are not in use. E-mail reminders to workers to turn off unnecessary equipment have also proven to be successful. Power strips are available with timers and/or occupant sensors that will turn off desk lamps, monitors, and other devices when the workspace is not occupied. These power strips have constant-on outlets for the computer and other devices that need to remain powered.[20]

Hardware replacement can also have a significant impact on plug loads. The US Environmental Protection Agency estimates that computers, monitors, printers, and other office equipment that qualify for their ENERGY STAR program use 40 percent less energy than conventional equipment.[21] Corporations, school districts, governments, and other entities have adopted policies to purchase only ENERGY STAR equipment, and this can make a big difference. For speculative or multi-tenant buildings, requirements to use ENERGY STAR equipment can be written into the leases and/or included as part of the tenant improvement standards.

Servers offer a special opportunity for savings that can be achieved through a practice called *virtualization*, which offers a way to consolidate servers by allowing multiple workloads to run on one machine (see fig. 5-8). Conventional practice has been for businesses to install a separate machine to serve each application, such as e-mail, database, printing, etc. IT professionals are very conservative, because a crash can be disastrous. As a result, multiple machines are often provided for redundancy, staging and recovery. The conventional one-workload-one-box approach means that most servers run at a very low "utilization rate"—the fraction of total computing resources engaged in useful work. Average server utilization rate has been estimated to be in the range of 6–12 percent.[22] The problem is that while these machines have a utilization rate of 10 percent or less, they use a lot more than 10 percent of their maximum power. At 10 percent utilization, they commonly use between 60 and 90 percent of maximum power. Many software vendors have products to achieve virtualization. Virtualization is commonplace in large data centers, but far less common for small server rooms.

Clearly, there are many opportunities to reduce and manage plug-load energy. The challenge for owners and managers of buildings that have ZNE as their goal is to motivate the businesses and organizations that use the building as well as their employees to engage in the process of meeting

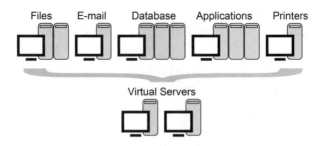

Figure 5-8: Server Virtualization

With virtualization, one or two machines are operated during periods of low use to perform the functions normally handled by many.

the goal. The users of the building, not the designers and constructors, have the ability to address plug loads. There are low-cost or no-cost opportunities to manage the power usage of equipment, occupant and load-sensing plug strips, connections to security systems, etc. Opportunities also exist to upgrade the hardware through purchasing programs that require only ENERGY STAR or other energy-efficient equipment. Savings can also be had by administering programs to encourage behavioral changes through social media, recognition programs, awards, and advisory notices.

Some building owners and managers are reluctant to place new requirements on tenants, especially in a tight rental market, but the management team must take a proactive approach in order to achieve ZNE. Owner-occupied buildings can be proactive through binding resolutions, executive orders, and/or legislative mandates. Leased spaces can achieve savings through tenant improvement specifications and corporate-responsibility policies.

The Bullitt Center has terms in its leasing contract that gives tenants an energy budget, including plug loads. Each tenant pays the landlord for electricity each month but is reimbursed at the end of the year if they meet their budget, which is based on the total building-wide PV production for that calendar year. If a tenant has 10 percent of the building and the PV production for the year is 250,000 kWh, then the electricity budget for that tenant is one-tenth of the total, or 25,000 kWh. Their budget includes the electricity they use not just for plug loads, but also for lighting, data, HVAC, ventilation, and a share of the energy used in common areas. If a tenant does not meet their budget, they are reimbursed less. The reimbursement can be a rent credit or cash.[23] The power allotment for plug loads at the Bullitt Center works is significantly lower than the COMNET defaults for a typical office.

CHAPTER 6

Metrics and Boundaries: What Exactly Is a Zero Net Energy Building?

Zero net energy is a powerful goal for buildings. The concept energizes just about everyone in the energy-efficiency community, from design professionals and policy wonks to environmentalists of every stripe. The Architecture 2030 Challenge calls for new commercial buildings to be zero net energy by 2030, and this challenge has been widely adopted as a policy goal. At first blush, the concept of zero net energy seems simple. The concept is strong and compelling, but there are lots of significant issues that surface as you dig deeper into the details.

As discussed in the introduction, a zero net energy (ZNE) building is one that uses no more energy on an annual basis than it produces (see fig. 1-4). The sum of all the energy delivered across the property line must be less than or equal to the sum of all the energy that is exported from the site. But the delivered energy does not have to pass through a single utility meter. Nor does the exported energy have to pass through the same meter as the delivered energy. When multiple meters are located within the property boundary, these may be combined into a virtual meter for the purposes of ZNE accounting. A *virtual meter*, as the name suggests, is not a real meter, but rather a collection of meters that are evaluated as one for the purposes of establishing zero net energy. There are many instances when it is necessary to apply the concept of a virtual meter. The most typical situation is residential condominiums, where each dwelling unit may have its own electric meter.[1] It rarely makes sense for each individual dwelling unit to have its own renewable-energy system as well, but a common system that serves all the dwelling units in the building may be very practical. In evaluating such a condominium project, the solar system would be on its own meter and the virtual meter would include this meter plus the meters for each of the dwelling units. ZNE would be achieved when the net energy use of the collection of meters is zero or negative. Other examples where virtual meters would be applicable are shopping centers and multi-tenant office buildings.

Operational vs. Asset Assessments

ZNE buildings are commonly verified by looking at the utility bills. If the building has a net-metering arrangement, the electricity meter will record both delivered energy and exported energy; otherwise, the renewable-energy system may be on its own meter and will supply energy to the grid through a feed-in tariff. Either way, the delivered energy must be less than the exported energy. Natural gas and other non-electricity forms of energy are typically only delivered to the site and not exported. Other than electricity, an example of possible exported energy is chilled water or hot water that is generated within the site boundary and pumped off-site to cool or warm another building. If electric vehicles are charged on-site and the cars are used for off-site transportation, then this too should be considered exported energy.

When building performance is measured after a building is built and occupied, this is known as an *operational assessment*. An operational assessment takes everything into account, since the test is performed by looking at the utility bills. Delivered energy is affected not only by the quality of the windows and the efficiency of the lighting system but also by the time of day the tenants come to work and how long they stay, whether they work on weekends, how many computers and servers they use, and how they set their thermostats. Weather is also a factor, as some years are colder, hotter, or cloudier than others. An operational assessment of ZNE can only be performed after the building has been constructed and has operated for at least a twelve-month period, in order to capture seasonal operational and weather patterns. However, in reality it usually takes longer than twelve months because it takes a while for the building to be fully occupied and all the systems properly commissioned. The results of an operational assessment will change each year, of course, depending on the occupants and the weather. Chapter 5, on energy modeling, recommends scenario analysis to make sure that a building is capable of achieving ZNE for all the reasonable patterns of building operation.

Figure 6-1 shows 2013 monthly use through the net meter at our home. We are net users of electricity in November, December, and January, and we are net producers for the months of April through August. February, March, September, and October can go either way, depending on weather conditions and how much we are at home using the house. Zero net energy means that the total lengths of all the bars that extend below zero are at least as long as the ones that extend above the line. For most years, we make more electricity than we use and achieve ZNE for electricity use, but some years we don't because of cold conditions, more houseguests, or more entertaining.

An *asset assessment*, by contrast, isolates the impact of the building assets. The assets in this context are the features of the building that survive a change of occupancy. Assets include the building envelope; the lighting systems; the systems that provide heating, cooling, and ventila-

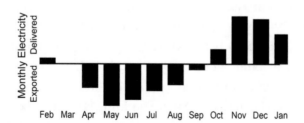

Figure 6-1: Monthly Electricity Use of a Zero Net Energy Residence
In this example, photovoltaic (PV) production exceeds usage for the months of April through August. Usage exceeds PV production for October through January. February, March, and September can go either way, depending on weather and building use.

tion; elevators; parking garages; and outdoor lighting. The assets do not include things the tenants would take with them when they leave, such as desk lamps, computers, servers, printers, and copy machines.

For an asset assessment, standard assumptions are made about the number of occupants and the energy used by their equipment and also about the annual weather, the hours of building operation, the thermostat settings, and other operational factors. The test track that EPA uses to rate the mileage of cars is a good metaphor for the test conditions used for an asset assessment. Buildings that are subjected to these standard test conditions can be effectively compared with each other.

Of course, it is not possible to subject a real building to a year of standard conditions like a car can be tested. We can't control the weather, and forcing all the occupants to work the same hours and use the same computers is not the least bit reasonable. For these and other reasons, asset assessments are made through energy modeling (see ch. 4). With energy modeling, it is easy to subject all buildings to the same operating conditions and weather patterns. Models can also predict the production from renewable-energy systems for standard weather conditions, and with this information the potential for achieving ZNE can be assessed. Of course, the typical operating conditions for a restaurant or retail shop are very different from those of an office, so standard conditions are defined separately for major building types. The Commercial Energy Services Network (COMNET) publishes standard conditions that may be used for comparative building asset assessments.[2]

An operational assessment is the true measure of whether a building is achieving ZNE, but sometimes it is necessary to use an asset assessment instead. For instance, when ZNE is a requirement of building codes, an assessment of whether a building will achieve ZNE must be made when the building plans are approved for construction and before the certificate of occupancy has been issued. Such a building is designed to achieve ZNE, but the true test will come later, once it is up and running. When energy modeling with standard conditions shows that a building is expected to achieve ZNE but has not yet proven it, the ZNE label should be qualified with a designation such as "Modeled-ZNE."

Accounting for Energy Other than Electricity

Understanding zero net energy is a lot easier for buildings that only use electricity, like the Bullitt Center and many of the other ZNE examples discussed in this book. Since both wind and photovoltaic (PV) systems make electricity, and the building uses only electricity as a power source, the accounting is pretty simple. You count the kilowatt-hours of electricity that are produced and you count the kWh of electricity that are used, and when more are produced than used on an annual basis, the building has achieved zero net energy.

On-site renewable-energy systems can produce electricity, but they can't make more natural gas, oil, propane, or any other kind of fossil fuel, for that matter. For some, this fact contributes to a line of reasoning that ZNE buildings should be all-electric; in other words, the principles of zero net energy do not apply to the direct use of depletable fossil fuels. When we burn oil or natural gas, that store of energy is lost forever and can never be recovered. Burning fuels in a building also results in emissions to the outside air, which, without proper ventilation, can affect indoor air quality. The ZNE certification program operated by the International Living Future Institute prohibits any type of on-site combustion.

Since almost all ZNE buildings are connected to the grid and use the grid to provide power at night and on cloudy days, and to accept excess power when the building has a surplus, such buildings (even if they are all-electric) indirectly use some form of fossil fuel. Virtually all electric utilities currently use coal and/or natural gas to some extent in their generating mix. Until we have utilities that operate entirely on renewable energy, this will always be the case. Nevertheless, even if grid power is provided from renewable energy or carbon-free sources (an example is the EverGreen offering by Sonoma Clean Power), reducing energy use and achieving on-site ZNE still has benefits, because SCP would not have to buy as much renewable energy from third-party generators and that renewable energy would be available for purchase by another utility, effectively reducing fossil-fuel use somewhere else.

With some net-metering tariffs, compensation for electricity produced in excess of what is used may be discounted. For instance, Pacific

Gas and Electric (my utility) buys back power at the retail rate unless you export more than is delivered on an annual basis, in which case, their rate of compensation for the excess is closer to the wholesale rate. This reduces the cost-effectiveness of ZNE buildings that use natural gas.[3]

Zero-energy accounting becomes more complex when buildings also use natural gas or other fossil fuels in addition to electricity. In rural areas, propane is often used for space heating, hot water, and cooking. In the eastern United States, fuel oil is trucked in for some buildings. And some buildings buy energy in the form of hot water, steam, or chilled water that is piped directly into the building from neighborhood-scale or campus systems (more on this later). Natural gas use is measured in therms, fuel oil and propane are measured in gallons, and various other units are used for hot and chilled water. Since renewable-energy systems typically only produce electricity, in order to get to zero net energy, additional electricity must be generated and pumped into the grid to make up for the natural gas or other fuels that are being used in the building.[4] So the question is how do we account for energy other than electricity when we determine whether or not a building is zero net energy? What's needed is a common currency, energy-accounting system, or metric for adding up all the energy delivered to a building and comparing this sum to the renewable energy that is exported.

SITE ENERGY

Electricity, oil, gas, etc. can all be converted to common energy units — for instance, British thermal units (Btu). A Btu of energy is roughly the amount of energy needed to raise the temperature of a pint of beer 1°F, or the energy released when one kitchen match is burned. In other parts of the world, a common unit of energy is the joule (J) or kilojoule (kJ), named after James Prescott Joule, a pioneer in the fields of energy and thermodynamics. A Btu is equal to 1,055 joules, or roughly one kJ. The units watt-hour (Wh) and kilowatt-hour (kWh) are used primarily for electricity, but other forms of energy can also be converted to kWh. A kWh is equal to 3,412 Btu, or 3,600 kJ. Every form of energy from oil and natural

Table 6-1 — Energy Equivalents for Calculating Site Energy

This table shows the conversion factors for common measures of energy with no consideration of upstream energy losses related to the generation of electricity or its delivery to the site.

British thermal unit (Btu)		kilowatt-hour (kWh)		kilojoule (kJ)
1 Btu	=	.000293 kWh	=	1.055 kJ
3,412 Btu	=	1 kWh	=	3,600 kJ
0.948 Btu	=	.000278 kWh	=	1 kJ

gas to electricity and chilled water can be converted to one of these common units. The total energy can then be added up and compared with the Btu of electricity production from solar or wind systems to determine if a building has achieved zero net energy.

This metric is called *site energy* because the accounting occurs at the building site. Site energy does not include the energy used upstream to produce electricity and deliver it to the site, and this omission can distort the process. The energy burned at a typical fossil-fuel-fired electricity-generation plant is about three times greater than the electric energy that is delivered to buildings. Site energy counts only the Btu that cross the property line or flow through the building meters, not the energy that is actually mined from the earth, burned at the generation plant, and lost through the transmission and distribution network. Nonetheless, site energy utilization index (EUI) expressed in site $kBtu/ft^2 \cdot yr$ is the most common metric for evaluating ZNE buildings and is used to present most of the data in this book.

Site energy is a simple metric, but it undervalues electricity relative to other fuels. Electricity is a much more versatile and useful form of energy than all other forms, and the market prices it three to five times higher on a common energy (Btu) basis. Furthermore, electricity is not really a source of energy like oil or natural gas, but rather a medium for transporting energy. There are no stores of electricity buried beneath the surface of the earth and it does not occur naturally in our environment, except in lightning strikes. Other forms of energy are required to produce it and distribute it to building sites.

SOURCE ENERGY

Source energy is another common currency for adding up energy from multiple sources. Source energy is used by the US Environmental Protection Agency (EPA) in its ENERGY STAR building programs and by the US Department of Energy (DOE) in its "Common Definition for ZEB." California used source energy to evaluate whole-building performance until about 2005, when it shifted to a more advanced metric called *time-dependent-valued* or TDV energy (more on this later). Source energy includes not just the energy that crosses the building property line but also the energy consumed in the extraction, processing, and transport of primary fuels such as coal, oil, and natural gas; energy losses at electricity-generation power plants; and energy losses in transmission and distribution to the building site.[5] The principal impact of using source energy instead of site energy is with regard to electricity, since the process of burning a fossil fuel such as natural gas or coal to make electricity

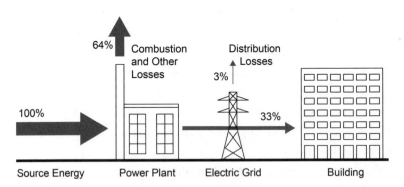

Figure 6-2: Source Energy for Electricity

The conversion efficiencies and losses are improving as utilities retire old coal and gas plants and replace them with renewable energy and modern combined-cycle gas plants. The values shown here are based on EIA data as compiled by Lawrence Livermore National Laboratory (see fig. 1-2). However, the values are adjusted to use the "captured energy" approach for noncombustible renewable energy as opposed to the "fossil-fuel equivalency" approach used in the past.

is fairly inefficient. Source energy is sometimes called "primary energy." The terms mean the same.

The efficiency of electricity generation and distribution is the ratio of usable energy that actually reaches the building in the form of electricity divided by the total amount of energy that feeds into the process. Modern combined-cycle gas plants can operate at efficiencies greater than 50 percent, but the mix of generating equipment that is now on-line in the United States is far less efficient; for the entire United States electric system, the efficiency is about 33 percent.[6] This means that for every Btu or joule of electrical energy that is used at a building site, about three Btu or joules are used upstream in the generation and distribution process.

There are upstream energy uses and losses related to delivering natural gas, oil, and other fuels to a building, but these are not nearly as large as they are for electricity. For natural gas, energy is used to pressurize the gas and move it through pipelines, and along the way, there are a few leaks and losses. All total, a source-site multiplier of 1.09 is assigned to natural gas, which represents a delivery efficiency of 92 percent, which is significant, but not nearly as low as for electricity.

Comparing overall energy use and greenhouse-gas emissions using source energy leads to a completely different result than site energy. Site energy can lead to misguided actions. Converting electricity directly to heat is a process that is essentially 100 percent efficient (except for tank or storage losses). Modern gas water heaters and boilers, on the other hand, operate at efficiencies in the range of 70–95 percent, i.e., 70–95 percent of the energy in the fuel being burned is converted to useable heat and 5–30 percent is lost as waste heat up the flue. An electric water heater or boiler uses less site energy than a comparable oil or natural gas product, but it would use more source energy and cost more to operate. If source energy is considered, the electric equipment really operates at an efficiency of only about 35 percent, on an average basis nationally, while the efficiency of the gas equipment is degraded only slightly to a range of 67–91 percent, which is still two to three times more efficient than electric resistance.[7] This is more than a theoretical point. In 1977, President Jimmy Carter directed energy managers to reduce site-energy use in federal buildings,[8] and many complied by replacing efficient gas equipment with electric equipment, thereby increasing overall United States energy use and cost.

The source energy conversion factors in table 6-2 are averages for the United States. Using national averages is recommended by DOE in its "Common Definition" in order to ensure that no specific building is credited (or penalized) for the relative efficiency of its energy provider. Furthermore, the United States is divided into just three power grids: the eastern interconnection (Nebraska, Kansas, and everything east), the western interconnection (Colorado, Wyoming, and everything west), and Texas.[9] Power is traded within each grid, so what really matters is the mix of generating sources within the grid. Supply and demand in the power markets results in the most-expensive generation plants being trimmed and the least expensive being brought on-line. A kilowatt-hour

Table 6-2 — Source-Site Multipliers for the United States

These values are based on the "fossil fuel equivalency" approach. The source multiplier for electricity will be lower if the "captured energy" approach is used. (Source: ASHRAE Standard 105-2014 and "A Common Definition for Zero Energy Buildings," USDOE, September 2015.)

Energy Type	Source Multiplier	Common Units	Site Btu/unit	Source Btu/unit
Imported Electricity	3.15	kWh	3,412	10,751
Exported Renewable Electricity	3.15	kWh	3,412	10,751
Natural Gas	1.09	Therms	100,000	109,000
Fuel Oil, Diesel, Kerosene	1.19	Gallons	138,000	164,220
Propane & Liquid Propane	1.15	Gallons	91,000	104,650
Steam	1.45	lb	1,000	1,450
Hot Water	1.35	millions Btu	1,000,000	1,350,000
Chilled Water	1.04	millions Btu	1,000,000	1,040,000
Coal or Other	1.05	short ton	19,210,000	20,170,000

Notes: The Btu per lb. of steam will vary depending on how much the steam is superheated.

saved in Seattle (where hydro is dominant) could result in less coal being burned in Montana.

ENERGY COST

Cost is another metric that is commonly used to add up the total energy for electricity and other fuels: electricity costs so much per kilowatt-hour, natural gas costs so much per therm, fuel oil costs so much per gallon, etc. Using this metric to determine ZNE, the dollar value of electric energy sold back to the utility would have to be greater than the dollar value of all energy (both electricity and natural gas) purchased from the utilities.[10] When cost is used, zero net energy is a bit of misnomer, since it is not really energy that is zero, but cost; a more accurate term, then, would be *zero net cost*.

The emergence of cost as a metric for evaluating energy performance in buildings came about as a compromise between source energy and site energy. The American Society of Heating, Refrigeration, and Air-Conditioning Engineers (ASHRAE), which develops Standard 90.1 as the technical basis for most energy codes around the world, was being pressured by the Edison Electric Institute (one of their prominent members) to use site energy as the metric for building performance, while the natural gas industry and others on the development committee were committed to source energy. After years of debate and bloody battles,[11] cost became the compromise metric in Standard 90.1 and thus cost also became the metric for many standards and programs that are derived from Standard 90.1. Cost has been adopted as the metric for energy performance in many building codes and recognition programs, such as LEED.[12]

If our energy markets are working properly, the price we pay for various forms of energy will reflect its relative energy content, its cost of production, and its usefulness. A perfect market would also price environmental impacts such as carbon emissions, air pollution, and water pollution associated with energy production. Our markets do work, but they are far from perfect. The use of common goods like air and water is rarely priced, and electricity prices are often distorted by government investments in hydro-generation dams as well as liability limits for nuclear plants, the cost of which is not recovered in the price charged for electricity.[13] Nevertheless, for most of the country, cost is a reasonable metric for evaluating whole-building energy performance.

A benefit of using cost is that it tracks source energy fairly closely, relative to other fuels. The ratio of electricity cost to gas cost on a per-Btu basis using national average prices is 3.06,[14] which compares closely with the ratio of the source multipliers for electricity and gas, which is 2.89 (that is, 3.15 : 1.09). As long as exported energy is valued the same as delivered energy, the impact of using national average cost rather than source energy is pretty small. For all-electric buildings, there would be no difference at all as long as fixed energy costs are used and the same value is assigned to delivered and exported electricity.

However, the price for electricity can vary by season and by time of day. The price of natural gas and other fuels can vary by season, but typically not by time of day. Also, the price that the utility pays for electricity that is exported from the building to the grid may be lower than the price charged for delivered electricity. These variations in energy prices can result in a quite different outcome relative to the use of source energy. Depending on the tariff that applies, this could make it easier or more difficult to achieve ZNE using cost as the metric. Time-of-use (TOU) pricing and net-metering, where the utility purchases exported energy at retail rates, could make it easier to achieve ZNE, since prices for electricity are generally higher during summer afternoons when PV systems are producing at a maximum. If the pricing works correctly, this could be a benefit and give the right signals. For large utilities, the mix of electricity generation will change throughout the day. Nuclear or coal may provide a base load and hydro or natural gas may be used to meet the peaks. The plants that are brought on last are usually the least efficient and the dirtiest, so saving energy during these peak periods can have a greater environmental impact. However, cost can also make it more difficult to achieve ZNE if the value of exported electricity is discounted or if the overall price is subsidized through federal investments.

TIME-DEPENDENT-VALUED (TDV) ENERGY

Site, source, and cost are the most widely used metrics for evaluating whole-building performance, but there are other metrics that deserve some discussion. California uses time-dependent-valued (TDV) energy as its metric. This addresses one of the weaknesses of the other three metrics, which is their inability to factor in peak demand for electricity. Electric utilities have to plan for and have the capacity to supply electricity for those few hours during the year when demand from all its customers is at a peak. This is known as the *system peak*. For most utilities the system peak occurs on summer afternoons, usually during the workweek, when commercial buildings are all open for business and the demand for air-conditioning is the highest. During this peak event, which may occur more than once but lasts for only a few hours each time, the utility has to put all or most of its generating capacity on-line, and if possible buy additional power from independent producers. In addition, the transmission and distribution network is often stressed during the peak, which can trigger failures (blackouts). As a result, saving energy during the system peak has much more value to the utility and to society than saving energy during periods when there is lots of spare capacity. When the system peak increases, the utility must build additional generation capacity or arrange to buy additional power from a third-party provider.

Figure 6-3 shows a typical demand curve for a small utility. The vertical axis of the graph is the total power that the utility must provide to its customers. The horizontal axis shows the percentage of time that this amount of generating capacity is needed. For this hypothetical utility, the median generation capacity is about 60 megawatts, but for a very short period of time (about 1 percent), more than 130 megawatts of capacity is needed. If the utility can "shave" the peak, then it can avoid having to build or acquire new generating capacity and the cost of its services will be lower, providing a societal benefit.

TDV energy addresses peak demand by placing a higher value on electricity used during the system peak and at other times when the grid is stressed. There are 8,760 hours in non-leap years—in other words, 365

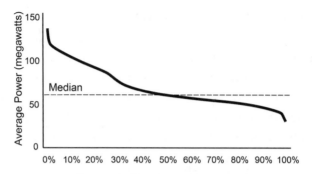

Figure 6-3: Typical Utility Demand Curve

For this hypothetical utility, the median generation capacity is about 60 MW, but it is more than double that for a few hours each year.

days times 24 hours per day. The California TDV system assigns a different electricity value for each of these hours and for each of the sixteen California climate zones. The highest values are on hot summer afternoons when many people are running their air conditioners and demand is greatest. During these periods, utilities are scrambling to dispatch all their reserve generating capacity and buying as much as they can from third-party generators.

To calculate TDV energy for a building, the electricity consumption for each hour of the year is multiplied by the time-dependent value for that hour and the results for all the hours in the year are added up. The schedule of TDV multipliers aligns with the standard weather files in California so that the maximum value coincides with the hottest and sunniest days, when air-conditioner usage is likely to be at a maximum.[15] Designing a building to have low TDV energy requires consideration not only of overall energy use, but also of when that energy is used. TDV typically values the contribution of solar PV systems more highly than other metrics do, because maximum production from PV systems aligns quite nicely with periods when the time-dependent value is greatest. TDV properly credits the time-dependency of energy use and embraces the carbon emissions and generation efficiency at various times during the year. While it is based on cost, it is normalized and expressed as a source-energy multiplier, whereas on-site gas use is assumed to be unity.

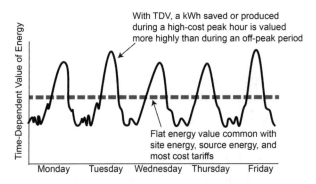

Figure 6-4: Time-Dependent-Valued (TDV) Energy
This is a conceptual diagram of TDV energy for a typical weekday.

California uses TDV for evaluating new zero net energy buildings, since TDV is already used as the metric for code compliance and utility programs. Extending TDV to other states or jurisdictions can be done, but this will require some research, since it is necessary to know the mix of generation sources in the electricity grid for different levels of demand and to understand how these are affected by weather and time of the week.[16] TDV energy values have been developed for natural gas and propane, but not steam, hot water, or chilled water. For natural gas and propane, the TDV multipliers are not hourly, but rather seasonal. TDV is intended for use with an asset assessment of ZNE and is to be evaluated through modeling. TDV does not work for an operational assessment, since the real weather does not align with the standard weather data or the TDV multipliers.

A simplified version of TDV energy is published for the entire United States within the COMNET Modeling Guidelines.[17] However, the COM-NET version of TDV is structured like a time-of-use energy tariff. The year is divided into two seasons: summer and winter. For each season, energy values are assigned for peak periods, shoulder periods, and off-peak periods, which are defined by time of day and day of the week. Each hour of the year falls into one of these periods, and for that hour a separate multiplier or energy cost applies. The system works a lot like California's TDV energy, but without the hourly detail. Separate tariffs are published for each of the sixteen DOE climate zones.

CARBON

With growing concern over global climate change, carbon emissions have become a metric of interest to many. Some green building standards have dual criteria, one applying to energy consumption and another applying to carbon emissions. ASHRAE Standard 189.1 and the International Green Construction Code (green building standards for new commercial buildings), for instance, require that both energy cost and carbon emissions be compared with a baseline. If carbon were used as the metric, then the zero net energy designation is no longer appropriate and should be changed to zero net carbon.

Source energy and carbon track each other very closely, so from a practical perspective, there is very little difference between the two. If you reduce source energy, you reduce carbon by roughly the same amount; if you reduce carbon, you reduce source energy.[18] There is a significant mismatch between carbon and site energy, however.

There are parallels between carbon and fossil fuels. When carbon dioxide is released into the atmosphere, it stays there for centuries. What matters is not our current rate of emissions but the cumulative emissions over time. Likewise, when we burn a fossil fuel like natural gas or oil, that resource is lost forever, so what matters for society in the long term is the cumulative amount used, not the rate of use.

Table 6-3 shows the national average carbon dioxide–equivalent (CO_2e) that is released into the atmosphere for each unit of energy that is consumed at a building site. CO_2e includes carbon dioxide, the primary greenhouse gas, but it also includes methane, nitrous oxide, and other, more-potent greenhouse gases.[19] Carbon dioxide is the primary emission from buildings.

COMPARING THE METRICS

ZNE is easier to achieve with some metrics and more difficult with others. There are also policy issues at stake. If our goal is to minimize energy use at the national level, it is best to consider *all* energy, including that which is lost at power plants that generate electricity. The same is true if our goal is to reduce carbon emissions. For these reasons, source energy is

Table 6-3 — Carbon Emissions from Energy Sources Delivered to the Building Site

(Source: ASHRAE Standard 189.1-2014.)

Building Project Energy Source	Carbon Dioxide Equivalent (CO_2e) Emissions (lb/kWh)	
	(lb/kWh)	(lb/kBtu)
Electricity (grid-delivered)*	1.39	4.73
LPG or propane	0.60	2.05
Fuel Oil (residual)	0.75	2.56
Fuel Oil (distillate)	0.71	2.41
Coal	0.84	2.85
Gasoline	0.69	2.35
Natural Gas	0.48	1.65
District Chilled Water	0.33	1.13
District Steam	0.81	2.77
District Hot Water	0.77	2.62

* The emission factors for electricity represent national averages.

the favored metric for evaluating ZNE, which is why it is recommended by the US Department of Energy in its common definition of ZNE buildings and why it is used by the US Environmental Protection Agency in its ENERGY STAR buildings program.

The ease or difficulty of achieving ZNE with the various metrics depends on the mix of fuels in the building. If a building only uses electricity, there is little difference between site energy, source energy, or cost when comparing design alternatives. However, it will be easier to achieve ZNE if the cost metric is based on a time-of-use rate, or TDV, in which electricity prices are higher on summer afternoons when PV systems are producing at their maximum.

The choice of a metric has a much larger impact, however, when buildings use a mix of fuels. In these cases, ZNE would be most difficult with

Table 6-4 — A Comparison of Energy Metrics for Evaluating ZNE Buildings

Metrics like time-of-use energy cost or TDV weight PV production greater and make it easier to achieve ZNE. For all-electric buildings, there is little difference between site, source, and energy cost.

	All-Electric Buildings	Mixed-Fuel Buildings
Site Energy		Most difficult to achieve ZNE
Source Energy (recommended)	Equal difficulty in achieving ZNE	
Energy Cost (flat rate)		Easier to achieve ZNE
TDV or Energy Cost (time-of-use)	Easiest to achieve ZNE	

site energy because the value of electricity production from PV systems is lowest relative to other fuels. With both source energy and cost, electricity is weighted almost three times greater than natural gas, so less PV capacity is needed to offset the gas use. With TDV energy or energy cost based on a time-of-use tariff, electricity from PV production is weighted even higher because it coincides with higher prices for electricity during the peak period. On the other hand, if the electric utility buys exported energy from a customer at a lower rate than what is charged for delivered energy, using cost as the metric could make it extremely difficult to achieve ZNE.

Defining Renewable Energy

Renewable energy technically includes biomass, hydro, geothermal, solar, wind, ocean thermal, wave action, and tidal action, but for almost all buildings, on-site renewable energy will include only wind and solar. It might be possible for large sites on the coast to take advantage of ocean thermal, wave action, or tidal action, but it would be rare situation for this to be considered on-site. Also, it might be possible for large sites to include a small hydro-electric plant, but again this would be rare. And in order for biomass to count as on-site renewable energy, the biomass would need to be grown and processed on the site in a sustainable manner. If the biomass is delivered to the site from another location, it is tallied as delivered energy, just like electricity or natural gas.[20]

REGENERATIVE ENERGY SOURCES

Wind power and solar power are inexhaustible. We convert the sun's energy into electricity by spinning turbines or using the photovoltaic effect, and we can do this as long as the sun is shining or the wind is blowing. It is not possible to use solar energy or wind at a rate greater than it is replenished. There is no significant time lag between when the solar or wind arrives at the building site and its conversion to electricity.

Wood and biomass are different. These forms of energy are potentially renewable, but only if certain conditions are met. I prefer to use the term *regenerative* to describe wood and biomass, as opposed to *renewable*. In order for biomass to be regenerative, our forests or crops must be properly managed so that they are sustainable. It is quite possible, and history has proven that it is even likely, that wood will be extracted at a faster rate than it is regenerated. At the global scale, we are harvesting wood products from our forests at a rate much greater than the ability of our forests to regenerate. Consider the following facts:[21]

- There were 6–7 billion hectares of forest before the agricultural revolution, roughly 10,000 years ago. We now have 3.9 billion hectares, a little more than half.
- More than half of the loss of natural forests has occurred since 1950. Between 1990 and 2000, we lost 160 million hectares, or 4 percent. This is an average of 16 million hectares per year, or about 0.5 percent per year. Most of this loss was in tropical forests.
- The United States, excluding Alaska, has lost 95 percent of its original (pre-Columbian) forest coverage.
- The quality of forests is just as important as forest area, or even more so. Much quality has also been lost, as many natural forests have been replaced by tree plantations (roughly 200 million hectares).
- Vast forest areas are presently threatened by logging claims, mines, agricultural clearing, and human settlements. Only about 300 million hectares (8 percent) of our current forests are formally protected in some way.

In spite of the global situation, some individual forests are being sustainably managed, but these are uncommon. The Forest Stewardship

Council is an organization that evaluates forest management practices and issues a certificate for forests that are sustainably managed.[22] Only 30 million hectares of forests (less than 1 percent of the total) have received this certification.

Demand for forest products is growing, and this will place additional stress on our forests. On a global basis, about half (50 percent) of what we take from our forests is burned as fuel. The majority of this is in developing and undeveloped parts of the world. In the United States, wood products provide less than 5 percent of our energy needs. Globally, saw logs and veneers represent about 30 percent of the global demand for forest products. The remaining 20 percent or so is used for pulpwood and other industrial uses.[23]

Our forests have many more benefits besides supplying us with fuel, timber, and pulpwood. They help regulate our climate by absorbing carbon dioxide and generating oxygen. They purify and regulate the flow of water. They have spiritual, religious, recreational, aesthetic, educational, and cultural value. They are essential to the formation of new soil, and they cycle and recycle nutrients.

Tropical forests represent 7 percent of the earth's surface but are home to at least 50 percent of the earth's plant and animal species.[24] Tropical rain forests have 170,000 of the world's 250,000 known plant species.[25] Many species in the rain forest, especially insects and fungi, have not even been discovered yet by scientists. Every year new species of mammals, birds, frogs, and reptiles are found in rain forests and cataloged. Tropical forests convert carbon dioxide to oxygen, help regenerate freshwater, provide a wealth of diverse plants and animals for medical research, and perform many other functions that have real and tangible value.

The DOE "common definition" for ZNE buildings requires that wood or biomass be grown and processed on-site. As a rule of thumb, an acre of land is needed to sustainably produce about one cord of wood per year. A cord of wood contains between 15 and 25 million Btu of energy, depending on the species. A maximum technical potential office building will have a site EUI of about 12,000 Btu/ft²·yr (see table 2-7). Running through the numbers, this means that for each square foot of building floor area, about forty square feet of sustainably managed forest would be needed to achieve ZNE if biomass were the only source of renewable energy.[26] A relatively small (10,000 square-foot) building would require about nine acres of land. If PV panels were installed over that same nine acres of land, the renewable-energy production would be about 200 times greater than the building's needs.[27] Looking at it another way, nine acres of PV could achieve ZNE for a 2 million square-foot office building.

From the numbers above, it is clear that the requirement that the biomass be grown and processed on-site eliminates its consideration as a renewable energy for achieving ZNE for all but the most unusual sites. For these rare sites, forests should also be sustainably managed and verified by a third party, like the Forest Stewardship Council (FSC). There should be little or no risk that the use of wood or biomass will revert to fossil-fuel or electricity use at some time in the future.[28] Moreover, emissions from the on-site combustion of the wood or biomass should not significantly worsen air quality.

ON-SITE SOLAR-THERMAL SYSTEMS

On-site solar-thermal systems have been around for quite a while and certainly qualify as renewable energy. They are called *solar thermal* because they produce heat (or thermal) energy, not electricity. The most common use is to heat water. The typical configuration is a panel located on the roof or other area that is exposed to rays from the sun. The panel consists of a sheet of metal (usually copper) that is coated black and sealed behind one or more panes of glass. Metal pipes are bonded to the metal panel. As sunlight heats the metal panel, that heat is transferred to water (or water mixed with glycol) that is pumped through the pipes. The heated water is stored in a tank that is typically located in a mechanical room inside the building. If it is possible to locate the tank at an elevation higher than the solar collectors, the pumps can be eliminated since water will flow through the collectors by gravity; such systems are called *thermosyphoning collectors*. Some solar-thermal systems heat air instead of water, but these are far less common.

The heated water that is stored in the tank can then be used for service uses like showers and washing hands, dishes, and clothes. It can also be used for space heating, but this application is less common. Some buildings such as hotels and hospitals use a lot of hot water, so solar-thermal systems can be very important in achieving zero net energy. Solar-thermal systems almost always have some form of gas or electric backup heat for cloudy days and for times when the storage tank is not hot enough.

Solar-thermal systems can significantly reduce the energy used for water heating and/or space heating.[29] However, they do not entirely eliminate the energy use, because of the requirement for backup. While it is possible that hot water can be exported across the property line to another building, this is rare.

Assessing ZNE for Multiple Buildings

The discussion so far is in the context of a single ZNE building, but the concept can also be applied to multiple buildings.

ZNE CAMPUSES

Large renewable-energy systems are less expensive per unit of output than smaller systems; they follow the principle of economy of scale. For this reason, college campuses, corporate headquarters, and other facilities that consist of multiple buildings on a single site and under single ownership may find it more cost-effective to have one large renewable-energy system that serves multiple buildings than to install a renewable-energy system on each individual building. Every building on a ZNE campus does not have to be ZNE, but the delivered source energy to the whole collection of buildings on campus must be less than or equal to the exported source energy. The campus can then be designated a ZNE campus. While not yet a ZNE campus, Foothill College in Los Altos Hills, California, installed PV systems in three parking lots that generate 1.4 million kWh/yr of electricity to offset campus energy use.[30] The University of California campus at Merced has committed to becoming a ZNE campus. Buildings are being designed to be energy-efficient, and there are plans to gradually introduce on-site solar PV, wind turbines, biomass, and geothermal systems to offset building energy use.[31]

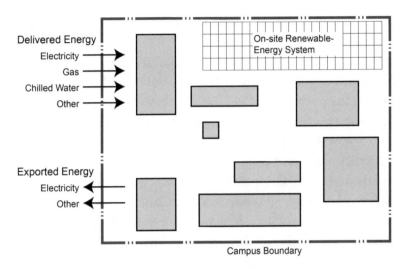

Figure 6-5: ZNE Campus

ZNE accounting for a campus occurs at the campus level. Each building may not achieve ZNE on its own, but the collection of buildings within the campus boundaries do.

Another case is a single building on a campus that has a large common renewable-energy system. In order for this one building to achieve ZNE (but not the whole campus), the production from the common renewable-energy system should be fairly allocated among all the buildings on the campus. The simplest (and recommended) approach is to prorate production on the basis of floor area. If allocation were based on energy use, energy-intensive buildings like laboratories would be allocated a larger share on a floor-area basis than less intensive buildings like classrooms. A new building that is striving for ZNE recognition would likely have a more difficult time with this secondary allocation if its EUI were lower. The lower its EUI, the smaller its share of renewable energy from the campus system.

ZNE PORTFOLIOS

A portfolio is a collection of buildings that are owned or leased by a single entity. It is similar to a campus, except that with a portfolio, the building sites are not all together. A good example of a portfolio would be the various schools within a school district. ZNE school portfolios are sometimes called "ZNE districts." If the sum of all the delivered energy to individual buildings in the portfolio is less than the sum of all the exported energy from the buildings, then the portfolio of buildings has achieved ZNE. While the portfolio is ZNE, this does not mean that each individual building in the portfolio is ZNE, e.g., a school district could become ZNE, without each individual school achieving ZNE on its own. Some schools in the district may have poor solar access or be located on a cramped or shaded site that makes it difficult or even impossible to achieve zero net energy, while other sites have an abundance of land, and renewable-energy-generation capacity can be installed that exceeds what is needed on the site. By combining all the meters within a school district into a single virtual meter, it might be possible for the district to be zero net energy, even if some individual schools are not. Some school sites would be net producers while others would be net users, but the district as a whole could be zero net energy.

Another case where virtual meters would give building owners more options for achieving zero net energy is a portfolio of related build-

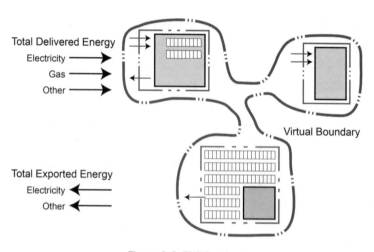

Figure 6-6: ZNE Portfolio

ZNE accounting for a portfolio, such as a school district, occurs within a virtual (discontinuous) boundary that includes multiple properties. The buildings within the virtual boundary are under the same ownership or control.

ings such as restaurants or retail stores and the distribution centers that serve them. Some retail stores, like supermarkets, are among the most energy-intensive buildings types, because of refrigeration loads for produce, chilled goods, and frozen goods. Restaurants are also very energy-intensive, because of both refrigeration and cooking. It may be difficult or even impossible for supermarkets and restaurants to become zero net energy on their own, but if they are combined with the distribution centers that serve them, they might stand a chance. The distribution centers are typically large warehouse-type facilities with the potential for large PV arrays and, in some cases, wind turbines. The distribution centers might be net producers while the stores are net users, but together (considering the whole operation or portfolio), the business operations of the company might achieve zero net energy.

ZNE COMMUNITIES

A ZNE community is similar to a portfolio except that the properties within the community are individually owned, whereas, with a portfolio, all the properties are owned or managed by the same entity. A com-

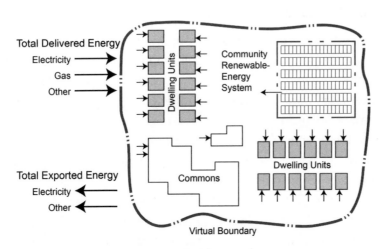

Figure 6-7: ZNE Community

ZNE accounting for a community includes multiple buildings under different ownership in combination with a community-level renewable-energy system. The virtual boundary need not be contiguous.

munity can be contiguous or non-contiguous. ZNE communities can be at the scale of an entire town or they can be at the scale of a residential development. Either way, one or more large renewable-energy systems would be installed to take advantage of the economies of scale. These renewable-energy systems would generate as much source energy as is used within the community. When the sum of all the source energy delivered to the community is less than that exported on an annual basis, the community has achieved ZNE.

For ZNE portfolios and ZNE communities alike, a virtual meter would aggregate the meters of the individual properties and the test for ZNE would be applied to this virtual meter. Utility policies on virtual meters are varied and sometimes restrictive.[32] California permits virtual meters, but all the actual meters must be located at the same service point, which basically limits the program to residential condominiums. But there are other options. Community solar systems and renewable-energy self-generation bill credit-transfer programs that can be used in many states to facilitate ZNE portfolios and ZNE communities. These options are discussed more in the next section.

Expanding the Boundary

There are a number of energy-intensive building types and site-constrained buildings where achieving on-site ZNE will be a challenge. Examples of energy-intensive buildings include data centers, supermarkets, restaurants, hospitals, and laboratories. Multistory or high-rise buildings in urban environments are site-constrained because space for solar panels, relative to the floor area, is limited. Northern climates may also be a challenge, since the days are shorter and the sun is lower in the sky. Table 3-5 identifies cases where on-site ZNE will be especially difficult.

To achieve ZNE for these difficult situations, the boundary for ZNE accounting must be expanded to include off-site renewable energy. The common boundary for a ZNE assessment is either the building itself or the site. When the renewable-energy system is located on the building itself, the National Renewable Energy Laboratory (NREL) refers to this as ZNE-A. When the renewable-energy system is located on the site, NREL calls this ZNE-B.[33] ZNE-A and ZNE-B are both considered on-site, but NREL identifies two other off-site boundary conditions for ZNE accounting:

- *ZNE-C — Renewable-energy systems are located on remote sites.* In this case, renewable-energy systems can be owned or leased on remote sites separate from the building. For example, an office tower in a downtown setting leases or buys land at a remote location and installs wind or PV panels to offset energy delivered to the office tower. A building owner might also buy a share in an off-site community solar farm (more on this later). In this case, the building owner makes an investment in a specific off-site renewable-energy system. The owner can point to the farm or community solar system and say, "This is where our power is coming from."

- *ZNE-D — Building owners and managers purchase renewable-energy certificates (RECs) on the open market or take into account renewable energy purchased by their local utility or community-choice aggregator.* In this case, the building owner or manager does not own or lease a specific renewable-energy system. In the case of RECs, the owner purchases the environmental attributes from renewable-energy producers on the open market. The RECs could be sold into the open market by wind generators in Iowa and purchased by a building owner in Los Angeles. Markets for renewable-energy credits are beginning to surface with the price determined by supply and demand. The US Department of Energy lists twenty-six brokers or exchanges that deal with RECs.[34] In the case of renewable energy provided by utilities and community-choice aggregators, the renewable energy is part of the mix of energy provided to the customer. The customer may have a choice of rates with different levels of renewable-energy content.

When PV is provided as part of a construction project, new renewable-energy capacity is being added simultaneously along with the additional demand for energy created by the new building. This can also be the case with remote renewable-energy systems. You can see the new solar panels being installed and monitor the additional clean energy they produce. This is referred to as *additionality* and means that new renewable-energy-generating capacity is being added to match the additional demand for electricity that is being added.[35] If a corporation building a new headquarters in a downtown tower buys an existing wind farm to offset its energy use, additionality may not be attained; they are just buying renewable power that was already being produced. Their transaction will create new demand, which in the long term could result in additionality, but in the short term no new renewable-energy systems are being added as a result of the construction project. Likewise, if a company simply outbids another for RECs, additionality may not be realized.

REMOTE SOLAR

Stanford University is a large campus, with over 8,000 acres (and just 7,000 undergraduates). There is probably enough room on campus to install enough renewable-energy to achieve campus-level on-site ZNE, but the trustees and administrators took a different approach. They are in the process of installing a 73-megawatt solar farm at a remote location in the California desert that will offset half of all electricity use on campus. Their campus will draw from the electric grid, but, as an offset, their solar power plant will supply energy to the grid. They are also installing rooftop and parking-area PV on campus, but this will be minor compared to the large, remotely located solar farm.

Fahmida Ahmed, director of the campus Office of Sustainability, reports that the remote solar farm is just one part of their plans. Stanford has accepted the challenge of climate change and is moving toward becoming a carbon-free and ZNE campus. It is implementing energy efficiency in all its classrooms, offices, laboratories, and housing. Most of these buildings receive heating and cooling from a campus-level central plant that has morphed into a cutting-edge energy-supply system known as the Stanford Energy System Innovations (SESI) project. SESI represents a transformation of university energy supply from a 100 percent fossil-fuel-based combined heat and power plant to a grid-sourced electric plant with an efficient heat-recovery system. The central plant represents about a third of campus-wide electricity, so the 73-megawatt remote solar farm (which powers half of the whole campus) will offset all the electricity use operating the plant and leave additional renewable energy for other purposes. This new system, along with Stanford's solar-power procurement, is anticipated to reduce campus emissions approximately 68 percent from current levels and save 15 percent of campus potable water.[36]

To facilitate remote renewable-energy systems, California has a program called Renewable-Energy Self-Generation Bill Credit Transfer (RES-BCT) that allows municipal governments and school districts to install an eligible renewable-energy generator on property located within its geographic boundary and under its ownership or control. The utility will install a meter at the remote generator to measure electricity exported to the grid. The exported energy is automatically credited to up to fifty separate electricity accounts. The benefiting accounts must be within the local government's geographic boundaries, and on property that the government entity owns, operates, or controls.[37] This program is limited to renewable-energy generators that are no larger than five megawatts.

COMMUNITY RENEWABLE ENERGY

Stanford is a special situation. The institution is large, tech-savvy, and generously endowed. They have the wherewithal to buy land and to finance, construct, and operate a large remote solar farm. What they are doing is not an option for the average Joe, but there are other options that are similar in concept but much more accessible to mainstream building owners. With community renewable-energy systems, a building owner can subscribe to or buy a stake in an off-site renewable-energy system and credit the production from this system to their electric bill just as if the system were located on their rooftop or over their parking lot. A community solar system is similar in concept to the Stanford system in the desert, except that its benefits are shared with the "community." If a building owner needs 200 kilowatts of panels to achieve ZNE, the owner can subscribe to or buy a 200-kilowatt share in a community solar system and avoid the complexities of building their own system on a remote site. Most community systems are developed through a partnership between utilities and developers, but there are also co-ops, utility-owned systems, and municipal systems.[38]

The Sacramento Municipal Utility District (SMUD) initiated a pioneering program in 2007 called SolarShares. Through this program, any customer (even renters) can pay a fixed monthly fee that entitles them to a share of the energy and environmental benefits of a local one-megawatt solar farm operated and managed by SMUD.[39] The participating customer is in effect leasing a portion of the community solar system and receives the energy and environmental benefits of the system, just as they would if the system existed on their own property. Their monthly utility bill has a credit for the energy produced. The credit they receive changes each month depending on how much energy is actually produced at the community solar system. The credits are larger in the summer and lower in the winter. The size of the system offered to a participating customer depends on the customer's annual electricity consumption for the previous twelve months. Smaller users are restricted to smaller shares in order to prevent over-generation and to make the program available to a greater number of customers.

The concept of community solar is growing. According to Joy Hughes, the founder of SolarGardens.org, a group that promotes community solar systems across the country, systems generating over fifty megawatts, collectively, are now in operation and she expects to see remarkable growth in the coming years. Over the last two years, community solar programs have nearly doubled in number, with forty-two utility-sponsored community solar programs now active. Ten states and the District of Columbia have crafted legislation to encourage community solar program development.[40] The size limit is on the order of 20–25 megawatts of capacity. Almost all community systems are solar, although most of the statutes would permit wind and other forms of renewable energy as well. Some predict that there will be more than 500 megawatts of community solar by 2020.[41]

There are two participation models commonly used for community solar. The first is a capacity offering. A participant pays money up front (or arranges financing) to lease a certain number of panels. The lease is usually for twenty-five years. Each community solar system has an arrangement with the local utility so that the energy and environmental benefits are automatically credited to the customer's account with each monthly utility bill. The local utility is generally a partner in the community solar program or operates it outright. The second compensation model is to purchase output from the system on a monthly basis, but these programs require a contract for at least twelve months because of seasonal variability in output. This is the model used by the SMUD SolarShares program.

RENEWABLE-ENERGY CERTIFICATES (RECS)

Renewable-Energy Certificates (RECs), also known as Green tags, Renewable-Energy Credits, Renewable-Electricity Certificates, or Tradable Renewable Certificates (TRCs), are tradable, non-tangible energy commodities in the United States that represent proof that one megawatt-hour of electricity was generated from an eligible renewable-energy resource. The REC is a separate asset from the actual energy production. It represents the environmental, social, and other non-energy-related attributes of one megawatt-hour of renewable electricity generation. The REC is sold separately from the electricity generated by a renewable-based source. The annual revenues from a renewable generating source are the sum of the electricity sales and the REC sales. The economic value of a renewable generating source is the net present value of the electricity sales over the life of the asset plus the net present value of future REC sales over the life of the asset (see table 6-5). When on-site renewable energy is used to achieve ZNE, the RECs must be retained for the life of the project and may not be sold; otherwise making a claim of being a ZNE building would be deceptive and would violate Federal Trade Commission (FTC) guidelines.[42]

Not all RECs are the same, and their price varies depending on their attributes. The main attributes are the year the megawatt-hours of electricity were produced, the generation technology (solar, wind, etc.), and the location of the generator. Solar renewable-energy certificates (sRECs) are RECs that are specifically generated by solar energy, and these command a higher price than RECs from other renewable-energy-generation sources because of greater demand. Demand may also vary from year to year. Achieving ZNE through the purchase of RECs should only be done when it is not possible or feasible to achieve ZNE with on-site or remote

Table 6-5 — Value of Renewable-Energy Asset

Renewable energy certificates are a separate tradable asset from the power that is produced by renewable-energy systems.

Per Year

Annual Revenue/Cost	=	Electricity Sales/Cost	+	Renewable-Energy Certificate Sales/Cost

For the Life of the System

Value of Renewable-Generation Asset	=	Net Present Value of Electricity Production	+	Net Present Value of Future RECs

renewable-energy generation. Once power enters the grid, the electrons are indistinguishable, so RECs provide a means of giving more value to those generated by renewable-energy sources, and they offer a means for some utilities to meet their RPS requirement.[43]

Demand for RECs is driven in large part by renewable portfolio standards (RPS), which require that a minimum amount of utility energy sales be provided by renewable energy. Some states require that a certain percentage of the renewable power be solar, which bumps up the price of sRECs. Some states require that generators be located within the state, which gives more value to those geographic locations. In California, the price of RECs may increase as that state's RPS requirement becomes more stringent, but this is highly uncertain.[44] When generating capacity is added to meet the RPS requirements, the RECs associated with that power must be retained or purchased by the utility and must be unavailable to others in the market.

The US Department of Energy's common definition for ZNE buildings allows RECs to be used to attain ZNE, but it requires a special designation or qualifier when this is the case. They recommend that the acronym "REC" be placed in front of the ZNE or ZEB designation. RECs may be the only way for some buildings to achieve ZNE, but there are many issues related to RECs: there are many types of RECs and the prices vary significantly; many people question whether RECs actually result in additional renewable-energy generation being installed; the investment is small compared with on-site renewables; there is no national clearing-house or exchange to regulate the market; and RECs provide a way for developers to pass the cost of achieving ZNE along to future tenants.

Additionality is one of the biggest issues with RECs. Many argue that the price of a REC is too low and is not a significant factor for developers of solar or wind generators. The critics argue that RECs are irrelevant in comparison with other factors such as natural gas prices, technology prices, and federal tax incentives. They argue that "cheap RECs actually make the climate problem worse because they distract us from real solutions."[45] Some even say that it would be better to make a donation to a nonprofit group that promotes clean energy rather than to buy RECs. Others have compared RECs to indulgences sold by the Catholic Church during the Middle Ages.[46] Words such as "scam" are often used.

Compared with installing on-site renewable energy, costs for RECs are unquestionably low. United States EIA data shows that the national average price for unqualified RECs has been generally less than $1/megawatt-hour since 2010. To understand what this means, consider a 10,000 square-foot building with a site EUI of 12 kBtu/ft^2·yr, as discussed earlier. The owner would need to purchase about 35 RECs each year in order to achieve ZNE.[47] At $1/megawatt-hour, the annual cost would only be about $35. If the owner pre-purchased RECs for an estimated thirty-year life of the building, the net present value would be less than $700. By comparison, installing an on-site PV system to achieve ZNE would cost over $90,000.[48] The cost of buying RECs is pocket change compared to the cost of installing an on-site PV system.

In the instance discussed above, however, $700 vs. $90,000 is not a direct comparison because those buying RECs, whether the owner or the tenants, would still need to purchase electricity from the local utility. Nevertheless, the $35 annual cost for the RECs is an insignificant fraction of the entire operational budget of the building and would likely not result in any new investment in renewable-energy generation. Furthermore, this is an annual cost that could be tagged onto the utility bill and passed on to the tenants. The owner/developer can "wear the halo" for achieving ZNE, but the tenants pay the bill. This is a reverse instance of the classic

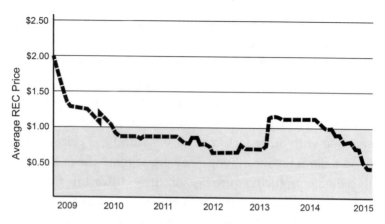

Figure 6-8: Voluntary REC Prices

These prices are a nationwide average for all energy-generation technologies, vintages, and locations. (Source: US Energy Information Agency; see: http://apps3.eere.energy.gov/green power/markets/certificates.shtml?page=5.)

split-incentives between the owner/developer and the building tenants.[49]

Another problem is that the market for RECs is not well regulated or controlled. The Center for Resource Solutions operates the Green-e organization and does a great job of putting some level of order into the market for RECs by certifying renewable-energy generators and by making sure that there is no double counting,[50] but there is no regulated market for the sale of RECs comparable to, say, the New York Stock Exchange.[51] Building owners and homeowners who install rooftop systems through power purchase agreements often don't understand RECs. The RECs are commonly retained by the companies that install the systems, and these renewable-energy certificates are sold in the open market to utilities or others to meet their RPS requirements, creating a situation of double counting.[52]

The market for renewable-energy certificates is far from perfect, but for energy-intensive buildings, office towers, and buildings on site-constrained sites, expanding the boundary for ZNE accounting through remote renewable energy, community solar, or RECs may be the only hope; it is probably not possible to achieve on-site ZNE. The concept of RECs is sound, but the market needs to be made to work better through regulation at the national level. Building owners need to be able to set up an annuity that will buy RECs for future tenants over the life of the building so that the cost is part of the capital-improvements budget and not the operating budget. The price needs to be significant enough to encourage (or enable) additional investment and construction of PV and wind systems. Moreover, the products offered in the marketplace need to be simplified so that the choices are clearer and more understandable.

RENEWABLE GRID POWER

Investor-owned utilities in California are currently required to secure 20 percent of their power from eligible renewable generators.[53] This increases to 33 percent by 2020 and to 50 percent by 2030. About thirty other states also have mandatory renewable portfolio standards (RPS) for their electric utilities, and a half dozen other states have voluntary goals.[54] Utilities may meet a portion of their RPS requirement by purchasing unbundled RECs from owners of rooftop systems, but in California this is limited to a maximum of 10 percent of the RPS requirement.[55]

Nationwide, the renewable energy used for electricity generation is pretty small: solar, wind, hydro, and geothermal account for 4.97 quads of the 38.0 quads of energy used to generate electricity, representing about 13 percent.[56] However, in the state of Washington, over 75 percent of electricity is generated by hydro, mainly because of federal investments in large hydro-electric plants.[57] In some states, the contribution from renewable energy is practically zero.

More than thirty states have adopted renewable portfolio standards that require utilities to generate a specified percentage of their power from renewable-energy sources. In meeting the RPS requirements in California, utilities can count small hydro (thirty megawatts or less), but large hydro plants are not counted for compliance with the RPS requirement, since the purpose of the standards is to encourage more renewable energy, not to credit legacy hydro plants for which there is little opportunity for expansion.[58] The definition of what renewable energy qualifies to meet the RPS varies from state to state.

Community-choice aggregation (CCA) is a system, used in seven states, that allows governmental organizations to buy power in the whole-

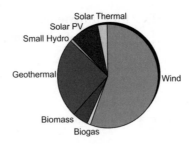

Figure 6-9: California Grid-Level Renewable Energy
Note: Large hydroelectric generation is not included. (Source: California Public Utilities Commission.)

sale market for their constituents. The power is delivered over the transportation and distribution networks of the local utility, and customers continue to get their monthly bill from the utility. CCAs negotiate with generators on behalf of their constituents to obtain a cost-competitive supply of energy that meets renewable-energy, local-generation, and other criteria. The price charged to customers includes the cost of energy but also a charge to cover the utility's costs for amortizing and maintaining the distribution network, for billing, and other expenses.[59] As of 2014, CCAs serve nearly 5 percent of Americans in over 1,300 municipalities.[60]

Most CCAs offer their customers a choice of energy products. For example, Sonoma Clean Power has two programs. CleanStart is their basic program and currently has a renewable-energy content of 36 percent, but this will increase to 50 percent by 2020.[61] EverGreen, their premium program, provides customers with 100 percent renewable energy, completely from local generators located within Sonoma County. Customers can also choose to opt out of the SCP and buy their power from PG&E, the local utility. A choice of energy products is also offered directly by some public utilities, municipal utilities, and electric cooperatives.

Summary

The most common means of measuring energy usage is *operational* assessment, which means that the test for ZNE is achieved simply by looking at the utility bills. However, for code compliance and other cases, an *asset* assessment may be used whereby the test is made through energy modeling using standard operational and weather conditions.

The ZNE concepts work clearly with source energy as the metric. With source energy, ZNE assessment is independent of the rates charged or paid for electricity. Unlike using cost as a metric, achieving ZNE is unaffected by the politics and whims of public utility commissions and sometimes complicated utility tariffs and rate structures. Source energy also tracks carbon emissions very closely.

The boundary for ZNE assessment can include the property line of a single building, an entire corporate or collegiate campus, a portfolio of buildings on discrete sites, or a community of property owners or citizens who band together to construct and manage a common renewable-energy system that serves them all. In all cases, the boundary for ZNE assessment must be carefully defined. For buildings and campuses, the boundary will typically be the property line, but for portfolios and communities the boundary can be discontinuous whereby multiple properties are grouped together by a virtual boundary.

The basic definition of on-site ZNE (see fig. 1-4) considers only what enters and leaves the property. Electricity is either delivered or exported. There is no consideration of the renewable generation sources upstream that produce the delivered electricity. With the basic definition, there is no credit for any of the off-site energy production options discussed above.

If a building can't achieve ZNE with on-site renewable energy, then the first off-site option to explore is a wholly owned renewable-energy system on a remote site or a long-term lease arrangement for renewable-energy-generating capacity from a community renewable-energy system. Both of these options have a high or certain probability of additional renewable energy being added as a result of the construction project. These options will typically be funded from the capital improvement budget rather than the operating budget. They also specify a fixed amount of renewable-energy capacity, and its production can be compared with the energy delivered to the building. In some states, school districts and governmental entities can link the remotely located renewable-energy system with one or more utility accounts through the RES-BCT method so that a net-metering tariff can apply to the joined properties as if they were together.[62] Community renewable-energy systems also directly associate output from the remote or community system with one or more utility accounts.

The ability to lease capacity from community renewable-energy systems will not always be available, and buying or securing land and installing a remote system will not be feasible for many building owners. In these cases, the second off-site option would be to purchase renewable-energy certificates or output from community renewable-energy systems. This is a less desirable option, because the cost burden is shifted from the capital improvement budget to the operating budget. There is also a low probability (especially with RECs) that additional renewable energy will be added as a result of these purchases. The quantity of RECs or renewable energy from a community system can change over time to accommodate more or less energy being delivered to the building; this is both good news and bad. The good is that it provides flexibility for legitimate changes in energy service. The bad is that it does not hold the building to a budget set by renewable-energy production.

The third off-site option is to purchase renewable energy through the utility or a community-choice aggregator. This is a reliable source of renewable energy that comes to buildings over the wires, but there is little probability of additionality unless the owner subscribes to a premium program. Also, this option can be used to achieve ZNE only if the agreement is to buy 100 percent renewable energy. If the delivered energy less the on-site and off-site renewables is greater than zero and the RPS of the energy provider is less than 100 percent, the building will always be using some amount of nonrenewable energy. The other options should be maximized before exercising the third option.

These three off-site options are summarized in table 6-6. The first off-site option is highly recommended because it provides additionality and is paid for from the capital improvement budget.

Tariffs and rate structures are a critical factor in the cost-effectiveness of ZNE projects. Utilities and their regulators need to establish clear and stable rules with regard to net-metering and feed-in tariffs upon which

Table 6-6 — Summary of Off-Site Renewable-Energy Options

This table shows the order in which off-site renewable energy should be explored when it is not possible to achieve on-site ZNE.

1	On-Site Test				
2	First Off-Site Option				The Zero Net Energy Criteria
3	Second Off-Site Option				
4	Third Off-Site Option				

$[Q_{Delivered} - Q_{Exported}$	$-Q_{Own\text{-}Lease}$	$-Q_{RECs\text{-}Subscribe}]$	$\times\ (1-\%RPS)$	≤ 0
Description Basic definition of on-site zero net energy building	Energy from wholly owned, remotely located systems and community systems arranged through a capacity agreement	Energy purchased through renewable-energy certificates and community systems arranged through a subscription	Renewable energy supplied through the grid	
Additionality New renewable energy is added as part of the construction project	High probability of additionality	Low probability that additional renewable energy will be added	New renewable energy will not be added except for premium offerings (low probability)	
Funding Capital Improvement Budget	Capital Improvement Budget	Operating Budget	Operating Budget	

investors can make their decisions. For school districts and other portfolio managers as well as ZNE communities, we need rules for when it is reasonable to aggregate meters into a virtual meter for ZNE accounting. For portfolios, the meters that need to be combined are often under a single account and paid for by the same customer. However, for ZNE communities or condominiums, multiple accounts would need to be combined.

Net-metering is not the only solution. Medium to large renewable-energy systems can connect to the grid through a meter separate from the buildings that are served, and the portfolio or community can be compensated through a feed-in tariff. In the European Union, feed-in tariffs are much more common than net-metering. Germany, Italy, Spain, and other EU countries have successfully used feed-in tariffs to promote renewable energy, and on a per-capita basis they are leading the world. Community solar systems are another option. These are each limited to about twenty megawatts of generating capacity, but they can be directly linked to utility accounts. This may be a solution for restaurants, super-

Table 6-7 — ZNE Qualifiers

To completely describe the claim of a ZNE building, a choice should be made for each of the following qualifiers.

Qualifier	Choices	Description
Assessment	Operational (recommended)	ZNE is verified by looking at the energy bills.
	Asset	ZNE is determined through modeling with standard operation and weather.
Metric	Source (recommended)	All energy is counted, including that used to generate electricity.
	Site	The efficiency of electricity production is ignored.
	Cost	Energy from multiple sources is converted to cost.
	TDV	Energy from multiple sources is converted to TDV, which is real-time cost.
	Carbon	Energy from multiple sources is converted to equivalent carbon emissions.
Boundary	Single Building	Energy accounting occurs at the building property line.
	Campus	All buildings and renewable-energy systems on campus are assessed.
	Portfolio	A group of separate buildings under the same management is assessed.
	Community	A group of homes or buildings under separate ownership is assessed.

Table 6-7 — continued

Qualifier	Choices		Description
Source of Renewable Energy	On-site (recommended)		The renewable-energy system is located on the roof or parking lot.
	Off-site capacity arrangement	Ownership	Wholly owned renewable-energy system on remote site.
		Lease	Long-term lease of capacity at community solar system.
	Renewable-energy purchase	Subscription	Subscription to buy renewable energy from community solar system.
		RECs	Purchase of renewable-energy certificates (RECs).
	Grid-supplied renewable energy		Renewable-energy content from the grid is considered.

markets, and other energy-intensive buildings that are managed by the same corporation.

Developing the rules will be tough, but having the flexibility of using feed-in tariffs, community solar, or virtual meters will likely be necessary in order for many energy-intensive and site-constrained buildings to achieve zero net energy.

CHAPTER 7

ZNE for the Mainstream: Scaling Up the Concept

The world is full of innovators who are bucking the norm and showing us that energy efficiency, renewable energy, and zero net energy buildings can be achieved. These individuals, nonprofit organizations, corporations, and governments are to be embraced and celebrated. They are having an impact. They are showing us tangible ways in which ZNE buildings can help us achieve a sustainable society. It's difficult for skeptics to say it can't be done when there are concrete examples we can point to that show that it can.

Many of the current examples of ZNE buildings are owned and/or operated by foundations, universities, research laboratories, and other "special clients" who are motivated to be environmentally responsible and who have the resources to make the necessary investment in energy efficiency and renewable energy. Some are premium buildings. However, the "real world" consists of school districts strapped for funds, shopping-center developers out for a quick buck, and speculative builders who plan to sell or lease their buildings shortly after they are constructed (and saddling someone else with the operating costs and energy bills). This chapter is about how, through smart and cost-effective policies and regulations, and transitioning to a smart grid, we can bring ZNE to these mainstream buildings.

All change or innovation occurs in phases, and there is a science to it. Some innovations, like the adoption of smart phones over the old flip-phone variety, happen very rapidly. Other changes happen much more slowly. Whether the change is slow or fast, it is first adopted by the leading-edge innovators who represent only 2.5 percent or so of the market. This is where we are now with ZNE buildings. The innovators are followed by early adopters, then the early majority, the late majority, and finally by the laggards. The population distribution of innovators through laggards looks like a bell-shaped curve (see fig. 7-1). The innovators and early adopters represent about 16 percent of the population; these groups are sometimes called the visionaries. The population of the early and late majorities is about two-thirds of the total (plus and minus one standard deviation), with the laggards representing the last 16 percent to embrace the change. The innovation–adoption life cycle is called the *diffusion process*; it is documented in numerous academic papers and can be applied to just about any change from ZNE buildings to electric vehicles.[1]

ZNE buildings are still very much the business of innovators, but the concept is ready to move further along the curve. There are several factors that will cause this to happen:

Building energy codes are establishing a very efficient level of energy performance. This sets a floor for building insulation, window

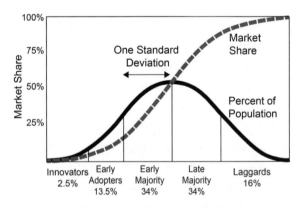

Figure 7-1: Innovation Diffusion Curves
(Source of Concept: Everett Rodgers, Diffusion of Innovations, 5th ed. [Glencoe, IL: Free Press, 2003].)

performance, equipment efficiency, lighting power, and controls. Some of the latest codes even require daylighting. When codes are effectively enforced, all buildings will be closer to the level of efficiency needed to achieve ZNE.

The cost of renewable-energy systems has declined significantly in the last decade, and additional cost reductions are anticipated. The industry is also offering innovative financing schemes like power-purchase agreements such that on-site renewable-energy systems can be added at little or no additional cost. However, the cost-effectiveness of renewable energy is still highly dependent on net-metering, utility feed-in tariffs, and tax incentives.

Tablet computers and other mobile devices are replacing notebook computers. Notebook computers are replacing desktop computers. These and other innovations, like virtualization of servers, are driving down equipment power use in buildings.

Building technologies are continuing to improve, especially with regard to LED lighting, advanced controls, user interaction with mobile devices, fenestration, and HVAC equipment. Some of these improvements are being driven by tough energy standards, so there is a symbiotic relationship between codes and technology improvements.

Commissioning is becoming more common, which is an essential element for achieving ZNE. The profession is maturing. Owners and developers are seeing the value and are including commissioning services in their standard procurement packages.

Scott Shell, a principal at EHDD Architecture, believes that these and other factors are pushing his firm to consider ZNE for every building they design, not just premium buildings like the Packard Foundation. EHDD is designing a market-rate, multi-tenant office building in Colorado that will be ZNE. Scott believes that all of their schools can be ZNE, even those constructed with public funding. Scott acknowledges that on-site ZNE is still a challenge for energy-intensive buildings like restaurants and hospitals, but he argues that we should move forward with the vast majority of buildings where on-site ZNE *is* possible and not stress over the few that we have trouble with.

Designing and constructing a building is a complicated process. At every phase of the process, decisions are made that affect the energy efficiency of the building and its potential to achieve ZNE. The decisions made near the beginning of the process are often the most important, because they establish the form and configuration of the building, which in turn enables or excludes other design opportunities later in the process, like daylighting and natural ventilation.

Cole Roberts, who leads the energy and resource sustainability business in Arup's San Francisco office, believes that most design decisions are made on the basis of precedent. He refers to this as the default condition and estimates that two-thirds or more of design decisions simply accept the default, with few questions asked. He estimates that about a third of the remaining design decisions are made through rational analysis and careful evaluation of alternatives, but that two-thirds of the remaining decisions are made irrationally. The architect likes a particular building shape. The owners saw something in Paris that they would like to replicate. If Cole is right, only about 10 percent or so of design decisions are made on the basis of rational thought.

If most design decisions are based on precedent, we must find a way to reset the default to include the energy efficiency technologies, design strategies, and renewable-energy systems needed to achieve ZNE. The existing market does not provide the majority of commercial-building owners and developers with a strong enough economic motive to pursue low-energy buildings and zero net energy buildings, but we can mitigate some of these market failures through government programs to develop promising technologies, place a price on pollution, and/or set minimum standards for energy efficiency.

My state of California has been one of the leaders in developing and enforcing tough energy standards for new buildings and providing economic incentives for energy efficiency. Through the ups and downs of oil prices over the last few decades, California and a few other states continued to develop stringent energy standards for buildings and appliances. The state also transformed the profit motive for investor-owned electric and gas utilities so that they enjoy financial benefits from helping their customers save energy in the same way that they enjoy financial benefits from selling electricity and gas. The result has been remarkable. Since 1975, about the time the California Energy Commission was first created, per-capita electricity consumption in California has been flat, while growth in the rest of the United States has increased by more than 60 percent. This has occurred in spite of trends for more air-conditioning, larger homes, larger refrigerators, more electronic devices, and a higher-quality lifestyle in general.

California's success comes from a combination of policies that involve both the carrot and the stick. It has adopted and enforced tough energy standards for the construction of new buildings, but it is also working to implement programs to help the market for energy efficiency function better. One of the most ambitious programs is a cap-and-trade system on carbon emissions, which began in 2012. This program started with large emitters but now applies to transportation fuels as well. It puts a price on emissions that will push the markets in a low-carbon direction. Another program, a declining set of incentives to encourage rooftop PV installations, helped develop the industry, create jobs, and drive down solar-energy prices. California is also working to require that information on energy efficiency be provided to companies and individuals who are buying or leasing property. It is impossible to take energy efficiency into

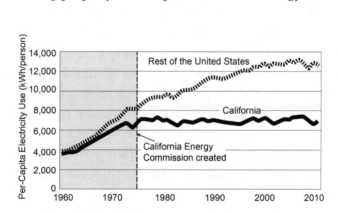

Figure 7-2: The Rosenfeld Curve

This chart is attributed to Dr. Art Rosenfeld, a leader in energy efficiency both in California and at the national level.

account if consumers don't have the information they need to make smart decisions. California is not alone in these efforts; similar programs are being implemented in many other states and cities.

Standards

Energy codes and standards are an effective tool used by California and other states to achieve a high level of energy efficiency in our buildings. Standards are not the perfect solution because they impose the same requirements on all buildings, without consideration of local site conditions, the microclimate, or the special needs of the building users. Creative designers sometimes find them a burden; standards impose design decisions with no appreciation of context. Yet they work. They have been a key element of California's success in stabilizing per-capita electricity use and producing buildings that are capable of achieving ZNE with the simple addition of renewable-energy systems.

APPLIANCE STANDARDS

There are two types of standards—appliance standards and building standards—and they are both important in our quest for ZNE. Appliance standards apply to a specific piece of equipment, such as a refrigerator, an air conditioner, or a water heater. Appliance standards are enforced at the point of manufacture or, for foreign products, at the port of entry. If a product does not comply with the applicable standard, then selling it is illegal. Since there are fewer entities to regulate (manufacturers of products being far fewer in number, that is, than the number of builders) and the point of enforcement is the manufacturing process, appliance standards have a much higher rate of enforcement than do building standards. Competition in the market is an effective enforcement mechanism; manufacturers watch their competitors closely and expose their failure to comply in order to increase their own market share.

The federal government has the authority to develop appliance standards for refrigerators, water heaters, air conditioners, and many other appliances. This authority rests with the US Department of Energy and was granted through the National Appliance Energy Conservation Act (NAECA), which was signed into law in 1975 and amended multiple times since.[2] The law is intended to provide uniform standards for energy efficiency that are "technically feasible and economically justified."

Another purpose of the law (and an important factor for manufacturers) is to preempt state and local governments from adopting their own appliance standards. This is both a positive and a negative feature of NAECA. On the positive side, it makes no sense for manufacturers to make a different product for each state. On the negative side, the feds have not always kept the NAECA standards up to date. For instance, the basic storage water-heater standard was adopted in 1989 and not updated until the 2000s. At the time the standard was updated, the efficiency of average water heaters in the market greatly exceeded the requirements of the standard, so it was having little or no impact. Meanwhile, states that wanted a meaningful standard were prohibited by law from adopting a more stringent set of requirements.[3]

BUILDING STANDARDS

Building standards, on the other hand, apply to the entire building, which may include hundreds of items that are covered by separate appliance standards. Building standards are enforced during the construction process, which makes enforcement much more difficult. A building permit application is submitted to the authority having jurisdiction (AHJ) which may be a city, county, state, or other entity. The plans and specifications submitted with the application are checked for compliance with the standards before the building permit is issued. Often the design team has to make corrections and/or additions that result from the plan check. Field inspections are performed once the building permit is issued and while the building is under construction. A certificate of occupancy is issued after construction is complete and after the AHJ has completed the necessary inspections. At least, this is how it is supposed to work; but in fact enforcement is lax in many areas.

ASHRAE Standard 90.1 is the model standard for commercial buildings and is the basis of most commercial energy standards. However, some states like California, Florida, and Washington adopt their own standards. But even in these cases, many of the requirements are similar. Standard 90.1 is a national consensus standard. This means that the standard and any changes to it must undergo an open public review. All substantive comments on the standard must be formally addressed by the adopting committee. The first version of Standard 90.1 was adopted in 1975, on the heels of the 1973 oil embargo. The next major update did not occur until 1989, fourteen years later. This was followed a decade later by version 1999. At that point, the standard ceased to go out for public review as a whole and instead only the pieces that changed were subjected to public review.

Since 1999, the standard has been under continuous maintenance. This means that it is changed piecemeal. The standard is republished every three years, but in each three-year period scores of individual addenda are separately developed, reviewed, and approved. Each new publication is simply a compilation of all the adopted addenda at the date of publication. This has sped up the process and enabled the standard to make remarkable improvements since 1999 in terms of its stringency (see fig. 7-3).

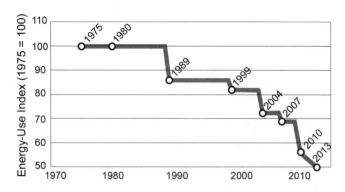

Figure 7-3: Stringency Improvements to ASHRAE Standard 90.1
In this figure, the building energy performance required by the first standard in 1975 is normalized at 100. Modern standards have an energy-use index of about 50, which means that buildings built in compliance with the latest standards would use half the energy of buildings in compliance with the 1975 standard. (Source: Pacific Northwest National Laboratory.)

MANDATORY MEASURES, PRESCRIPTIVE STANDARDS, AND PERFORMANCE STANDARDS

Building energy standards contain *mandatory measures* that are basic requirements applicable to all buildings, with few exceptions. A good example of a mandatory measure is a requirement that every room have at least one light switch. *Prescriptive standards* are simple rules or prescriptions for achieving energy efficiency. For instance, walls shall be insulated with a minimum of R-19 insulation. Lighting power shall not exceed 0.8 watts per square foot of area. Furnaces shall have an efficiency of at least 85 percent. Prescriptive standards apply separately to each building system or component, and only indirectly affect overall building performance. By contrast, *performance standards* apply to the whole building and may be used in lieu of the prescriptive standards. Compliance with performance standards is achieved through energy modeling that shows that a proposed building design uses less energy than a baseline building, which usually is one that is in minimum compliance with the prescriptive standards, although this is changing (see fig. 4-4).

As the standards become more stringent and we move toward ZNE, performance standards will be used more and prescriptive standards will be used less. Performance standards are based on energy modeling, which gives an estimate of energy use and enables on-site renewable-energy systems to be sized to offset this need. Performance standards also provide much more design flexibility and enable creative solutions that might be hindered by the prescriptive standards. As the baseline for performance standards becomes stable, software will automate the process of creating the baseline building, which will further ease the process. (See chapter 4 on energy modeling for a discussion of zEPI and PCI.)

The California building standards will require that all new low-rise residential construction be designed to achieve ZNE by 2020 and that all new nonresidential construction be designed to achieve ZNE by 2030. These will be asset assessments of ZNE, since compliance must be verified before utility bills are available.

THE COST-EFFECTIVENESS TEST

Statutes require that both appliance standards and building standards be cost-effective. The enabling legislation for the California standards requires that "the standards be cost-effective when taken in their entirety and amortized over the economic life of the building."[4] Cost-effectiveness is also a factor in the development of Standard 90.1, but the methodology is different. The committee is currently using a scalar ratio criterion of 21.4 for natural gas savings and 18.2 for electric savings.[5] The scalar ratio is similar to a simple payback, but accounts for the price of electricity and gas and increases over time, a discount rate for future savings, and assumptions on the economic life of energy-efficiency features. A measure is considered cost-effective if the annual energy savings multiplied times the scalar ratio are greater than the cost premium for the measure. Environmental externalities like carbon emissions are not factored into the scalar ratios. If they were, the standards would be even more stringent.

ADOPTION AND ENFORCEMENT

Model standards like ASHRAE 90.1 don't save energy until they are adopted by a state or local jurisdiction and effectively enforced. Some states adopt Standard 90.1 directly but many adopt the International Energy Conservation Code (IECC), based on Standard 90.1 and published by the International Code Congress (ICC). Figure 7-4 is a map of the United States that shows the version of Standard 90.1 (or the equivalent IECC standard or local standard) that is adopted by each state.[6] Compare this to the Energy-Use Index for various versions of Standard 90.1 from figure 7-3. Adopting a standard and enforcing it are two different things. Many building departments are strapped for funds and don't assign a high priority to codes that are not directly related to life-safety issues. Enforcement is very spotty.

Making the Market Work

Standards are a rather iron-fisted way to correct for market imperfections. Standards have immediate impact, but they impose the decisions of the

Figure 7-4: Adoption of Commercial Energy Standards, by State

For an interactive version of this map, see: http://bcap-energy.org/code-status/commercial/.
At this site you can click on a state and get a status summary of the energy codes in effect.
(Source: Building Codes Assistance Project, BCAP.)

code writers on all designers, constructors, and building owners. At the same time, soft approaches are also available to correct market failures. These include putting a price on pollution and waste through taxes or cap-and-trade systems, requiring that the energy efficiency of buildings be disclosed at the time or sale or lease, and providing incentives to jump-start promising technologies. Recognition programs also provide additional incentives by giving a nod to energy efficiency and ZNE buildings.

Every day, each of us makes decisions that use energy, create waste, and have other environmental impacts. These decisions seem trivial and inconsequential, but when added to the individual decisions of our 7 billion neighbors, the impact becomes enormous. Individual actions make up the whole, and the whole is currently leading us in a direction that will eventually exhaust depletable resources, pollute our planet, and change the climate.

The decisions we make are motivated by market considerations. The market sets the price for the things we purchase and for the services and products we sell, including our labor. Most of us are motivated by price; if two items are similar in quality, we will purchase the one that has the lower cost. If we are offered two similar jobs and one pays more, well, that is a no-brainer. The problem is that the market does not always price things appropriately. Pollution and waste are rarely included in the prices we pay. Economists call these "externalities." When externalities are ignored (which, by definition, they are), common resources like fisheries can be over-harvested and common sinks like our atmosphere can be over-polluted.

A working group of federal agencies led by the US Environmental Protection Agency estimates that the social cost related to carbon emissions—which includes the impact on agricultural productivity, human health, property damages from increased flood risk, reduced costs for heating, and increased costs for air-conditioning—is on the order of $60 per ton.[7] If these costs were included in the price we pay for electricity, the price would increase by about $0.037/kWh.[8] This represents a 33 percent increase in the current average cost of electricity in the United States. Other studies that focus just on coal estimate that coal-generated-electricity prices would more than triple if externalities were included.[9] If these premiums were included in our energy costs, we would have a much stronger incentive to save energy and design our buildings to achieve ZNE. Furthermore, renewable energy would be even more cost-effective, since the cost of conventional electricity would be higher.

Another problem with our markets is that we don't always have adequate information to compare products we are buying. For most of us, buying a home is the most significant purchase we make in our lifetime. We saddle ourselves with debt for decades and we go ahead and make this purchase with little or no information about the size of our monthly utility bill or how much we will pay for energy. Leasing or purchasing decisions made by companies choosing to relocate are also commonly made without information about how big the monthly energy bills will be.

Uncertainty is another issue. If we already own a building and we are considering energy-efficiency improvements or a solar system, there is often uncertainty about what the future benefits will be and sometimes about what the cost will be to implement the improvements. Even when the information is reliable, some of us assign little weight to future energy savings and instead spend our money on granite countertops which we can enjoy right away.

Externalities, incomplete information, uncertainty about future energy savings, and inattentiveness to future energy savings when purchasing energy-consuming products are all, to one degree or another, market failures. Collectively, they are one of the serious problems we face as we move toward zero net energy buildings and communities. As long as these failures exist, our markets will not adequately motivate us to save energy and invest in the future.

CAP AND TRADE

One of the most innovative programs under way in California is its cap-and-trade program on greenhouse gases. The goal of this program is to place a price on carbon dioxide pollution so that markets will pull us in the right direction. California's ambitious goal is to reduce greenhouse gases to 1990 levels by 2020 and to 20 percent of 1990 levels by 2050 (1990 is used for the reference year to be consistent with the Kyoto protocol). Initially, the program applied only to large facilities but was recently extended (in January 2015) to encompass around 360 businesses throughout California and nearly 85 percent of the state's total greenhouse-gas emissions. In the northeast United States, the Regional Greenhouse Gas Initiative (RGGI) is also a cap-and-trade system covering nine states: Connecticut, Delaware, Maine, Maryland, Massachusetts, New Hampshire, New York, Rhode Island, and Vermont.

Each facility that is regulated by the California program must monitor its emissions and obtain emission allowances to cover those emissions. A set quota of emission allocations are free, and additional allowances may be purchased from the state at its quarterly auctions or they may be purchased in the secondary market. If a facility takes measures to reduce its carbon dioxide emissions, and it is left with extra emission allowances, it can sell those emission allowances to another facility that is unable to reduce its emissions. Investors can also purchase the emission allowances, bank them for a period of time and sell them to industries that need them.

Another way to comply with the program is to purchase offset credits. An offset credit represents the removal of one tonne of CO_2e generated by a project separate from the operations of the regulated facility. Offset credits may be substituted for emission allowances on a one-for-one basis. Offset credits are limited to specific projects that are defined by the CARB's cap-and-trade regulations. The more-common projects that qualify are forestry and livestock projects. The offset projects do not have to be located in California to qualify; they can located anywhere in the United States, Canada, or Mexico.

A cap-and-trade system to control power-plant pollutants responsible for acid rain has been in place for several decades and is responsible for significantly reducing this impact. A form of cap and trade is also used to manage fisheries in Iceland, Alaska, and other areas. The concept is solid and has great potential. The California economy is large—about the same size as Italy's—but for cap and trade to be truly successful, it needs to be extended globally, or at least nationally. The benefits of California's program are enjoyed by all people of the world, but California pays the price through higher prices on energy and products that release a lot of carbon dioxide in their manufacture. This equity imbalance will be corrected as more states and countries sign on to cap and trade.

CARBON TAXES

Levying taxes on carbon emissions is another way to put a price on carbon pollution and to help the markets work better. In 2012, Australia introduced a carbon tax of A\$23 per tonne and became a world leader on climate-change action.[10] Unfortunately, there was a change of government and the tax only lasted for two years. Al Gore and other writers favor a carbon tax over cap and trade because it is simpler to administer.[11] Both serve to increase the price of goods and services that are carbon-intensive and to lower the price of goods and services that are less carbon-intensive.

Yet, a tax lacks flexibility and fails to spur creative solutions in the same way as a program of cap and trade. When carbon offsets have a value, entrepreneurs will use their ingenuity to find cost-effective ways to make reductions. The market is turned around and used to *reduce* pollution, not *increase* it.

SUBSIDIZING RENEWABLE ENERGY

The California Solar Initiative (CSI) is a successful program that helped nurture a robust solar industry, drive down the cost of solar power, and create jobs. The program, created in 2007 and now wrapping up, was funded through utility rates at a level of about $2 billion with the goal of installing 3,000 MW of solar-power generation in the state. Incentives to commercial customers were paid on a one-time basis, beginning at the rate of $2.50 per installed watt and declining to just $0.20 per watt as installations begin to reach the program capacity. As a result of the program, prices have declined (see fig. 3-11), the industry has matured, jobs have been created, and financial products like PPAs have been developed such that the program is no longer needed. Countries in the European Union have taken a different approach to encouraging the development of renewable energy. Instead of paying an up-front incentive, they encourage development by agreeing to buy renewable-energy production at a premium through a feed-in tariff.

At the federal level, the tax incentives for solar and wind have been extended through at least 2020.[12] For solar, the 30 percent investment tax credit (ITC) will continue at 30 percent levels for both commercial and residential systems through 2018, then taper off in yearly increments to settle at 10 percent in 2022. For wind, the 2.3¢-per-kilowatt-hour production tax credit (PTC) for wind power will continue through 2016, followed by incremental reductions in value for 2017, 2018, and 2019 before expiring in January 2020. The Solar Energy Industries Association estimates that the solar market will add roughly 72 gigawatts (GW) of new capacity between 2016 and 2020, pushing the country's net solar capacity to more than 100 GW, or roughly 3.5 percent of all electricity produced in the United States. The declining structure of the federal tax credits provides predictability to the solar and wind industries as we transition toward a cleaner economy.

REDUCING SUBSIDIES FOR FOSSIL FUELS

The companies that find and develop oil and gas reserves, operate the refineries, and distribute oil and gas are some of the wealthiest and most powerful entities in the world. The market value of the top four companies (Exxon Mobile, PetroChina, Chevron, and Shell) is over $1 trillion.[13] The top five coal companies have a market value of over $400 billion.[14] Yet, worldwide, these industries receive $452 billion per year in subsidies in the form of direct spending, tax breaks, and investments.[15] Subsidies in the United States are more than $20 billion per year. The top twenty industrial nations (G20) are encouraging us to use more fossil fuels by subsidizing the cost, but this is just the direct subsidy. Amory Lovins is quoted in the movie *Pump* that the United States spends $500 billion dollars a year to defend oil fields in the Middle East, which he notes is ten times what we pay for the petroleum we buy there.

Subsidies to the fossil-fuel industries far exceed government support for renewable energy. The subsidies allow coal- and gas-fired power plants to deliver electricity below the true cost, making it more difficult for renewable energy to compete in the marketplace. Instead of pricing the externalities, we offset the costs for oil and gas exploration through tax breaks and direct investment. Reducing subsidies for oil, gas, and coal has the same effect in the market as adding subsidies for renewable energy.

LABELING PROGRAMS AND MANDATORY DISCLOSURE

Buyers, sellers, and leasers of buildings have detailed information about the basic assets, but oftentimes very little is known about their energy efficiency and potential to achieve ZNE. To address this issue, various levels of government and professional associations are developing ways to rate the energy efficiency of buildings so that this information can be provided to buyers and leasers at the time of major real estate transactions. These programs influence public opinion about buildings through recognition and shame.

The most widely used labeling program is the US EPA's ENERGY STAR program. This voluntary program compares your utility bills with other similar buildings, makes adjustments for weather and operating conditions, and gives you a score. The score is a percentile that shows where you rank compared with other buildings. To be an ENERGY STAR building you need a score of 75, which means that you are in the top twenty-fifth percentile of energy-efficient buildings (75 percent are worse). If a building qualifies, the building owner can get a plaque to display in the lobby.

The ENERGY STAR program is voluntary and the information submitted to it is confidential and not shared, but a number of local governments are changing this. The Institute of Market Transformation, a Washington, DC, nonprofit, reports that "fourteen cities, two states, and one county in the U.S. have passed policies requiring benchmarking and transparency for large buildings. These policies will soon affect almost 5 billion square feet of floor space in major real estate markets—making them powerful catalysts for energy efficiency in the built environment."[16] These programs are all based on ENERGY STAR and would require that energy use and benchmarking information be publicly disclosed. The market can't work to promote energy efficiency if buyers and sellers don't have the necessary information. The goal of these programs is to correct this shortcoming.[17]

ENERGY STAR is an operational rating. As such, a building can earn the ENERGY STAR plaque because of the inherent energy efficiency of the building, because it is well maintained and operated, or because the tenants require fewer energy services. Asset-rating systems are also being developed to enable buyers and sellers to compare the energy-efficient assets of buildings they are considering for lease or purchase. Asset ratings are like the EPA mileage ratings for cars. They rate buildings using the same climate and operating conditions so they can be effectively compared. The US Department of Energy (DOE), through the Pacific Northwest National Laboratory (PNNL), recently released the DOE Building Energy Asset Score tool for assessing the physical and structural energy efficiency of commercial and multifamily residential buildings.[18] The Asset Score generates a simple energy efficiency rating that enables comparison among buildings and identifies opportunities to invest in energy-efficiency upgrades. California and other states are also developing tools to evaluate and rate the energy assets of buildings.

RECOGNITION PROGRAMS

Recognition programs shine light on the good buildings, but don't expose the bad ones. Nevertheless, they can be effective in promoting energy efficiency and encouraging zero net energy. The Leadership in Energy and Environmental Design (LEED) program by the US Green Building Council is one of the most successful programs. Since its initiation in 2000, more than 18,000 buildings have been certified. LEED is about more than just energy efficiency. It also has criteria for sites, water, materials, and indoor environmental quality. It consists of mandatory requirements and optional credits. The more credits that are earned, the more prestigious the rating: certified (formerly silver), gold, or platinum.

There are several organizations that have certification programs for ZNE buildings. One of the most rigorous is the *Zero Energy Building Certification* offered by Living Building Future.[19] The core requirement is that "one hundred percent of the project's energy needs must be supplied by on-site renewable energy on a net annual basis, without the use of on-site combustion." The Living Building Future program is an operational assessment. An independent auditor reviews utility bills for a minimum twelve-month period before the zero energy certification is issued. The assessment is based on site energy, but since all buildings that qualify for its program are all-electric (on-site combustion is not allowed), there is little difference between site energy and source energy for their assessment.

In addition to its certification program for ZNE buildings, the Living Building Future has a green building certification program that is also very rigorous. Some of the mandatory requirements of their green building program also apply to ZNE certification; they call these mandatory requirements "imperatives." The ones that apply to ZNE buildings include: (Imperative 1) appropriate siting of buildings to avoid floodplains, marshland, and other environmentally sensitive areas; (Imperative 19) features intended solely for human delight and the celebration of culture, spirit, and place; and (Imperative 20) programs to communicate the benefits and educate the public of the project.

Living Building Future does not recognize RECs or green tags in achieving ZNE. All renewable-energy production must be on-site. However, the program does recognize what they call "scale jumping" that allows the boundary for ZNE assessment to extend beyond the individual building. Scale jumping allows multiple sites to be aggregated for ZNE accounting. Living Building Future charges a registration fee and an additional certification fee that depends on the size of the building. At the time of this writing, twenty-one projects had achieved certification.

The New Buildings Institute maintains a list of Verified Zero Energy Buildings.[20] Buildings can use sources of energy other than electricity and be listed by NBI. The NBI program is an operational assessment based on site energy. Building owners or managers submit their utility bills for a twelve-month period and NBI verifies that they have achieved ZNE. The NBI 2015 report included thirty-nine buildings that had achieved ZNE. Neither the Living Building Future nor the NBI programs require that the assessment be updated as new utility data becomes available. NBI also maintains a list of Emerging Zero Energy Buildings. These are buildings with the stated goal of achieving ZNE, but cannot yet be verified. Some are still in the design stage or under construction, while others have been in operation for less than a year. This list presently includes 152 buildings.

ZNE and the Future of Electric Utilities

During some periods, ZNE buildings are producing more power than the building is using and the extra power is absorbed by the electric grid and sold to other customers. At other periods of time, the building is drawing more power from the grid than is being produced. The typical zero net energy building uses a photovoltaic (PV) system to produce power, which means that the building is a net producer during the day and a net consumer at night and on cloudy days. Many commercial buildings, like offices and schools, do not operate on weekends but the PV systems are still generating power that the utility buys.

The electric grid serves as a kind of rechargeable storage battery for zero net energy buildings, taking in the extra energy when it is available and serving it back to the building at night or at other times. For readers who are financially inclined, you can also think of the utility as a bank account: you can put money in and you can take it out. But the rechargeable storage battery is a better metaphor. If the electric grid did not do this job, then zero net energy buildings would need large racks of batteries or some other form of energy storage to serve this function. This would increase the cost of zero net energy buildings but enable them to be off the grid—that is, not connected at all to the electric utility. A ZNE building is not an off-the-grid building, but an off-the-grid building could be a ZNE building if it does not use any fossil fuels.

Owners of zero net energy buildings still pay a utility bill for storage services provided by the utility. This fee also includes costs to maintain and support the distribution system, read the meters, and be ready to provide power to the building when the renewable systems are not producing enough or are down for maintenance.

UTILITY TARIFFS AND NET-METERING POLICIES

A key requirement for the financial viability of zero net energy buildings is a reasonable utility policy for net-metering or for a feed-in tariff. If the utility does not accept surplus power from the building at times when the building is making more electricity than it is using, the cost-effectiveness of zero net energy buildings is seriously impeded.

With net-metering, the electric utility agrees to purchase excess electricity, usually at the retail rate that applies at the time the renewable energy is being added to the grid. The electric meter records the flow of electricity in both directions, entering the building and leaving the building (entering the grid). Each month, the net electricity is tallied and the customer is billed for the net amount. Most zero net energy buildings are net producers in the summer months and net users in the winter months, when days are shorter.

Pacific Gas and Electric Company, one of the largest utilities in the United States, has a net-metering policy that compensates customers at the retail rate for energy that flows into the grid, but there is a limit. If the customer puts more electricity into the grid on an annual basis than is used, the additional energy is purchased at a lower price, something closer to the wholesale rate. With net-metering, the renewable-energy system is generally located on the building side of the meter, but there are situations when the renewable-energy system can have its own meter, which is linked to the building meter for billing and accounting purposes.[21]

Feed-in tariffs are another way that utilities purchase solar and wind power. Feed-in tariffs are far more common in Europe and other countries, but are still used in the United States for large systems. With this arrangement, the renewable-energy system has its own meter connected directly to the electric grid. The utility agrees to purchase power from the renewable-energy system and a feed-in tariff applies to the power that is sold. In Europe, the rate at which the utility buys power from renewable-energy systems is often greater than the retail rate in order to provide an incentive for the design, construction, and management of the systems. A feed-in tariff has been an effective incentive in Germany, Spain, and other countries, and is largely responsible for their high concentration of wind turbines and solar panels.

Enlightened policies for net-metering and/or feed-in tariffs are critically important to the cost-effectiveness of renewable energy, but these policies, especially net-metering, have been under fire in recent years.[22] Most utilities don't want to pay retail rates for the power that they buy back from customers. Some critics make the case that net-metering is a benefit offered to wealthy building owners who can afford to install solar and this benefit is paid for by non-solar customers. There can be merit to this argument. Grid-tied solar customers need the same infrastructure as non-solar customers, because their peak demand for electricity is equal to or maybe even higher than that of non-solar customers. Plus, the hourly pattern of energy use typical of a solar customer places a larger burden on the electric grid and is more difficult and expensive for the utility to provide (more on this later).

Furthermore, not all ZNE buildings are the same, yet with most net-metering arrangements, they all pay the same kind of bill. Consider two ZNE buildings. One is very energy-efficient, with an EUI in the range of 15 kBtu/ft²·yr. This building achieves ZNE with a 20-kW PV system. The second ZNE building is the same size, but with conventional construction and an EUI of 45 kBtu/ft²·yr. This building requires a 60-kW PV system to achieve ZNE. The second building requires an electric service three times larger, and the transition between when the building is exporting power and when it is importing power is far more extreme, requiring that the utility quickly bring on more conventional generation as the sun goes down. Clearly, the second building should pay more to the utility, because it receives more services, but the way most net-metering tariffs are structured, both buildings pay the same.

As long as there are only a few ZNE buildings, most utilities can serve the storage-battery function at a very low cost. In fact, a limited number of ZNE buildings can be a benefit to most utilities. The peak demand for power that most utilities experience occurs on hot sunny afternoons, and this coincides quite nicely with the times when PV systems are producing at their maximum. In these cases, the extra production from ZNE buildings can help the utility company to manage its peak.

The potential problem comes when we get far away from the margin (as economists call it). At the extreme, what would happen if all buildings were zero net energy? In this case, the utility might have more power than it could use on sunny afternoons. PV systems would all be cranking out electricity and there would be no one to buy it because everyone would be making their own. The time of the utility peak would shift from the afternoon, when PV systems are producing, to the early evening, when buildings are still operating, but the sun has gone down. Power-plant capacity might need to be as great in an all-ZNE net-metering world as it would be with no ZNE buildings at all.

ELEPHANTS, CAMELS, AND DUCKS

The California Independent System Operator (CaISO) manages the flow of electricity across the high-voltage, long-distance power lines that make up 80 percent of California's and a small part of Nevada's power grid. CaISO serves 30 million customers and grants equal access to 26,000 circuit miles of power lines. It also facilitates a competitive wholesale power market designed to diversify resources and lower prices. Every five minutes the ISO forecasts electrical demand, accounts for operating reserves, and dispatches the lowest-cost power plants available for the upcoming five-minute interval. CaISO ensures that enough transmission capacity is available to deliver the power needed. To maintain reliability, the ISO must continuously match the demand for electricity with supply on a second-by-second basis. It serves the critical function of balancing supply with demand, an essential task performed by all utilities.

In 2012, CaISO issued a report on the impact of solar and wind on the California grid. They looked at net load, which represents the variable portion of electrical load that CaISO must meet in real time.[23] For a high-load January day, the demand for electricity ramps up in the morning, stays relatively flat until sundown, and then ramps up again as workers arrive home to turn on lights and appliances. Demand slowly ramps down after about 7:00 p.m. Without solar and wind, the CaISO would bring new generation into service in the morning, run the plants pretty much steadily all day long, bring on a few more between about 4:30 p.m. and 7:00 p.m., and then gradually shut them down after 7:00 p.m. This is for a typical day in January, but every day is different because of weather and other factors.

The contribution of wind and solar is increasing in California, and as it does it has a big impact on the net load that CaISO must meet. Figure 7-5 shows the contribution that the CaISO expects from wind and solar in 2020 for this same January day. The net load (the part that CaISO must provide) is much more variable. Wind is expected to be fairly steady, providing between 2,000 and 3,000 megawatts of power for the whole twenty-four-hour period, but solar is a different story. Solar production will ramp up in the morning from zero to over 9,000 megawatts and fall again in the afternoon. The load profile without wind and solar is shaped like an elephant. With wind and solar it is shaped like a camel with two humps. For this high-load January day, CaISO would need to bring on 8,000 megawatts in the morning before sunrise and then shed most of this generation capacity a few hours later after the sun is up and solar production kicks in. But the biggest challenge is at dusk. Demand will increase

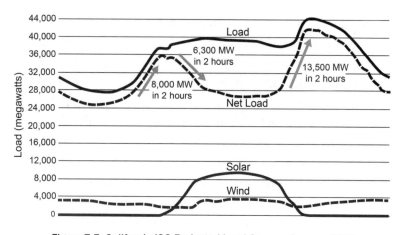

Figure 7-5: California ISO Projected Load Curves—January 2020
The net load is the load that must be satisfied with conventional generators like natural gas, coal, or nuclear.

as residents get home and turn on their lights, and at about the same time, solar production is falling off very quickly. CaISO would need to bring on 13,500 megawatts of generation capacity in about two hours.

The information provided by CaISO can be displayed in lots of different ways and for different days of the week and months of the year. One of the graphs that has caused quite a stir is their "duck chart" (see fig. 7-6). This shows the net load (the part that CaISO must meet) for a typical March day. The various lines on the chart represent what will happen as we have more ZNE buildings and renewable energy on the grid. Together, the lines resemble a duck with its tail to the left and its head to the right. As we add more renewable energy, the belly of the duck gets fatter and its neck gets longer. It is the neck that is the potential problem. For this March day in 2020, CaISO would need to bring on 13,000 megawatts of additional generating capacity in about three hours.

Another potential problem that CaISO could face is over-generation. With more wind and solar feeding into the grid in combination with more energy-efficient buildings and base-load generators that can't be trimmed back, there could be periods of time (the belly of the duck) when there is too much generation capacity. This is a different kind of problem for the

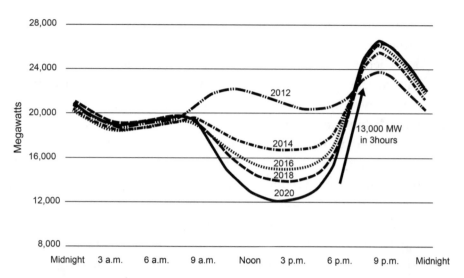

Figure 7-6: California ISO "Duck Chart"

As more solar is added in California, the belly of the "duck" gets fatter and the neck gets steeper. The steepness of the neck is the potential problem, as system operators have to bring on a lot of conventional generators in a short period of time.

CaISO, and it will require a different kind of solution. The most straightforward solution is to shut down some of the renewable-energy generators (more on this later).

Obviously, it is much easier to meet a steady load throughout the day than one that has big swings. Coal and nuclear generators run at a constant rate to meet the base load and can't be easily trimmed; natural gas and hydro generators are more flexible and can be brought on-line more quickly. As more renewable energy, especially solar, is brought on through ZNE buildings, there will be a greater need for more-flexible backup generators, which is the main point of the CaISO study.

NEW CHALLENGES

More wind and solar power will create challenges to balancing the grid, but there are solutions. These solutions will change the way CaISO and other electric markets buy energy, but will also affect how we design and construct ZNE buildings.

At the grid level, one solution is to export power to other regions when there is an over-generation problem or import power from other regions when it is necessary to bring on more generation capacity in order to climb the humps on the camel's back. This works best when different regions have different load profiles because of time zones, climate, or demand. Implementing this strategy will require that interstate and interregional transmission lines be upgraded in many areas.

Another solution is to implement more energy efficiency and demand response, which would reduce the overall size of the demand curve and help smooth it out. As discussed in chapter 5, the future will bring systems of communication between the utility and buildings and appliances, whereby demand for energy can be automatically trimmed during critical periods without causing inconvenience or discomfort to building managers or the occupants. There are thousands of opportunities in this area, some large and some small, but when considered in aggregate they can reshape the basic demand curve.

Energy storage is another opportunity for reshaping the load curve. This can be implemented both on the supply side at the grid level and on the demand side at the building level. Pumped storage has been used by utilities for decades. Water is pumped to a higher-elevation reservoir when power is plentiful and used to generate power when power demand is high.[24] Utilities are also evaluating battery storage.[25]

At the building level, thermal storage has been used for decades to shift air-conditioning loads from the afternoon to night; chillers create a store of chilled water at night when temperature conditions are more favorable and this chilled water is used the next day to cool the building without running the chillers during periods of peak electric demand. Battery storage at the building level will also become a more important part of building design. I anticipate that buildings will still be connected to the grid, but that batteries will be able to store some of the solar energy generated during the day and use it in the early evening. This will require much smaller batteries than what is needed to go off the grid completely. Tesla, the car company, is building a huge battery plant near Reno, Nevada. Their batteries will be used not only for cars but also for stationary storage. They already offer a home battery that charges using electricity generated from solar panels, or when utility rates are low, and this battery powers the building in the evening.[26] The RMI Innovation Center (see appendix) incorporates a 45-kilowatt-hour battery to reduce peak load and carry out other functions. Battery storage is not the perfect solution, since the efficiency of charging and then discharging a battery is only about 80 percent, but with an abundance of solar energy, batteries still make sense.

Electric vehicles (EVs) present another opportunity to manage the electric load. Goef Syphers, the CEO of Sonoma Clean Power, is evaluating the possibility of installing 10,000-EV charging stations in the county, which they can control to help manage their load. Southern California Edison (California's second-largest utility) is initiating a pilot program with EV owners to manage the times when EVs are charged.[27] Right now, the only load-management opportunity is to schedule the times for charging and the rate of charging. Eventually, it may be possible for EVs to provide genuine electric storage capabilities if they are able to add power to the grid through VtoG (vehicle to grid) technology. There are lots of issues related to battery warranties and owner acceptance, but the expected growth of EVs presents a huge opportunity.

Finally, there will be times when renewable-energy production is simply not needed. The best way to address over-generation caused by too much solar-power production is to turn off the solar plants. Other options, like burning off the extra power in a load bank, are much less desirable. Modern inverters will have the ability to communicate with the grid and shut down or scale back PV production when power is being exported from the building and the grid is experiencing an over-generation problem. However, stationary batteries, if they exist, could be charged with this extra power. Already many wind generators and large solar farms are controlled in this manner.

THE SMART GRID AND DYNAMIC PRICING

A smart grid will help implement the solutions listed above and more. A smart grid combines dynamic pricing with buildings, EVs, appliances, and renewable-energy systems that can automatically respond to the price signals. The system operators at the CaISO and other networks will still have to balance the system, but much of the job would be performed through price signals. When prices are at a peak, buildings would automatically dim the lights and perhaps raise the cooling setpoint. Refrigeration equipment would run at a lower speed, still maintaining temperature, but taking advantage of the thermal storage of all the refrigerated or frozen items. An orb would glow red to warn occupants of the high prices so they can turn off equipment that they don't need. These and other actions would occur automatically or with a little occupant intervention and would assist in balancing the system.

Appliances like water heaters, clothes washers, and dishwashers would be able to communicate with the smart grid and automatically schedule their operation for periods when electricity prices are low. Electric vehicles would be programmed to charge their batteries in the afternoon when the sun is out, prices are low, and there is an abundance of solar energy.[28] But EVs would be smart enough to provide a minimum charge or range to get their owners where they need to go. Homeowners and building managers would have an economic incentive to invest in batteries or other electric storage systems in order to shift their use of electricity to periods when prices are low. With dynamic pricing, an inefficient ZNE building with a large PV system would pay more for grid storage and backup than an efficient ZNE building with a smaller PV system.

Electricity prices at the wholesale level are already dynamic. The TDV curves (see fig. 6-4) are based on real-time pricing in California. PJM is an East Coast regional electric transmission organization that coordinates the movement of wholesale electricity in all or parts of thirteen states and the District of Columbia.[29] Similar markets exist in other areas. PJM's tools give members access to a continuous flow of up-to-the-minute energy price data that enables them to make business decisions and manage their transactions in real time. These price signals work for large customers and utilities but are generally not passed on to building owners and managers. However, with a smart grid, they would. Building-management systems would also have machine-learning algorithms to automatically respond to these signals.

For markets to function effectively, the participants need information and the ability to act on it quickly. Real-time price information will allow building managers to follow market fluctuations and make rapid decisions on how to operate their buildings and renewable-energy systems: when to export power, when to charge their batteries, when to curtail use and draw from their storage.

THE UTILITY OF THE FUTURE

The electric grid itself and the role of utilities that manage it will change as more of our buildings become ZNE. Most utilities are now large one-way distribution systems. Massive power plants generate electricity that is carried in one direction to customers down the line. The traditional role of utilities as power producers and sellers will morph into one of managers of a smart and intelligent electric grid. Instead of having a few really big power plants producing all the power, each connection to the grid would function as both a buyer and a seller of power. The Internet is a good analogy. Every connection to the Internet can both provide content and receive content. In a similar manner, utility customers will both purchase electricity from the grid and sell it to the grid. This will be managed by a smart grid, and buildings, appliances, renewable-energy systems, and storage systems will respond automatically to dynamic price signals.

Peter Fox-Penner, a consultant to electric utilities and an Island Press author, believes that the utility company of the future will take one of two directions, depending on the regulatory climate of the state or region where they operate.[30] In regions that have opted for open competition in the wholesale power market, he believes that utilities will become smart integrators. "The smart integrator (SI) is a utility that operates the power grid and its information and control systems but does not actually own or sell the power delivered by the grid. Its mission will be to deliver electricity with superb reliability from a wide variety of sources, from upstream plants to in-home solar cells, all at prices set by regulator-approved market mechanisms."[31] The smart integrator will manage the grid to accommodate two-way flows of electricity, since each customer can be both a supplier and a user. It will manage an open platform for information on electricity prices so that customers can decide to buy or sell on an hourly (or even sub-hourly) basis. Regulators will approve a system for setting prices, but prices will be set by the approved market mechanisms once they are in place.

In regions where utilities continue to be vertically integrated (i.e., they own most of the power plants, manage the transmission and distribution network, and sell power to customers), Fox-Penner believes that utilities will morph into energy services utilities (ESUs). "An ESU is a regulated entity whose prices and profits are controlled, though not without major changes to traditional cost-of-service regulation. It is responsible for supplying customers' demand with high reliability. It can own the generators that provide its supply, whether large upstream plants or small local ones, but is also required to purchase or transmit power from others attached to its wires."[32] The ESU model differs from the smart integrator model in two important ways: First, the ESU has little incentive to cooperate with local generators or ZNE buildings that want to sell power into the smart grid. It may view them as competition to its own generating sources. Second, it has little incentive to help customers reduce their energy use, since this would erode their sales. Regulators would have a larger role with the ESU model to manage these disincentives through decoupling the utilities' profits from their sales and/or through other means.

With either model of the future utility, the smart grid will be an important feature to help balance the system and more fairly charge customers for the services provided. Several utilities have begun to pilot dynamic pricing and smart meters. The systems can work with different levels of customer technology. The most basic method of communication is an orb that glows red when prices are high and green when prices are low. More-enhanced technologies include energy-management dashboards, smart plugs, and programmable communicating thermostats. Advanced technologies include responsive building-management systems, smart appliances, special controls for electric vehicles, and devices to enable integrated distributed generation and storage.[33] National Grid, one of the largest utilities, has launched a smart grid pilot project that will make quasi-dynamic pricing available to 15,000 residents in Worcester, Massachusetts. Participating customers will be charged daytime rates that are lower than their current basic service rate for most of the year. In return, customers will be asked to conserve energy on thirty peak-demand days each year, and they will face higher prices on those days. This is not true dynamic pricing like what exists at the wholesale market, but it is a step in the right direction.

Utilities are natural monopolies and as such are regulated by the public. This gives the public some leverage over utilities and some level of input into the policies they implement. The dynamic rates and tariff structures they adopt, as well as the policies they promote, will be determined through negotiations or imposed by their regulators. In the short term, utilities need to encourage the development of distributed renewable-power generation through appropriate feed-in tariffs or net-metering, but in the long term, dynamic pricing will provide incentives to make our ZNE buildings as energy-efficient as possible and to incorporate small renewable-energy systems as opposed to having inefficient buildings with large PV systems.

Electric and gas utilities have a critical role in promoting ZNE buildings and addressing climate change. As players in the market, they must internalize the externalities of pollution and waste and include these costs in the prices they charge for energy. They must cease to function as one-way power suppliers and become managers of the grid and power brokers between buyers and sellers. The future of mainstream ZNE buildings depends in large part on the direction taken by power utilities.

CHAPTER 8

Beyond ZNE:
The World of Our Grandchildren

Zero net energy buildings are an important part of a strategy to prevent the worst impacts of climate change, but there are many more opportunities related to our buildings and the built environment that we can address as design and construction professionals.

Indirect Building Energy Use

The concept of ZNE buildings is to produce enough energy from on-site renewable-energy sources to offset the energy use that is directly used for heating, cooling, lighting, and plug loads. But it also takes energy to construct buildings in the first place, to meet their transportation needs, and to provide water and other services. There are opportunities to save indirect energy as well as the direct energy.

EMBODIED ENERGY

Constructing buildings requires vast resources and energy use. Timber is harvested from forests, milled or otherwise processed, delivered to the building site, and assembled into walls, floors, or other building components. Raw materials for concrete, steel, and glass are mined from the earth, manufactured into building products, transported to the construction site, and assembled. Energy is used throughout the construction process, from resource extraction to refinement, product manufacturing,

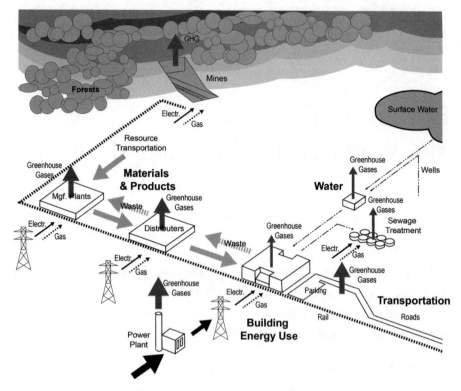

Figure 8-1: Total Environmental Impact of Buildings

The environmental impact of buildings includes not only the energy that is used directly but also the "upstream" energy needed to power the grid. Materials and products used to construct each building add to the impact, as well as materials and products used during building operation. Water for irrigation and service use adds to the impact. One of the largest impacts is the transportation needs of building users getting to and from the building.

and transport to the site, as well as for tools and equipment used in construction. The sum of this energy is referred to as *embodied energy*. It is the total energy needed to prepare a new building for occupancy or to renovate an existing building. Most of the embodied energy is expended when the building is initially constructed, but this process continues to some extent throughout the life of the building as it is renovated and modified. If embodied energy were taken into account in our definition of ZNE buildings, each building would begin its life deep in debt and would have to function as a net energy producer for many years in order to make up for the energy used to build it.

The concept of embodied energy can be applied to every product we buy, from cars to toothbrushes, and should be a consideration when we make a purchase, if we only had the information. Information on embodied energy of building construction is fairly sparse, but the Athena Sustainable Materials Institute has some very interesting tools.[1] The embodied energy for buildings varies, depending on the type of construction and many other factors, but Athena's EcoCalculator tool suggests a range between about 250 and 400 kBtu/ft^2 of source energy.[2] Depending on the EUI of the building, the embodied energy could represent many multiples of the operational energy.

Once a building is occupied, there is a continuous stream of supplies, materials, and products that enter the building and a continuous stream of waste that leaves the building. Every sheet of paper and every computer monitor requires energy to produce and energy to recycle at the end of its life. Building equipment and systems need to be maintained, which also requires energy. This component of energy use is affected only partially by the design of the building. It has much more to do with the operations and activities taking place inside. However, buildings have an influence on how we use them. As Winston Churchill once said, "We shape our buildings; thereafter they shape us."[3]

There are, of course, impacts other than energy that result from the making of a product, such as air pollution, water pollution, and resource depletion. The science of accounting for all environmental impacts from the birth of a product through its use and final disposal or recycling is called *life-cycle assessment*, and advances are being made in LCA methodologies and data collection techniques.

TRANSPORTATION

Transportation is another large and quite significant indirect energy use related to buildings. People need to get to and from buildings. Where buildings are located in the community, the proximity of commercial buildings to employees or customers, the availability of services near residential areas, pedestrian friendliness, and transit opportunities all affect the type and magnitude of transportation that is needed. In compact neighborhoods like San Francisco's North Beach, the average car miles per year per household is less than 8,000 because so many services, jobs, and friends are within walking distance or an easy bus ride. Residential suburbs like San Ramon, California, just across the Bay, require more than 30,000 car miles per year per household because a car trip is needed for just about every activity.[4]

On its website, the National Academy of Sciences, Technology, and Medicine explains:

> In the United States we use 28 percent of our energy to move people and goods from one place to another. The transportation sector includes all modes of transportation—from personal vehicles (cars, light trucks) to public transportation (buses, trains) to airplanes, freight trains, barges, and pipelines. One might think that airplanes, trains, and buses would consume most of the energy used in this sector but, in fact, their percentages are relatively small—about 9 percent for aircraft and about 3 percent for trains and buses. Personal vehicles, on the other hand, consume more than 60 percent of the energy used for transportation.[5]

A few years ago I did a sustainability study for the San Francisco school that educated our children. The facilities are very efficient, earning high marks on the ENERGY STAR scale. However, the largest component of energy use was transportation. By looking at the zip codes of the students, we could determine more or less where they lived. We made estimates, through surveys, to see how the kids got to school, and found that, due to their young age, most of the students were driven by their parents. After accounting for car-pooling and ride sharing, we determined that transportation accounted for about two-thirds (67 percent) of the energy use and carbon footprint of the school.[6]

The newsletter *Environmental Building News* published a piece a few years back titled "Driving to Green Buildings."[7] The well-written piece by Alex Wilson points out the irony that the energy used to serve the transportation needs of many green buildings dwarfs the energy that the building directly uses for lighting, heating, cooling, and equipment. For typical buildings, the transportation energy is 30 percent greater, and for newer buildings that meet more-stringent energy-efficiency codes, the transportation energy is more than double.

WATER

Water is another indirect building-energy use. Buildings have water requirements for both irrigation of the site surrounding the building and for interior uses. Irrigation needs vary with size, the type of plants used, and the climate. Interior water needs depend primarily on the building use, with hotels, restaurants, and health clubs having the greatest water-use intensity and offices and other work environments having the least.

Water is a valuable resource on its own, but it also has significant energy implications. Energy is used to pump water out of the ground, treat it at purification sites, and distribute it to buildings. Additional energy is used to collect and treat wastewater and discharge it back to rivers or lakes. Some wastewater is recycled and distributed for use as irrigation water; this also takes energy. In Northern California, each acre-foot of water used for agricultural, residential, or commercial use requires about 12,000 kilowatt-hours (kWh) of energy. In Southern California, the energy consumption for an acre-foot of water is close to 40,000 kWh, more than three times greater, primarily because much of the water is pumped from the Colorado River, on the eastern boundary of the state, over the Tehachapi Mountains at a peak elevation of 8,000 feet.[8]

The process of generating electricity also uses an enormous amount of water. About 90 percent of electricity in the United States is generated with steam turbines; water is used to condense the steam and cool the generating equipment. In 2005, over 200 billion gallons (613,000 acre-feet) of water each day were used to produce electricity (excluding hydroelectric power).[9] Hydro plants also indirectly use water because, once a dam is built, the water surface area increases and the rate of evaporation to the atmosphere is increased. Surface water is used to cool most power plants, which is the reason they are commonly located near rivers or along the coast. Electric-power generation accounts for almost half of all withdrawals of water from surface sources, even more than irrigation. The energy required to withdraw the water, process it, use it, cool it back down, and release it into the river or lake is quite significant and is one of the factors that determines the efficiency of a power plant.

Water and electricity are interdependent. They both need each other. Making electricity takes water and providing water to our buildings takes energy.

New Urbanism

ZNE buildings are a means to a more sustainable world, but they are a milestone—not an end in and of themselves. Buildings are elements in the larger urban fabric within which we live and work. By addressing human needs in the broader context, we can provide more walkable communities where we can get by without a car; where we can support our buildings with a simpler and more inexpensive infrastructure; where we can preserve more land for recreation, agriculture, and wilderness; and where we can reduce urban sprawl and move more toward transit-oriented developments.

New Urbanism is an urban design movement that encourages walkable neighborhoods containing a diverse range of housing, commerce, and employment. It is about raising our quality of life and standard of living by creating better places to live, but the beauty of New Urbanism is that such places do all this with less energy and a vastly smaller environmental footprint. This is another example of how we can improve our living conditions while at the same time addressing climate change and other pressing global environmental issues.

ZNE buildings, in the context of transit-oriented compact communities are an important element, but it is the urban fabric that enables us to go about our lives without driving so much, using as many resources, or generating as much carbon dioxide. Streets are narrower and lined with trees. Sites are more constrained and achieving on-site ZNE may be more difficult, but opportunities for community solar abound. Buildings can still achieve ZNE, but they can also significantly reduce transportation energy and embodied energy (since buildings are more compact), and water can be conserved because irrigated areas are smaller and more focused on human needs.

Bold new community design holds great promise, and leaders like Peter Calthorpe are making great progress, but ZNE buildings represent something we can all do right now on an incremental basis. We presently have the knowledge and technology to design the vast majority of our buildings to produce as much energy as they use. We don't have to wait for transit-oriented communities. We don't have to wait for the development of new technologies or products. We don't have to wait for our government leaders, politicians, and policy makers to provide more economic incentives or to correct market imperfections. We don't have to wait for the smart grid or dynamic electricity pricing. We don't have to wait at all. We can do it now.

A Vision for Our Grandchildren

The principles outlined in this book can lead to a more sustainable future for our children and grandchildren. Here is the vision I dream of:

Our buildings will be enclosed by smartly designed building envelopes that are highly insulated, decked out in light colors to reflect the sun, and have windows strategically placed to maximize daylighting, provide ventilation air and cooling, and connect us to the out-of-doors. Heating and cooling systems will use a minimal amount of energy through efficient equipment, design, and controls. Lighting will be provided primarily from the sun (daylighting), and efficient electric lights will be used, sparingly, to supplement the primary daylighting source. Computers, appliances, and other equipment will be energy-efficient and have controls to shut down unnecessary components when they are not needed.

Appliances will have sophisticated control chips that can communicate with the grid and avoid energy consumption when energy prices are high. If you attempt to start a washer or dryer when rates are high, a message will appear to let you know that if you wait a couple of hours, the cost will be much lower. You will be presented with an option whereby you can let the machine start automatically when the cost of electricity has declined. If you want to endure the higher rates because little Joey needs his jersey for a soccer game, you will also have this option, but you will pay extra.

Each building will be a both a supplier and consumer of electricity from the grid. Rooftops and parking lots will be covered with solar panels to produce electricity. Most buildings will achieve zero net energy and generate as much electric power on an annual basis as they use. The other buildings will subscribe to community solar systems that will add as much power to the grid as those buildings use. As the saturation of ZNE buildings increases, buildings will incorporate energy-storage technologies to provide more control for when they draw power from the grid and when they supply it.

Our utility companies will cease to be one-way power suppliers that operate huge fossil-fuel-fired plants and deliver electricity in one direction from these plants to our homes and businesses. Instead, they will operate a multi-directional electric grid where each connection to the grid is both a supplier and a seller. Utility rates will be dynamic and vary by time of day and by day of the year, encouraging participants in the grid (they are no longer strictly customers), to produce power and sell it into the grid when rates are high and take power from the grid when rates are low.

Existing buildings will be seen as assets that not only reflect our history and celebrate our heritage, but also represent vast stores of embodied energy. Saving them and restoring them enhances our lives and avoids the energy penalty associated with tearing down an old building and constructing a new one. Our throwaway society will embrace permanence and durability. Wares will be designed to last a lifetime (or two) and be repairable. Packaging will be minimized. We will find better ways to share our tools, cars, homes, offices, and equipment so that our industries can produce less but all of us can still enjoy the benefits.

Gasoline-powered private vehicles will give away to electric vehicles, and these vehicles will be programmed to charge themselves from the grid and provide power to the grid when they are able. Parking lots and garages will be fitted with smart charger outlets. It won't be necessary to put in a credit card or pay with cash; the smart charger will recognize the car and the associated payment method. Drivers in the United States presently own about 250 million cars and trucks, or about 2.3 such vehicles per household. At any given time, most of these are parked—and if they were electric, they could provide the grid with an enormous storage capacity. Either after work or in the morning, car owners would be able to participate in the grid by digitally entering the minimum distance they need to drive. The car would have the smarts to either charge itself or release its energy, depending on the price of electricity that day and how much reserve must be left in the battery.

Our communities will become more compact, with the highest-density development clustered around light-rail transit stops. Single-family homeownership in suburbia will decline. Residents in the new transit-oriented communities will be able to walk to work, take public transit, or work from home and have nearby services, so that owning a car becomes optional. Many Americans will gain one to two hours per day by not having to commute to work on a congested freeway. In terms of leisure time, this is like getting six to twelve weeks of additional vacation each year.

This vision is technically achievable today. And it is cost-effective, especially if the cost of pollution and waste are included in the prices we pay. We can make it happen if designers, building owners, tenants, utility companies, and governments at all levels take a long-term view and build for our grandchildren. But don't wait. Do it now. We're running out of time.

Examples of ZNE and Energy-Efficient Buildings

BULLITT CENTER | Seattle, Washington | 52,000 ft²

PROJECT TEAM
Owner: Bullitt Foundation (www.bullitt.org)
Architect: Miller Hull Partnership, LLP (www.millhull.com)
MEP Engineer: PAE Engineers (www.pae-engineers.com)
Solar Design: Solar Design Associates (www.solardesign.com)
Lighting: Luma : Lighting Design (www.lumald.com)
Builder: Schuchart (www.schuchart.com)

ENERGY PERFORMANCE
Site EUI: 16 kBtu/ft²·yr designed (12 kBtu/ft²·yr actual)
Renewable energy: 15.1 kBtu/ft²·yr designed (16 Btu/ft²·yr actual, 244,000 kWh/yr)
In 2014, the building was net positive by 4 kBtu/ft²·yr

FOR MORE INFORMATION
https://www.youtube.com/watch?v=urNPqusW3cs
https://en.wikipedia.org/wiki/Bullitt_Center
http://www.bullittcenter.org/building/
http://corporatetechdecisions.com/article/the_tech_behind_the_bullitt_center_the_worlds
_greenest_office_building/Energy#

Bullitt Center exterior image. (© Brad Kahn, Flickr.)

DESIGN FEATURES
- Triple-pane glazing
- Automatic exterior window louvers
- Water-source heat pumps
- DOAS
- Radiant floor slabs
- 575 photovoltaic panels
- Advanced energy-management system
- "Irresistible" stairway to discourage elevator use
- Regenerative elevator turns braking into power
- Heat recovery

NREL RESEARCH SUPPORT FACILITY | Golden, Colorado | 220,000 ft²

PROJECT TEAM
Owner: National Renewable Energy Laboratory (www.nrel.gov)
Architect: RNL (www.rnldesign.com.)
MEP Engineer and Energy Modeling: Stantec (www.stantec.com)
Daylighting Consultant: Architectural Energy Corporation (www.noresco.com)
Builder: Haselden Construction (www.haselden.com)

PROJECT DELIVERY
Design built with an energy-performance clause in the contract

FOR MORE INFORMATION
https://www.youtube.com/watch?v=43dT66mhh0c
http://www.nrel.gov/sustainable_nrel/rsf.html
http://www.hpbmagazine.org/attachments/article/12170/12F-Department-of-Energys
-National-Renewable-Energy-Laboratory-Research-Support-Facility-Golden-CO.pdf

NREL Research Support Facility, two building wings with entrance. (Dennis Schroeder, NREL.)

DESIGN FEATURES
- Optimal orientation and office space layout
- Daylighting and efficient electric lighting
- Continuous-insulation precast wall panels
- Operable windows for natural ventilation
- Glazing optimized for each orientation
- Radiant heating and cooling
- DOAS with outdoor-air preheating
- Aggressive plug-load control strategies
- Data Center outdoor air economizer
- Thermal-storage labyrinth
- 449-kW photovoltaic system on roof
- 524-kW photovoltaic system over visitor parking
- 706-kW photovoltaic system over staff parking

NREL Research Support Facility wall detail. (Bill Gillies.)

IOWA UTILITIES BOARD AND OFFICE OF CONSUMER ADVOCATE
Des Moines, Iowa | 44,460 ft²

PROJECT TEAM
Owner: Iowa Utilities Board (https://iub.iowa.gov/)
Architect: BNIM (www.bnim.com)
MEP Engineer: KJWW Engineering Consultants (www.khww.com)
Energy Modeler: The Weidt Group (www.theweidtgroup.com)
Builder: J. P. Cullen (www.jpcullen.com)
Commissioning: Engineering Economics, Inc. (www.eeiengineers.com)

ENERGY PERFORMANCE
Site EUI: 21.2 kBtu/ft²·yr
Renewable energy: 4.5 kBtu/ft²·yr

FOR MORE INFORMATION
Video: tinyurl.com/k2x3ro2
http://issuu.com/bnim/docs/iubfinal_343fe1f1e990bd
http://www.hpbmagazine.org/attachments/article/12210/15Su-Iowa-Utilities-Board-and
-Office-of-Consumer-Advocate-Des-Moines-IA.pdf

Distant view of Iowa Utilities Board building and wall detail. (© Assassi, Courtesy BNIM.)

DESIGN FEATURES
- Narrow building profile oriented E–W
- Sunscreen/light louvers on south façade
- Mixed-mode ventilation with e-mail notifications
- Occupant engagement for plug-load management
- Advanced concrete sandwich panels
- Advanced glazing optimized for each orientation
- 95 percent of regularly occupied area has daylight and views
- Tubular skylights for interior spaces
- 45-kW crystalline photovoltaic system
- Geothermal heat-pump system
- ECM fan motors and variable-speed pumping
- Replicable design

THE DAVID & LUCILLE PACKARD FOUNDATION | Los Altos, California | 49,000 ft²

PROJECT TEAM
Owner: Packard Foundation (www.packard.org)
Architects: EHDD (www.ehdd.com)
Builder: DPR Construction (www.dpr.com)
MEP Engineer: Integral Group (www.integralgroup.com)
Daylighting: Loisos + Ubbelode (www.coolshadow.com)
Commissioning: Altura (www.alturaassociates.com)

ENERGY PERFORMANCE
Site EUI: 23.5 kBtu/ft²·yr
Renewable energy: 29.1 kBtu/ft²·yr

FOR MORE INFORMATION
https://www.youtube.com/watch?v=48VA83sOe7U
http://www.ehdd.com/work/the-david-and-lucile-packard-foundation
http://www.hpbmagazine.org/attachments/article/12152/15W-David-&-Lucile-Packard
-Foundation-Headquarters-Los%20Altos-California.pdf

Courtyard at the David & Lucille Packard Foundation building.
(© Jeremy Bittermann.)

DESIGN FEATURES
- Active chilled beams
- Dedicated outside-air system
- Triple glazing (eliminates need for perimeter heat)
- Automated exterior shades for glare control
- Motorized windows
- Natural ventilation with e-mail system for occupants
- Excellent daylighting
- Interior light shelves with radiant heat
- No chiller (oversized cooling tower)
- Thermal storage for both chilled and hot water

ROCKY MOUNTAIN INSTITUTE INNOVATION CENTER
Basalt, Colorado | 15,610 ft²

PROJECT TEAM
Owner: Rocky Mountain Institute (www.rmi.org)
Architects: ZGF Architects, Graybeal Architects, LLC (www.zgf.com)
Builder: JE Dunn Construction Group, Inc. (www.jedunn.com)
MEP Engineer: PAE Engineers (www.pae-engineers.com)
Lighting: David Nelson & Associates (www.dnalighting.com)
Commissioning: Resource Engineering Group (www.reginc.com)

PROJECT DELIVERY
Integrated project delivery with rewards and penalties offered based on meeting project goals. Bonus to design team for exceeding energy targets.

ENERGY PERFORMANCE
Site EUI: 17.2 kBtu/ft²·yr (estimated)
Renewable energy: 21 kBtu/ft²·yr (estimated)

FOR MORE INFORMATION
http://www.rmi.org/innovationcenter
http://mountaintownnews.net/2014/11/13/net-zero-small-office-building/

View of the RMI Innovation Center and wall detail. (Craig Schiller, Rocky Mountain Institute.)

DESIGN FEATURES
- E–W building orientation
- Resilient and adaptable for future changes
- Passive solar heating
- Light shelves and overhangs for solar control
- Hyperchairs and personal fans
- Natural ventilation (no mechanical cooling)
- Energy monitoring at each workstation
- Hoteling workstations to reduce building area
- 83-kW monocrystalline photovoltaic system on roof
- 45-kWh battery storage

STANFORD Y2E2 BUILDING | Palo Alto, California | 54,000 ft²

PROJECT TEAM
Owner: Stanford University (www.stanford.edu)
Architect: Bora Architects (bora.co)
MEP Engineer: Arup (www.arup.com)
Energy Modeler: Arup (www.arup.com)
Builder: Hathaway Dinwiddie (www.hdcco.com)

ENERGY PERFORMANCE
Site EUI: 127 kBtu/ft²·yr

On-site Renewable energy: 0.35 kBtu/ft²·yr (This is for demonstration only. Stanford has a large off-site PV system to offset on-site electricity use.)

FOR MORE INFORMATION
http://www.hpbmagazine.org/attachments/article/11976/11Su-Y2E2-Stanford-CA.pdf

Stanford Y2E2. (© Tim Griffith.)

DESIGN FEATURES
- Atrium used for natural ventilation and temperature through automated control
- Campus chilled water and steam from SESI plant
- Radiant floor conditioning
- Low-velocity exhaust in laboratories
- Management of office equipment loads
- Recessed and operable windows
- Natural ventilation cooling for one-third of space
- Mixed-mode natural ventilation for remaining non-lab areas
- Chilled beams in mixed-mode areas
- High-performance windows tailored to each orientation
- Heat recovery from laboratory exhaust air
- Multitasking fume hoods
- Heat pipes in lab airstream
- Natural smoke-ventilation system

RICHARDSVILLE ELEMENTARY SCHOOL | Richardsville, Kentucky | 72,285 ft²

PROJECT TEAM
Owner: Warren County Public Schools (www.warrencountyschools.org)
Architect: Sherman Carter Barnhart Architects (scbarchitects.com)
Builder: RG Anderson Company, Inc. (www.rgandersoncompany.com)
Mechanical/Electrical Engineer: CMTA Consulting Engineers (www.cmtaegrs.com)
Energy Modeler: CMTA Consulting Engineers (www.cmtaegrs.com)

ENERGY PERFORMANCE
Site EUI: 18.2 kBtu/ft²·yr
Renewable energy: 17.8 kBtu/ft²·yr

FOR MORE INFORMATION
http://www.hpbmagazine.org/attachments/article/11817/12F-Richardsville-Elementary
-School-Richardsville-KY.pdf

View across parking lot at Richardsville Elementary School. (© CMTA Inc.)

DESIGN FEATURES
- Interior and exterior light shelves on south windows
- Tubular skylights
- Insulated concrete form walls
- Efficient lighting
- Ground-source heat pumps

- Dedicated outdoor-air system (DOAS)
- Advanced CO_2 monitoring for outside-air ventilation
- 208-kW thin-film photovoltaic system on roof
- 140-kW crystalline photovoltaic system over parking

DPR CONSTRUCTION | Phoenix, Arizona | 16,533 ft²

PROJECT TEAM
Owner: DPR Construction (www.dpr.com)
Architect/Engineer: SmithGroupJJR (www.smithgroupjjr.com)
Builder: DRP Construction (www.dpr.com)
Consultant: DNV KEMA (now DNV-GL, www.dnvgl.com)

ENERGY PERFORMANCE
Site EUI: 29 kBtu/ft²·yr
Renewable energy: 30 kBtu/ft²·yr (in 2013)

FOR MORE INFORMATION
http://www.dpr.com/view/path-to-net-zero-energy

View across collectors at DPR Construction. (Gregg Mastorakos, courtesy DPR Construction and SmithGroupJJR.)

DESIGN FEATURES
- 82 Solatube® skylights for interior daylighting
- Natural ventilation through 87 operable windows, 3 roll-up doors, and 14 BigAss® fans
- Evaporative cooling through four "shower towers" and one zinc-clad solar chimney
- 79-kW(DC) photovoltaic system shades parking area
- ILFI Certified
- LEED Platinum

Additional case studies are available in two books written by Ed Dean and produced by Pacific Gas and Electric. They have case studies for eleven zero net energy buildings in Northern California. The first volume has six case studies (including the Packard Foundation); it is available at http://bit.ly/2a6J6v4. The second volume, featuring five case studies, is available at http://bit.ly/29VOVwx.

Endnotes

PREFACE

1. See, for example: http://www.pewresearch.org/fact-tank/2014/02/03/10-projections-for-the -global-population-in-2050/.

CHAPTER 1 NOTES

1. R. Buckminster Fuller, *Operating Manual for Spaceship Earth* (New York: Simon & Schuster, 1968).
2. It took about 100 million years for the Earth to build up our reserves of oil, gas, and coal. We have used about half in 150 years. Assume a 40-year career and the math works out as follows: (150 years/100,000,000 years) $\times$ 40 years $\times$ 8,760 hours/year $\times$ 60 minutes/hour = 31.5 minutes. At this rate half of the store is used up in 15 minutes.
3. W. Steffen, "Unburnable Carbon: Why We Need to Leave Fossil Fuels in the Ground," Climate Council Australia, April 23, 2015. See: http://www.climatecouncil.org.au/unburnable -carbon-why-we-need-to-leave-fossil-fuels-in-the-ground.
4. The United States population in 2012 was estimated to be 314 million, while the population of the entire world was estimated to be 7.05 billion.
5. In 2010, the worldwide total primary energy consumption was 511 quadrillion Btu. The United States' primary energy consumption was about 98 quadrillion Btu, nearly 19 percent of the worldwide total primary energy consumption. See: http://www.eia.gov/tools/faqs/faq .cfm?id=87&t=1.
6. A quad of energy is 10^{15} or 1,000,000,000,000,000 (1 quadrillion) Btu, enough energy to drive an average car to the moon and back 580,000 times (if there were roads).
7. From US Energy Information Administration (EIA) data as compiled by Lawrence Livermore National Laboratory (LLNL-MI-410527), 4.75 quads of natural gas are used in residential buildings and 3.30 quads are used in commercial buildings out of a total natural gas usage of 28.3 quads in 2015. This total of 8.05 quads represents 28 percent of total US natural gas use.
8. From EIA data as compiled by LLNL (LLNL-MI-410527), 4.78 quads of electricity are used

in residential buildings and 4.63 quads in commercial buildings out of a total of 12.6 quads produced. The total for buildings is 9.41 quads, or 75 percent of the total. The 12.6 quads of electricity produced in the United States required 36.3 quads of primary energy, mostly from coal, natural gas, and nuclear, with smaller contributions from wind, hydro, and other sources. In this calculation, the energy inputs for non-combustible renewable-energy sources use the captured-energy approach instead of the fossil-fuel-equivalent approach displayed in figure 1-2. See endnote 6 in chapter 6 for more detail.

9. Total energy use by buildings in 2015 included 8.05 quads of natural gas, 28.24 quads of electricity (9.41 site quads at 33 percent efficiency using the captured energy approach), 1.54 quads of petroleum, and 0.58 quads of biomass, for a grand sum at the building site of 38.41 quads. This represents 39 percent of the 97.5 quads of total US energy consumption in 2015.

10. A gigatonne is one billion (10^9) metric tons. A metric ton of CO_2 is 1,000 kilograms or 2,250 pounds, enough to carbonate about half a million 12-ounce cans of soda, given that one can of soda contains about 2.2 grams of CO_2.

11. Buildings used 75 percent of electricity, which represents 1,530 million metric tons of CO_2 emissions. In addition, direct emissions from combustion within the buildings represent 573 million metric tons. The total is 2,103 out of 5,410, or 39 percent.

12. CO_2 is a by-product of a chemical conversion process used to convert limestone to lime to produce clinker, a component of cement. See: http://www.ipcc-nggip.iges.or.jp/public/gp /bgp/3_1_Cement_Production.pdf.

13. Kira Gould wrote a great history of the AIA Committee on the Environment. See: http://www .aia.org/practicing/groups/kc/AIAS077347.

14. The US Department of Energy (DOE) and the National Institute of Building Sciences jointly published "A Common Definition for Zero Energy Buildings" in September 2015. See: http://energy.gov/sites/prod/files/2015/09/f26/bto_common_definition_zero_energy_build ings_093015.pdf.

15. This is the designation recommended by DOE in its "Common Definition." DOE dropped the word *net* because its focus groups found it confusing. See endnote 14.

CHAPTER 2 NOTES

1. Stewart Brand, *How Buildings Learn: What Happens After They're Built* (New York: Viking Press, 1994).

2. Keith Boswell, a partner at Skidmore Owens and Merrill in San Francisco, confirms this range but notes that there is considerable variation by the anticipated use and by city.

3. For details of the design-build process for the RSF, see: http://www.nrel.gov/docs/fy12osti /51387.pdf.

4. This is the average of post-1980 large, medium, and small office buildings in climate zone 5B (Denver). See: http://energy.gov/sites/prod/files/2013/12/f5/refbldgs_eui_tables_1-4_7-0 .pdf.

5. Michael Holtz reports that the form and configuration of the RSF was developed early in the process, in collaboration with Craig Randock of RNL Architects. Among other propos-als that were considered was a double-envelope solution, but this was rejected because of expense.

6. Mireya Navarro, "City's Law Tracking Energy Use Yields Some Surprises," *New York Times*, December 24, 2012.

7. Ran Liu, "The Impact of Operable Windows on a High-Performance Office Building in the U S Midwest," presented at the ASHRAE Winter Conference, Orlando, FL, January 25, 2016.

8. Lisa Heschong has conducted some of the more interesting and convincing work to show the relationship between daylighting and health as well as productivity. For a series of articles and interviews with her on the topic, see: http://h-m-g.com/projects/daylighting/pub licity%20daylighting.htm.

9. A. Gustavsen, B. P. Jelle, D. Arasteh, and C. Kohler, "State-of-the-Art Highly Insulating Window Frames—Research and Market Review," Project Report 6, SINTEF Building and Infrastructure, 2007.

10. Cara Carmichael reports that the center-of-glass COG R-value is 13.2 on the north, 12.2 on the south, and 12.8 on the east and west. The windows use aluminum frames with a thermal break.

11. Guardian Industries has a very interesting video that shows the process of coating glass; see: https://www.guardian.com/commercial/AboutGuardianSunGuard/AboutSunGuard Glass/PostTemperableSputterCoatingTechnology/index.htm.

12. For example, see section 5.4.3 of Standard 90.1-2013.

13. This estimate of lighting's share of total energy use is based on energy modeling of reference buildings by the National Renewable Energy Laboratory and Pacific Northwest National Laboratory.

14. Alessandro Volta demonstrated in 1800 that light could be produced by passing electricity through a wire and causing it to glow.

15. For a description of the Edge building, see: http://www.bloomberg.com/features/2015-the -edge-the-worlds-greenest-building/.

16. The Center for the Built Environment at UC Berkeley has an online Thermal Comfort Tool; see: http://comfort.cbe.berkeley.edu/.

17. With passive solar heating (and cooling), the temperature in the space needs to vary, and the more it varies, the more effectively heat is transferred into and out of thermal-mass elements such as concrete floors and walls.

18. Cara Carmichael reports that the personal comfort stations at RMI do not include foot warmers. They may add foot warmers and possibly wrist warmers if this proves necessary.

19. For more information about the personal comfort system developed by the UC Berkeley Center for the Built Environment, see: http://www.zdnet.com/article/iphone-7-its-time-for -innovation-and-reinvention-not-gimmicks/. See also: http://www.cbe.berkeley.edu/research /personal-comfort-systems.htm.

20. Electric-powered air conditioners were commercialized by Willis Carrier in 1902. Before that, cooling our buildings was rare and pretty basic. There are records of human-powered fans in China as early as AD 200 and various designs for evaporative cooling in medieval Persia. In the nineteenth century, winter ice was harvested and stored for summer cooling, mostly in theaters. This practice is why we measure the capacity of air conditioners in tons: a ton of air-conditioning capacity is roughly equal to the cooling capacity of a ton of ice.

21. A building that provides a high level of service operates for more hours, accommodates more people, and has a higher equipment load, i.e., more computers and other equipment. The concept was introduced by David Goldstein and myself in a paper titled "A Classification of Building Energy Performance Indices." See: Springer, Energy Efficiency, ISSN 1570-646X, doi 10.1007/s12053-013-9248-0; this is available at www.eley.com.

22. A good source of information is the California Energy Commission's "Advanced Variable

Air Volume System Design Guide," October 2003, http://www.energy.ca.gov/2003publica tions/CEC-500-2003-082/CEC-500-2003-082-A-11.pdf. See also: https://energydesignre sources.com/resources/publications/design-guidelines/design-guidelines-advanced-vari able-air-volume-(vav)-systems.aspx.

23. This is based on fluid in both the pipe and the duct having the same velocity. The volumetric heat capacity of water is about 62 Btu/ft^{3}·°F, while the volumetric heat capacity of air is about 0.018 Btu/ft^{3}·°F. The ratio is approximately 1:3,400, which is the ratio of the cross-sectional areas of a 1-in. pipe to a 60-in. duct.

24. The product used at RMI is manufactured by PhaseChange Energy Systems (see: www .phasechange.com). Formulations are available that "melt" at 23°C, 25°C, and 27°C (71°F, 77°F, and 81°F). The product used at RMI is intended to work primarily for cooling.

25. The engineers for the project are Deerns. For their description of the building, see: https: //www.deernsamerica.com/projects/real-estate/most-sustainable-office-building-in-the -world-the-edge-amsterdam-netherlands.

26. I am not aware of any ATES systems in the United States. For more information, see: https: //en.wikipedia.org/wiki/Aquifer_thermal_energy_storage. Jaap Hogeling of the Nether-lands reports that a large site is needed so the hot wells and the cold wells can be spaced a suitable distance apart. They must also be located so that the natural movement of water through the aquifer does not cause the warm well to heat the cold well (or vice versa).

27. Jason Glazer, GARD Analytics, "ASHRAE 1651-RP, Development of Maximum Technically Achievable Energy Targets for Commercial Buildings, Ultra-Low Energy Use Building," December 31, 2015.

28. See: http://greentechadvocates.com/2013/05/07/plug-loads-a-growing-concern/.

CHAPTER 3 NOTES

1. The Earth receives about 8.2 million quads of energy a year, or 936 quads per hour. The energy of the world economy is on the order of 400 quads per year. This means that in about 26 minutes (calculated as (400/936)×60), we receive all the energy we need.

2. The sun produces about 12.2 trillion watt-hours per year per square mile. This works out to be 0.042 quads of energy per year per square mile (12.2×10^{12} Wh × (3.412 Btu/Wh) / 10^{15} Btu/quad). Sunlight arriving over an area of 2,400 square miles is about equal to current United States energy consumption. This is an area about 50 miles square, or about 2 percent of the state of Colorado. For the source of the data on 12.2 trillion Wh per year, see: http: //www.ecoworld.com/energy-fuels/how-much-solar-energy-hits-earth.html.

3. Denholm and Margolis, "Land-Use Requirements and the Per-Capita Solar Footprint for PV Generation in the United States," *Energy Policy* 36 no. 9 (August 2008): 3531–43.

4. Electric vehicles (EVs) are currently designed to take power *from* the grid, but to date, none have the capability to provide power *to* the grid. Providing power in both directions would require a redesign of the current generation of EV chargers.

5. The Wind Energy Foundation publishes data from time to time on the industry. See: http: //www.windenergyfoundation.org/interesting-wind-energy-facts.

6. The widely used GE 1.5-MW model, for example, consists of 116-foot blades atop a 212-foot tower for a total height of 328 feet.

7. The French physicist Edmund Becquerel discovered in 1839 that a voltage appeared when he illuminated a metal electrode immersed in a weak electrolyte solution.

8. The Solar Energy Industries Association publishes data on the state of the industry. See: http://www.seia.org/research-resources/solar-industry-data.

9. Ibid.

10. For typical solar cell efficiencies, see: Godfrey Boyle, *Renewable Energy, Power for a Sustainable Future* (Oxford: Oxford University Press, 2004). For theoretical efficiency limits, see: William Shockley and Hans J. Queisser, "Detailed Balance Limit of Efficiency of pn Junction Solar Cells," *Journal of Applied Physics* 32 (1961).

11. The first step is to separate the silicon atoms from the oxygen atoms and remove other impurities. There are several methods for doing this, but melting the quartz at about 3,600°F (2,000°C) and adding carbon is the common method. The carbon reacts with the oxygen in the molten silica to produce carbon dioxide (a by-product of the process), leaving metallurgical-grade silicon. This in turn is ground into a fine powder and further treated to produce nearly perfectly pure silicon.

12. The sawing process involves a wire coated with an abrasive compound of glycol and silicon carbide. The wire is hundreds of miles long. About half the material is lost as the ingots are sliced, but the silicon is recycled and used to make more monocrystalline ingots.

13. The Florida Solar Energy Center publishes a test procedure for rating solar collectors; see: http://www.fsec.ucf.edu/en/publications/pdf/standards/FSECstd_202-10.pdf. For another document that looks at performance metrics, see: http://www.nrel.gov/docs/fy14osti/60628 .pdf.

14. PTC refers to PVUSA Test Conditions, which were developed to test and compare PV systems as part of the PVUSA (Photovoltaics for Utility-Scale Applications) project. The PTC test conditions are 1,000 W per square meter solar irradiance, 20°C air temperature, and wind speed of 1 meter per second at 10 meters above ground level.

15. A typical specification will include the following: System Rating, Wattage (PTC), Max Power Voltage (V_{mpp}), Max Power Current (I_{mpp}), Open-Circuit Voltage (V_{oc}), Short-Circuit Current (I_{sc}), Max System Voltage, Series Fuse Rating, and Module Efficiency.

16. The Enphase M215 is an example.

17. For comparisons between a two-axis tracking system and fixed panels that are sloped to the south, east, and west, see, for instance: http://www.eia.gov/todayinenergy/detail.cfm ?id=18871. Flat panels are also compared. For Los Angeles, annual production was 2,078 kWh for two-axis tracking, 1,566 kWh for south, 1,403 kWh for west, 1,332 kWh for east, and 1,402 kWh for flat.

18. The solar path finder has been used for decades to evaluate shading conditions at building sites. See: http://www.solarpathfinder.com/.

19. One of the more popular devices is the SunEye 210 Shade Tool by Solmetric, though it has been discontinued; see http://www.solmetric.com/buy210.html. For how to use a camera and fish-eye lens to do a solar study, see: http://www.pge.com/includes/docs/pdfs/about/ edusafety/training/pec/toolbox/tll/appnotes/taking_a_fisheye_photograph.pdf.

20. "Price Quotes," http://pv.energytrend.com/. Archived from the original on June 26, 2014. See: https://en.wikipedia.org/wiki/Cost_of_electricity_by_source.

21. See: https://www.eia.gov/forecasts/aeo/electricity_generation.cfm; for a summary description of LCOE, see: https://en.wikipedia.org/wiki/Cost_of_electricity_by_source.

22. The US EPA has a good description of solar-power purchase agreements; see: http://www .epa.gov/greenpower/buygp/solarpower.htm.

23. For a discussion of options regarding what to do at the end of the SPPA, see: http://breaking

energy.com/2012/09/26/a-guide-to-end-of-term-options-in-a-solar-ppa/.

24. For a good description of the differences between a solar-power purchase agreement (sPPA) and a solar lease, see: http://www.energysage.com/solar-lease/lease-ppa-whats-the-difference.

25. This is based on a solar panel with an area of 1.64 m² (17.5 ft²) that has an STC rating of 270 W.

CHAPTER 4 NOTES

1. The American Society of Heating, Refrigeration, and Air-Conditioning Engineers (ASHRAE) has a certification program for building-energy modelers. Qualified candidates sit for an exam, and when they pass, they become certified Building Energy Modeling Professionals (BEMP).

2. For an example of how a calibrated model can agree with utility bills, see: http://esl.tamu.edu/docs/terp/2002/ESL-HH-02-05-13.pdf. This is a case of the R. E. Johnson office building in Austin, Texas, where Jeff Haberl and others calibrated a model I developed during the design process. Another example is the Oakland Administration Building for which my former company did new building performance contracting; see: http://aceee.org/files/proceedings/2000/data/papers/SS00_Panel4_Paper27.pdf.

3. Ed Dean, "Zero Net Energy Case Study Buildings," Vol. 1, September 2014. This source contains six zero net-energy case studies (including the Packard Foundation) and is available at http://bit.ly/2a6J6v4. The second volume contains five zero net-energy case studies (including four retrofits) and is available at http://bit.ly/29VOVwx.

4. For instance, the first performance standards developed by the California Energy Commission in 1978 included a table of performance targets with building types in rows and climate zones in columns. The BEPS program developed by the federal government in about the same era included similar targets. The BEPS program never got off the ground, but the CEC standards existed until the mid-1980s in spite of many problems.

5. Zero-energy performance index (zEPI) is explained best in a research paper developed for Southern California Edison. See: http://eley.com/sites/default/files/pdfs/090722%20Rethinking%20Percent%20Savings%20Final.pdf. See also: http://newbuildings.org/sites/default/files/Rethinking_Percent_Savings.pdf.

6. CBECS 2003 is also the baseline for the ENERGY STAR program as well as the Architecture 2030 program, so the technical basis of zEPI is consistent with these programs.

7. Some incentive programs such as the early version of LEED offered credits for energy savings beyond code, but the savings percentages were calculated based only on regulated energy, which is the component of energy use for which the standard has requirements. Regulated energy includes lighting, HVAC, and water heating. Non-regulated components such as plug loads, elevators, and commercial refrigeration were not considered.

8. PCI is introduced in the performance rating method (appendix G) of Standard 90.1-2016, which was not yet released at the time of this writing. For a paper that discusses the benefits of the approach, see: http://eley.com/sites/default/files/pdfs/033-045_Rosenberg_WEB.pdf.

9. David B. Goldstein and Charles Eley, "A Classification of Building Energy-Performance Indices," Energy Efficiency (magazine), February 2014, ISS 1570-646X, doi:10.1007/s12053-013-9248-0, http://eley.com/sites/default/files/pdfs/10.1007_s12053-013-9248-0.pdf.

10. Many of the COMNET assumptions, for instance plug loads, are based on the national 2003 Commercial Building Energy Consumption (CBEC) survey.

11. For official ASHRAE schedules, see: http://sspc901.ashraepcs.org/content.html.

CHAPTER 5 NOTES

1. See: http://jobordercontracting.org/2013/08/06/moving-from-design-build-db-to-integrated -project-delivery-ipd/.
2. Ibid.
3. For the best description of the Oakland performance contracting effort, see: http://eley.com /sites/default/files/pdfs/energy_performance_contracting_for_new_buildings_rmi_ef.pdf. See also: http://www.eley.com/sites/default/files/pdfs/ACEEE98_Contracting_for_Energy _Performance_0311.pdf.
4. Jonathan W. Cohen, "Integrated Project Delivery Case Studies," January 2010, http://www .aia.org/aiaucmp/groups/aia/documents/pdf/aiab082051.pdf. See also: School of Architecture University of Minnesota, "IPD Case Studies," March 2012, http://www.aia.org/aiaucmp /groups/aia/documents/pdf/aiab093702.pdf#public.
5. See: http://bimandintegrateddesign.com/tag/clay-goser/. See also: http://www.gartner.com /technology/research/methodologies/hype-cycle.jsp.
6. See: "IPD Case Studies," School of Architecture University of Minnesota, March 2012, http: //www.aia.org/aiaucmp/groups/aia/documents/pdf/aiab093702.pdf#public.
7. Jonathan W. Cohen, "Integrated Project Delivery Case Studies," January 2010, http://www .aia.org/aiaucmp/groups/aia/documents/pdf/aiab082051.pdf.
8. Interview with Cara Carmichael, February 8, 2016.
9. For a good summary of the history of building commissioning, see: http://www.totalbuild ingcommissioning.com/2010/07/history-of-commissioning/.
10. E. Mills, H. Friedman, T. Powell, N. Bourassa, D. Claridge, T. Haasl, and M. A. Piette, "The Cost-Effectiveness of Commercial-Buildings Commissioning," Lawrence Berkeley National Laboratory, 2004, http://evanmills.lbl.gov/pubs/pdf/cx-costs-benefits.pdf.
11. Ibid. Energy benefits range between $0.02/ft^2$ and $0.19/ft^2$. Non-energy benefits range between $0.23/ft^2$ and $6.96/ft^2$. Costs range between $0.49/ft^2$ and $1.66/ft^2$. Using these figures, the simple payback for commissioning is, on the low side, $49/(2+23) = 1.96$ years, and, on the high side, $166/(19+696) = 0.23$ years (or 3 months).
12. Ibid. The breakdown is 18 percent for design review, 14 percent for construction observation, 64 percent for acceptance testing, and 4 percent for post-construction warranty issues.
13. See: http://www.iklimnet.com/expert_hvac/building_control.html.
14. See: http://www.bacnet.org/.
15. See: http://buildingrobotics.com/how-comfy-works/.
16. The Hawaii Public Utilities Commission filed a ruling to close Hawaiian Electric Company's net-metering program to new participants because of the extraordinarily high levels of renewable energy the state has already achieved. The utility will still purchase electricity from distributed systems, but not at the retail rate. For more details, see: http://www.green techmedia.com/articles/read/hawaii-regulators-shutdown-hecos-net-metering-program.
17. See: "Plug-In Equipment Efficiency: A Key Strategy to Help Achieve California's Carbon Reduction and Clean Energy Goals," http://www.nrdc.org/energy/files/home-idle-load -plug-in-efficiency-IB.pdf.
18. For the COMNET Technical Support Document on plug loads, see: http://www.comnet.org /mgp/sites/default/files/mgp_appendices/150928-Plug-Loads-TSD.pdf.

19. David Kaneda, Brad Jacobson, and Peter Rumsey, "Plug Load Reduction: The Next Big Hurdle for Net Zero Energy Building Design," ACEEE Summer Study, 2010. This paper documents 44 percent savings at the Packard Foundation building in San Francisco.

20. See: ECOS, "Commercial Office Plug Load Savings Assessment," Report 3.2, CEC PIER Program, #500-08-049, December 2011, http://www.newbuildings.org/sites/default/files /PlugLoadSavingsAssessment.pdf.

21. Source: EPA Office Equipment Calculator.xls, December 2014. Savings for computers are around 43 percent, monitors 36 percent, printers between 26 percent and 66 percent depending on size and duty, and copiers between 26 percent and 72 percent depending on size and duty.

22. See: https://www.energystar.gov/index.cfm?c=power_mgt.datacenter_efficiency_virtuali zation.

23. Interview and follow-up e-mail from Paul Schwer, February 19, 2016.

CHAPTER 6 NOTES

1. Solar Market Pathways, "Virtual Net-Metering Policy Background and Tariff Summary Report," June 30, 2015.

2. See: COMNET.org, http://www.comnet.org/mgp/content/appendices?purpose=0.

3. The California Energy Commission requires that their standards be cost-effective, but at the same time the standards encourage the use of natural gas for water heating and space heating. This creates a cost-effectiveness challenge, since current utility tariffs offer lower compensation for electricity exported in excess of electricity used, which is a requirement for ZNE buildings that use gas. There is less incentive to put in a larger PV system to make up for the gas use because the payback is reduced.

4. The term *grid neutral* is sometimes used to describe buildings that produce as much electricity as they use but don't make additional electricity to offset gas and other fuel use. The California Division of the State Architect promoted such a program for K–12 schools for a number of years.

5. US Department of Energy, op. cit.

6. This is calculated using EIA data shown in figure 1-2, but the energy inputs from noncombustible renewable energy are adjusted to use the "captured energy" approach described in the United States DOE Request for Information DE-FOA-0001512, February 2, 2016. The 4.97 quads of non-combustible renewable energy shown in figure 1-2 are reduced to 1.78 quads by multiplying by the ratio of the captured energy (3,412 Btu of heat content) to the typical fossil-fuel plant heat rate of 9,542 Btu/kWh. The fossil-fuel plant heat rate was taken from the above-referenced report. Transmission and distribution losses are assumed to be 1.0 quad, which is consistent with recent estimates by EPA. The generation efficiency of 33 percent is calculated as follows: energy inputs = 38.0 − (4.97 − 1.78) = 34.81; energy delivered = 12.6 − 1.0 = 11.6; efficiency = 11.6 / 34.81 = 33 percent.

7. The question of source energy vs. site energy is by far the most contentious issue that is debated in the energy development arena at the national level. The associations representing the electric and gas industries have battled over this for years. The ASHRAE Standard 90.1 committee compromised on energy cost as its metric in 1989, and this has survived to this day.

8. See: http://www.presidency.ucsb.edu/ws/?pid=7842.

9. See: http://energy.gov/articles/top-9-things-you-didnt-know-about-americas-power-grid.

10. Selling energy back to the utility is often constrained. California investor-owned utilities, for instance, will buy what you produce at retail rates until you produce more than you use. They buy the remaining electricity at a discounted rate, closer to the wholesale rate.

11. Some of the negotiations were brutal. In the 1990s, a related issue emerged over a dual-envelop standard, whereby the insulation requirements in the standard would be more stringent for buildings with more-expensive electric heat as opposed to buildings with gas heat or heat pumps. A number of environmentalists were dismissed from the project committee and new leadership was installed. The new leadership, in turn, was rejected by the IESNA, a co-sponsor of the standard.

12. LEED is the US Green Building Council's Leadership in Energy and Environmental Design (LEED) program.

13. The areas served by the Tennessee Valley Authority (TVA) and the Bonneville Power Administration (BPA) are cases where the price for electricity is held below market rate because of government investment.

14. The average electricity price used in standards development work is $0.1032/kWh ($0.03025/kBtu). The national average for natural gas is $0.99/therm ($0.0099/kBtu). These data are used in the Standard 90.1 development process.

15. For the actual TDV values used in California, see: https://ethree.com/public_projects/2013 _title24.php.

16. For more information, see: https://ethree.com/National_Time-Dependent_Values.html. EThree is the organization that developed the TDV values for California; at this site, you can download a spreadsheet that calculates TDV values for eight cities in the United States — Atlanta, Washington, New York, Phoenix, Fresno, St. Louis, Chicago, and Houston.

17. See: www.COMNET.org.

18. To verify that source energy and carbon track each other closely, compare the electricity-to-gas ratio for both source energy and carbon. For CO_2e emissions, the ratio is 1.39 : 0.48, or 2.90. For source energy, the ratio is 3.15:1.09, or 2.89, almost the same. If you reduce energy by 50 percent, you also reduce CO_2e by 50 percent, even if the mix of fuels changes between the baseline and the efficient building.

19. CO_2e assesses all greenhouse gases in terms of the equivalent emissions of CO_2. It is based on their global-warming potential (GWP), which is an index for estimating the relative global-warming contribution of atmospheric emissions of 1 kg of a particular greenhouse gas compared to emissions of 1 kg of CO_2.

20. See the United States DOE Common Definition for Zero Energy Buildings, op. cit.

21. Donella Meadows, Jorgen Randers, and Dennis Meadows, *Limits to Growth — The 30-Year Update* (White River Junction, VT: Chelsea Green Publishing, 2004).

22. See: https://us.fsc.org/.

23. Meadows, op. cit.

24. Ibid.

25. See: http://kids.mongabay.com/elementary/201.html.

26. These calculations are based on 67 percent conversion efficiency and 20 million Btu/cord of wood. Another key assumption is that a cord of wood can be sustainably produced for each acre of land. This will, of course, vary significantly by climate and the type of wood that is grown.

27. This is based on 1,200 kWh/y of PV production per kW (STC) of installed capacity and 68 ft^2

of collector area per kW (STC).

28. Some boilers are designed to take multiple fuels. They can operate with wood pellets, or they can alternatively use oil or even natural gas.

29. The performance of solar water heating systems is commonly expressed in terms of an energy factor (EF), which is the ratio of the energy that goes into the process divided by the heat delivered by the system. The EF for a typical gas water heater is in the range of 0.70–0.80. The EF of a typical electric-resistance water heater is close to 1.00, but this does not account for power generation and distribution losses. Solar systems with gas backup have an EF in the range of 2.5, while solar systems with electric backup have an EF in the range of 3.3. The EF is calculated using site energy, so as you compare electric and gas water heaters; keep in mind that the energy costs and source-energy values will be higher for the electric systems. Solar-thermal systems are also sometimes rated in terms of a solar-savings fraction (SSF), which is the amount of the heating load that is provided by the solar system. A solar savings fraction of 60 percent means that 60 percent of the load will be satisfied by the solar system and the remaining 40 percent will be satisfied by the backup system.

30. See: http://www.foothill.edu/news/newsfmt.php?sr=2&rec_id=3062.

31. The campus goals and plan is spelled out in some detail in the UC Merced Sustainability Strategic Plan (2010).

32. Solar Market Pathways, op. cit.

33. Shanti Pless and Paul Torcellini, "Net-Zero Energy Buildings: A Classification System Based on Renewable Energy Supply Options," Technical Report NREL/TP-550-44586, June 2010.

34. See: http://apps3.eere.energy.gov/greenpower/markets/certificates.shtml?page=2.

35. Additionality is the property of an activity being additional; it is determined according to whether an intervention has an effect compared to a baseline.

36. See: https://sustainable.stanford.edu/campus-action/stanford-energy-system-innovations -sesi.

37. For the PG&E tariff that applies in such an instance, see: http://www.pge.com/tariffs/tm2 /pdf/ELEC_SCHEDS_RES-BCT.pdf. For a description of the program, see: http://www.pge .com/en/b2b/energytransmissionstorage/newgenerator/ab2466/index.page.

38. Information from e-mail correspondence with Joy Hughes and from her website, www .SolarGardens.org. See also: http://www.utilitydive.com/news/why-utilities-across-the -nation-are-embracing-community-solar/354164/.

39. See: http://blog.solargardens.org/2011/06/guest-post-smud-solar-shares-in.html.

40. J. R. DeShazo, Alex Turek, and Michael Samulon, "Guide to Design Decisions for Utility-Sponsored Community Solar," Luskin Center for Innovation, UCLA, May 2015.

41. See: http://www.greentechmedia.com/articles/read/us-community-solar-market-to-grow -fivefold-in-2015-top-500-mw-in-2020.

42. See: https://www.ftc.gov/sites/default/files/documents/federal_register_notices/guides-use -environmental-marketing-claims-green-guides/greenguidesfrn.pdf.

43. The investor-owned utilities in California are allowed to use unbundled RECs to meet a maximum of 10 percent of their RPS commitment, but most use RECs for far less than this, partly because the California Air Resources Board (CARB) does not allow RECs at all and the utility will still have to buy carbon offsets to meet California's cap-and-trade program on carbon.

44. According to Geof Syphers, the CEO of Sonoma Clean Power (SCP), a community-choice aggregator in California, there is not much demand for unbundled RECs. SCP will have

none in its RPS portfolio after 2016, and Goef reports that the share of RECs in the PG&E RPS portfolio is around 1 percent, much lower than the 10 percent that is permitted.

45. One of the harshest critics of RECs is Auden Schendler, who has blogged about these issues in www.thinkprogress.org. See, for instance: http://thinkprogress.org/climate/2011/06/07 /238244/clean-energy-trainwreck-why-most-recs-are-bad-and-how-to-find-the-good-ones/.

46. During this period, the Roman Catholic Church would sell an indulgence that would absolve the purchaser from a sin that had been committed or even one that might be committed in the future. In 1517, Martin Luther denounced the Church for selling indulgences, and this was a factor in igniting the Protestant Reformation. See: Paul Vitello, "For Catholics, a Door to Absolution Is Reopened," *New York Times*, February 9, 2009, http://www.ny times.com/2009/02/10/nyregion/10indulgence.html?pagewanted=all&_r=0.

47. To achieve ZNE, a 10,000-square-foot building with an EUI of 12 kBtu/ft²·yr would require 120 million Btu/yr or 35 mWh of renewable energy production each year.

48. The estimated cost of the on-site PV system is based on a 30 kW system at a cost of $3/W.

49. The classic case of split incentives is that the owner is disinclined to invest in energy efficiency, since the benefits would accrue to the tenants who pay the utility bills.

50. See: http://www.green-e.org/.

51. Interview with Jennifer Martin, executive director of Green-e, January 13, 2016. See also: http://www.green-e.org/.

52. Severin Borenstein, "Feeling Smug about Your Solar Rooftop? Not So Fast" (blog posting), January 21, 2016, http://blogs.berkeley.edu/2016/01/21/feeling-smug-about-your-solar-roof top-not-so-fast/.

53. See: http://www.cpuc.ca.gov/PUC/energy/Renewables/. Most states exclude large hydro plants from eligible renewable-energy generators, since they are legacy plants and it is unlikely that any large new hydro plants will be constructed, both because the best sites have been taken and because of environmental and land-use problems.

54. See: https://www.eia.gov/todayinenergy/detail.cfm?id=4850. See also: http://www.cpuc.ca .gov/RPS_Homepage/.

55. The California RPS requirements define three different forms of renewable energy, which are called "buckets." For an explanation of the California buckets, see: http://www.cpuc.ca .gov/RPS_Procurement_Rules_33/. Most of the renewable energy must come from bucket one, which represents eligible renewable-energy systems that communicate directly with the California Independent System Operator (CaISO). The minimum amount in bucket one is 75 percent, beginning in 2017 (65 percent now). Bucket two includes renewable energy that may be substituted and "firmed and shaped." Note the following example: An IOU buys wind energy from a farm in Oregon, but that energy is substituted or augmented with energy from conventional generators so that it does not have the variability inherent with wind. This substituted energy is what actually arrives at CaISO. The third bucket are unbundled RECs. These can represent a maximum of 10 percent after 2017 (15 percent now).

56. Lawrence Livermore National Laboratory, op. cit. Solar = 0.532, hydro = 2.39, wind = 1.82 and geothermal = 0.224. The total is 4.97 quads, or 13 percent of the 38.0 quads of input to electric generation. (See fig. 1-2.)

57. Ibid. For the state of Washington in 2012, 1,100 trillion Btu was used to generate electricity. Hydro represented 850 trillion Btu, with another 63 trillion Btu from wind. See: https://flow charts.llnl.gov/content/assets/images/charts/Energy/Energy_2012_United-States_WA.png.

58. See: http://www.midwestenergynews.com/2012/01/13/renewable-or-not-how-states-count-hydropowe/.

59. For Sonoma Clean Power, PG&E adds a PCIA/FF, which represents the power charge indifference adjustment (PCIA) and the franchise fee surcharge (FF). The PCIA is a charge to cover PG&E's generation costs acquired prior to a customer's switch to a third-party electricity-generation provider. PG&E acts as a collection agent for the franchise fee surcharge, which is levied by cities and counties for all customers. These charges add $0.01234 per kWh of cost.

60. See: https://en.wikipedia.org/wiki/Community_Choice_Aggregation.

61. Conversation with Geof Syphers, CEO of Sonoma Clean Power, February 22, 2016.

62. Renewable Energy Self-Generation Bill Credit Transfer (RES-BCT). The capacity of the renewable-energy system is usually limited (less than 5 megawatts in California).

CHAPTER 7 NOTES

1. For the original presentation of the diffusion model, see: Everett M. Rogers, *Diffusion of Innovations* (Glencoe, IL: Free Press, 1962).

2. For a good history of the federal law, see: https://en.wikipedia.org/wiki/National_Appliance_Energy_Conservation_Act.

3. In September 2005, New York, California, and thirteen other states filed suit against the US Department of Energy, charging the agency with failure to meet deadlines to update the appliance standards. The complaint identified twenty-two violations. For a copy of the complaint, see: http://oag.ca.gov/system/files/attachments/press_releases/05-077_0a.pdf.

4. This requirement is from the Warren-Alquist Act, which created the California Energy Commission in 1975 and granted it authority to develop energy-efficiency standards for buildings and appliances.

5. The ASHRAE cost-effectiveness methodology and documentation can be reviewed at https://www.energycodes.gov/sites/default/files/documents/commercial_methodology.pdf.

6. The BCAP website has an interactive map, located at http://energycodesocean.org/code-status-commercial, where you can click on the state and get more-detailed information about the code that is in effect for that state.

7. Interagency Working Group on Social Cost of Carbon, United States Government, "Technical Support Document: Technical Update of the Social Cost of Carbon for Regulatory Impact Analysis Under Executive Order 12866," May 2013. The original TSD was published February 2010; see: http://www3.epa.gov/climatechange/EPAactivities/economics/scc.html.

8. Recent LLNL figures for 2015 show 12.6 quads of annual electricity consumption in the United States (3.7 trillion kWh). This resulted in a little over 2 trillion tonnes of CO_2. Using the EPA Social Cost for Carbon of $60/ton, this is a cost per year of $136 billion. This works out to be a premium of about $0.037/kWh, or an increase of about 50 percent over national average prices. The EPA figures vary by year and by discount rate.

9. In a report published in the *Annals of the New York Academy of Sciences*, Epstein et al. (2011) do a full-cost accounting for the life cycle of coal, taking externalities into account. Among the factors included in this analysis were government coal subsidies, increased illness and mortality due to mining pollution, climate change from greenhouse-gas emissions, particulates causing air pollution, loss of biodiversity, cost to taxpayers of environmental monitoring and cleanup, decreased property values, infrastructure damage from mudslides

resulting from mountaintop removal, infrastructure damage from mine blasting, impacts of acid rain resulting from coal-combustion by-products, and water pollution. They found that the externalities would add an average of $0.18/kWh to the price of electricity, but there was a range in their estimates from a low of about $0.09/kWh to a high of $0.27.

10. Tim Flannery, *Atmosphere of Hope: Searching for Solutions to the Climate Crisis* (New York: Atlantic Monthly Press, 2015). This discussion is on page 70.

11. Al Gore, *The Future: Six Drivers of Global Change* (New York: Random House, 2013).

12. See: http://www.scientificamerican.com/article/renewables-boom-expected-thanks-to-tax-credit/.

13. See: http://www.statista.com/statistics/272709/top-10-oil-and-gas-companies-worldwide-based-on-market-value/.

14. See: http://www.statista.com/statistics/272706/top-10-mining-companies-worldwide-based-on-market-value/.

15. Elizabeth Bast, Alex Doukas, Sam Pickard, Laurie van der Burg, and Shelagh Whitley, "Empty Promises: G20 Subsidies to Oil, Gas, and Coal Production," Oil Exchange International, November 2015, http://www.odi.org/sites/odi.org.uk/files/odi-assets/publications-opinion-files/9957.pdf.

16. See: http://www.imt.org/policy/building-energy-performance-policy.

17. One of the fiercest opponents of mandatory disclosure is the powerful real estate industry.

18. The DOE Building Energy Asset Score is an online tool. See http://energy.gov/eere/buildings/building-energy-asset-score.

19. For more details on this ZNE certification program, see: http://living-future.org/netzero.

20. For the most recent list, see: http://newbuildings.org/sites/default/files/2015ZNEbuildings List.pdf; this is updated each year.

21. These situations include RES-BCT and virtual metering (see discussion in ch. 6).

22. One of the most interesting battles has been between the solar industry and Arizona Public Service; see: http://www.azcentral.com/story/money/business/energy/2015/12/28/arizona-regulators-seek-solar-net-metering-compromise/77716104/. For documentation of the Hawaii issues, see: http://www.greentechmedia.com/articles/read/hawaii-regulators-shut-down-hecos-net-metering-program.

23. California ISO, "What the Duck Curve Tells Us about Managing a Green Grid," 2013, https://www.caiso.com/Documents/FlexibleResourcesHelpRenewables_FastFacts.pdf.

24. One of the earliest pump storage systems was completed by the Tennessee Valley Authority in 1978. Water is pumped from Nickajack Lake on the Tennessee River at the base of Raccoon Mountain to a 528-acre storage reservoir built at the top of the mountain. It takes twenty-eight hours to fill the upper reservoir. During periods of high electricity demand, water can be released from the reservoir through a tunnel drilled through the center of the mountain, driving electric generators in an underground hydroelectric plant. The plant has a capacity of 1,652 MW and can generate for up to twenty-two hours. The plant is used most days and serves as an important element for peak power generation and grid balancing in the TVA system. See: https://en.wikipedia.org/wiki/Raccoon_Mountain_Pumped-Storage_Plant.

25. Pacific Gas and Electric and the California Energy Commission are piloting a battery storage system in San Jose; see: http://www.pge.com/about/newsroom/newsreleases/20130523/pge_energy_commission_unveil_battery_energy_storage_in_san_jose.shtml.

26. This product is targeted for residences; see: https://www.teslamotors.com/powerwall.

27. Interview with Randall Higa, February 18, 2016.
28. EV manufacturers are working together to establish standards for EVs to communicate with the grid. This would enable the grid to schedule the charging time for cars and even to draw power from the batteries when this is feasible and the owners agree. See: http://www .pevcollaborative.org/sites/all/themes/pev/files/CPEV_annual_report_web.pdf.
29. See: http://www.pjm.com/markets-and-operations/energy.aspx.
30. Peter Fox-Penner, *Smart Power: Climate Change, the Smart Grid, and the Future of Electric Utilities* (Washington, DC: Island Press, 2010).
31. Ibid., 175.
32. Ibid., 189.
33. This is based on the Northeast Utilities pilot program; see: http://www.iso-ne.com/commit tees/comm_wkgrps/othr/clg/mtrls/2010/may62010/cserna_revised.pdf.

CHAPTER 8 NOTES

1. For information on Athena Sustainable Materials Institute, see: http://www.athenasmi.org.
2. The lower end of the range is a wood-framed building on a concrete slab. The high end of the range is an all-concrete building. Calculations performed by the author for Los Angeles.
3. See: http://www.brainyquote.com/quotes/quotes/w/winstonchu111316.html.
4. John Holtzclaw, Robert Clear, Hank Dittmar, David Goldstein, and Peter Haas. "Location Efficiency: Neighborhood and Socio-Economic Characteristics Determine Auto Ownership and Use: Studies in Chicago, Los Angeles, and San Francisco," *Transportation Planning and Technology* 25, no. 1 (March 2002): 1–27.
5. See: http://needtoknow.nas.edu/energy/energy-use/transportation/.
6. This is based on a presentation by the author to the San Francisco School in 2008 and a follow-up presentation at the California Energy Commission in 2009, with similar conclusions.
7. Alex Wilson and Rachel Navaro, "Driving to Green Buildings: The Transportation Energy Intensity of Buildings," *Building Green*, August 30, 2007, http://www2.buildinggreen.com /article/driving-green-buildings-transportation-energy-intensity-buildings.
8. Lorraine White and Gary Klein, "The Water–Energy Connection in California," ACEEE Summer Study, 2006, http://www.eceee.org/library/conference_proceedings/ACEEE_build ings/2006/Panel_12/p12_13/paper.
9. US Geological Survey, http://water.usgs.gov/edu/wupt.html.

Index